Praise for *The Good, the Bad, and the Dolce Vita*

"Mickey Knox has a wonderful story to te''   ~er of
a memoir. A young war veteran goe~   ~ce
to grab the brass ring of ce''   ~ed
down by the blacklist. The   ~s begun.
Then he gets up. And goes on   ~asterpiece: his
life. We move with him throug~   ~u and the New York
stage, across Europe (from his bas~ ~ome) in the great days of
post-war cinema, seeing the actors and directors and writers
close-up. There are beautiful women here, and wives, and various wounds, along with great meals in the best of company in
most of the capitals of the world. A splendid life, a splendid tale."
— Pete Hamill

"I knew Mickey Knox or, as it turns out, a bit of him, enough
though to confirm this astonishing *racconto* that was his life. The
sumptuous years career by in these pages. It's as if this little car
drives up. Get in, he simply says. It's a glorious ride."
— James Salter

The Good, the Bad, and the Dolce Vita

The Adventures of an Actor in Hollywood, Paris, and Rome

Mickey Knox

Preface by Norman Mailer

NATION BOOKS
NEW YORK

THE GOOD, THE BAD, AND THE DOLCE VITA: *The Adventures of an Actor in Hollywood, Paris and Rome*

Copyright © 2004 by Mickey Knox
Preface © 2004 by Norman Mailer

Published by
Nation Books
An Imprint of Avalon Publishing Group
245 West 17 St., 11th Floor
New York, NY 10011

Nation Books is a co-publishing venture of the Nation Institute and Avalon
Publishing Group Incorporated.

Library of Congress Cataloging-in-Publication Data is available.

ISBN 1-56025-575-7

9 8 7 6 5 4 3 2 1

Book design by Paul Paddock
Photographs courtesy of Photofest
Rome: First View by Norman Rosten © by the Norman Rosten Estate.
Reprinted by permission.

Printed in the United States of America
Distributed by Publishers Group West

For:

Valentina and Melissa, my beautiful daughters.

Carl and Seymour, my intelligent brothers.

And for the memory of Alex Nicol and George Rarey, unforgettable friends.

Preface
Norman Mailer

I t may be fair to say that I encountered Mickey Knox before I ever met him. That's because I saw him first in a movie called *City Across the River,* a B film made, if I recollect, back in 1948. It was about a Brooklyn gang called the Amboy Dukes, and Mickey played their leader, a small, trim, well-contained young hood with absolute authority over his cohorts despite the name he carried— Larry Tunafish. It was a riveting film to me, since I, too, came from Brooklyn, and was caught up with enjoying my tangential acquaintance with the subject.

At that time, I knew nothing about the art of the actor, and was quick to assume that the real Mickey Knox must be truly tough. Over the years, I came to learn that my friend was indeed tough in his own way—he had learned to survive in Hollywood and Rome where a player can hardly develop the confidence that his wallet and his ego will not be on the chopping block by evening. Given the ups and downs that he went through (and has now written about), a weaker man could have gone under.

I knew little of that, however, on the day we actually met, sometime in the summer of 1949. I came through the door of his house brought along by a mutual acquaintance, we shook hands and I said, "Hey, you're a real good actor." For there he was before me, my own size, and my own psychic weight, which is to say, not tough, not weak, just there, another friendly guy from Brooklyn ready, much like myself, to get along with anyone whose hand you were shaking for the first time. He was in person, therefore, a long distance away from the study in force he had presented as a gang leader, and so I said, "Hey, you're a real good actor," and our friendship was begun. He did, after all, love *The Naked and the Dead*.

Since then we've been around for each other as stand-up friends over more than five decades and each of us has learned a good deal about the permutations of lives that go in and out of parallel, into marriage and into divorce—hell, we were even brothers-in-law for a time, married to two sisters back in the late fifties, and we each became the father of two girls, beautiful girls then and beautiful now, a nice feat I cannot keep myself from declaring aloud.

I do not wish to give a sampling of what is to come in these pages (although the reader will encounter a host of movie stars with fresh anecdotes nicely attached to them) but I would underline how frustrating were the situations that were soon to come upon Mickey Knox after we met. Like many a young actor in his milieu, he was left-wing, and got trashed in the hysteria of the early fifties while the Hollywood red-hunt was going on. In a few months his fortunes shifted from being a young actor under contract who had already made ten movies over a brief two years, to a young actor who could not get any work. His career floundering, his French wife, Georgette, as practical as she was charming, broke up with him, and he was reduced to living on his wits with what must have been the unendurable ambiguity of not knowing whether the town had decided he was without the talent to become a real star, or was, rather, on an undeclared blacklist. Indeed, the blacklists in those days were, for the most part, secret, and the gray lists were even more numerous. I remember that with the exception of one month's work for Sam Goldwyn, I could get no jobs as a screenwriter, as this, after all, was in the year after the publication of *The Naked and the Dead*. Indeed, my agent at the time, a decent conservative man, could never understand why.

Mickey kept alive. He went back to New York, worked at Actor's Studio, did some TV and went back to L.A., where he developed a reputation I soon envied him for. It was as a lover. For a man who has no money and no prospects, that was not a small achievement in L.A. Indeed, there were periods where he had the back door key to more than one movie star's apartment, the same ladies who would be coupled in the gossip columns with their leading men. When you are not yet thirty, and a friend is having carnal success without fame or fortune to back him up, it is not routine to be free of envy. It was obvious that his sex life had more drama than my own.

Later, his movie career moving nowhere, he migrated to Rome and there he would live for much of his life while working on Italian films as an actor, translator, dramatic coach, and dialogue director. It was also a time when he coached Anna Magnani, Marcello Mastroianni, and acted with him and Sophia Loren. He also became so knowing about Rome, Roman ways, and the felicities of the Italian language, that indeed there was a long period when visiting Americans and even a few Italians would call him the mayor of Rome. To know Mickey Knox in those years was to be provided with all the guide that an average good American needed for the Via Veneto.

Occasionally, Mickey would come back to New York, and on one of those returns he saved my play of *The Deer Park* on opening night at the Theatre De Lys, which was then as royal a theatre as you could find off-Broadway, what with its proscenium stage and 299 seats all covered in red velvet.

We had had a month of previews. By opening night, therefore, all my friends, family, and theatre acquaintances were veteran audience. Nonetheless, I invited all one hundred back for the occasion. There were also a hundred seats for ticket buyers and finally a most formidable one hundred for the theatre critics who occupied most of the ten rows and proceeded after curtain-rise to sit there in a collective block of ice, one hundred frozen critical faculties all intact, and so powerful in their presence that for the first half hour, no one in the audience dared to laugh. My friends and relatives, having seen the play several times, could not be surprised into sufficient energy to laugh one more time at familiar lines, not in the chill of these critics. The hundred new theatergoers weren't ready to laugh at all, certainly not while the giant ice block up front neither squeaked nor groaned.

The play went on in agony then for the actors, the director, and the playwright. We had our thirty previews, and on decent nights we had aroused a good deal of laughter in the first thirty minutes; even on less-good evenings, one could feel some real merriment. But here, opening night, not a sound. My actors were like a team that was being badly outplayed, but managing to hold together just enough not to fall apart. It was a respectable feat under the circumstances.

Not until the fortieth minute did Mickey Knox make his entrance. He was playing Collie Munshin, a classic Hollywood producer of that period, a man who knew every good and evil nuance to be extracted from an unexpected opportunity, and he came onstage like a winner. There was a force in him reminiscent of his distant, long-gone film brother, Larry Tunafish, and he radiated such confidence that a first crack appeared in the ice block, and then the first laugh of the night actually rose up out of the frontal mass. In another two minutes everyone in the theatre was laughing, indeed, they didn't stop all the while Mickey was on. Good momentum—so much like the awakening of momentum in a football team—was back, and we succeeded in half-carrying the day. Our reviews ranged from good to fifty-fifty and the play survived for four months. I don't think we would have lasted four days without Mr. Knox.

He has had other great days in his life, and certainly some great nights, but this particular evening is the one I would honor the most, for he came out onstage knowing the stakes and the perils, and he took command. There are not many stage actors, no matter how stellar, who can rally their team in the manner of a great athlete. Part of the joy in remembering this hour is that it emerged from the sum of many frustrations in his career, and yet also was fueled by the bond of our friendship. It is not a small event when on separate rare occasions we succeed in doing something for oneself and yet do something more for a best friend. How agreeable that hope is not always ill-invested in a long friendship. You can see then that this preface is written in salute to a rare warrior of that rarely heroic world of stage and screen, honors to you, old friend Mickey.

—Norman Mailer

The Beginning

I was born a "love-child," as they sweetly used to describe a bastard. My birth was at home on Coney Island in Brooklyn where we lived, for the most part, until we moved to Washington, D.C. when I was fifteen, in 1937.

My mother and biological father were Russian Jews, my mother from Odessa and I'm ignorant of what town my father came from. My mother was a political Lefty and that's the way she brought me up— "a red-diaper baby." I barely knew my father and saw him about six times. He was a Yiddish poet and would send me his published (in Yiddish newspapers) short poems from time to time.

When I was five or six my mother married a young, hard-working Polish Jew. He proved to be a godsend for us. I had an older half brother and sister (from my mother's first marriage in Russia) and Nathan, my stepfather, worked during the toughest years of the depression as a house painter, often walking miles to and from work to save the carfare. I hated the father I barely knew and carried some of that over to my new father—unjustly. But most little kids are shits and I was no exception.

Up until Nate came along I was a lonely kid and avoided playmates because they had fathers and I didn't. I made my mother and sister miserable because I wouldn't eat, don't ask me why, and so was anemic and thin as a rail until I was thirteen when a year on a farm endowed me with a healthy appetite.

Coney Island, during the summertime, was a dreamland for kids: on the beach and in the ocean during the day and lounging on the boardwalk in our longies in the evenings.

It was a great life for a young teenager, but when I was fifteen the Great Depression of the thirties drove us (literally) to Washington, D.C., where my sister had married a young lawyer. We had an old Dodge and it took us over twenty hours to make the two hundred and forty-mile trip, due to half a dozen blowouts (the car was over-loaded with our belongings) and a malfunctioning electrical system.

Washington was a strange place for me, so different, certainly not as exciting as Coney Island. Then, out of the blue, I decided I wanted to be an actor. Just like that. Probably inspired by James Cagney and John Garfield—Cagney, small and tough as nails, Garfield, an outsider but loaded with passion.

I put myself on the line. I studied speech and drama at Catholic University, the best known school for drama in the country at the time. I worked in two summer stock companies, one in Maryland, the other in Virginia, acting and painting sets.

I had the will and persisted and it happened.

1941–42 New York

Broadway, here I come. Goodbye virginity,
with thanks to Brooke.

That unforgettable day! Leaving home at nineteen to begin my adventures as an actor. After sixty years I can still call up the elation, the excitement. Broadway was my target. I was too young to feel scared, but young enough to be optimistic: The theater would be my new home.

My mother didn't object to my going to New York or warn me of the difficulty in getting work on Broadway. She was Jewish, but not a "Jewish Mother." She gave me five bucks to take a bus, so I hitch-hiked.

My buddy George Rarey had gone to New York earlier and wrote that I could share his small apartment when and if I made the break. The offer fit nicely into my condition of poverty. Rarey was a talented cartoonist and a skillful artist. He carved Don Quixote, sword and all, out of a block of wood in one night as we sat facing the fireplace drinking beer, or as he called it, suds.

Rarey was rare. He was authentic, had no envy, no meanness or rancor toward anyone. He was open and affectionate to those he knew and spoke to people, radiating an aura of simple goodwill. He was a true "mensch."

My future home was in a small, three floor, building made of dark brick. It stood directly above the subway entrance on the northwest corner of Seventh Avenue and Eighteenth Street.

The apartments were unique, each one different in space and color. They had fireplaces and plumbing that broke every safety regulation in Manhattan. The floors, walls, and ceilings were wood and beams, whimsically painted or simply left unpainted, showing the beauty of the natural wood. Many of the rooms were oddly angled and all the floors slanted slightly.

Rarey had the "penthouse," fancifully called the "chicken coop." In winter it was bone-chillingly cold, in summer, miserably hot. But I loved the chicken coop. It had picture windows on three sides, a fireplace, a tiny kitchen, and a cube of a haphazardly put together bathroom.

The building was owned by a remarkable woman of indeterminate age, called Lady. To me, at nineteen, she looked ancient. On her own, without a helping hand, she had renovated all the apartments to conform, more or less, to her crazy imagination. In a way she was like a phantom, appearing out of nowhere, doing some fixing, then disappearing. She rarely spoke or smiled.

I arrived in New York in mid-September and immediately started to make the rounds of agencies, producers' offices and actors' hangouts in an effort to learn who was casting what.

By mid-November I was the envy of my fellow actors looking for their first Broadway job. I had a part in *Jason*, a new play by Samson Raphaelson, a well-known, successful playwright. George Abbott, one of the most potent director/producers on Broadway was producing it. However, Raphaelson insisted on directing his own play.

I had traveled light hitchhiking to New York and made the mistake of not packing my trusty harmonica. The part in *Jason* called for a young Irish kid to play the harmonica. I didn't have the money to buy one and, to tell the truth, it was a good reason to meet the famous harmonica virtuoso, Larry Adler.

I tracked down his address, rang his doorbell, and came face-to-face with my boyhood hero. He smiled and said, yes? I told him I was a harmonica player without my harmonica, but needed one to audition for a Broadway play. I couldn't afford to buy a decent harmonica. Could he lend me one? (What chutzpah!) He told me to wait a moment, left and returned with a Horner Chromatic. "Please bring it back," he said. Oh, of course, I promised. And after auditioning I returned it. He took the harmonica, smiled slightly and went back into his apartment.

I got the part of Nick Wiggins. I was to understudy the part of Mike Ambler, the young catalyst of the piece, based on William Saroyan. Nick Conte, later known as Richard Conte, was hired to play Ambler. Alexander Knox played the noted drama critic, Jason, and Helen Walker, a lovely young actress, played his wife.

I was in only one scene and had little to say, but it thrilled me to be rehearsing in a big-time Broadway play. The rehearsals lasted a month and it was the most exciting time of my life. I was a professional actor!

My enthusiasm faltered once—December 7, 1941. Pearl Harbor had been bombed. I heard the news blaring from storefront radios as I walked down Broadway on my way to rehearsal. Was it war? I feared the play would be cancelled. It was war all right, but the play went on.

We had our first run-through for George Abbott. He hadn't seen any of the rehearsals; he wanted a clean look. He got it, and so did Nick Conte. At the end of the run-through, Abbott had the actors sit onstage.

He spoke to each member of the cast briefly. He wasn't the most generous man and any praise was faint. He saved Conte for last. (Abbott originally wanted Burgess Meredith for the part of Mike Ambler, but Meredith was not free.) Abbott pointed a long finger at Conte and zeroed in like a laser beam: "Who the hell do you think you are? Burgess Meredith? You're not and never will be. But why do you mimic him in body and voice? It's the worst acting I have seen in all my years in the theater. Young man, have you no sense of yourself, must you try to be someone you can never be?"

Nick turned bloodless gray, rushed off the stage and into the theater's alley to vomit his guts out. Raphaelson followed and probably saved Nick's career. He told him to forget Abbott's criticism, that he would be Mike Ambler or the play would not go on. That was desperately needed oxygen for Nick's career and ego.

It was fascinating watching Conte's transformation during rehearsals. He had dropped the Burgess Meredith mannerisms, his distinctive way of speaking, the way he walked. Nick Conte became Mike Ambler. It didn't happen overnight. Raphaelson worked with Conte hour after hour to keep his performance authentic and not a transparent imitation. I realized Abbott knew exactly what he was doing by cruelly tearing Conte's interpretation to shreds.

The play opened January 15, 1942 at the Hudson Theater to lukewarm reviews. Alexander Knox took most of the hits and in due time left the play to be replaced by Lee J. Cobb.

Abbott had me change my name because Abraham Knox, he said, was too close to Alexander Knox. Or was it too Jewish for the part of an Irish kid? So I ended up on the playbill as Knox Stevens. A fancy name for an aspiring actor.

Cobb's wife also joined the cast, replacing, to my sorrow, Helen Walker. I had a crush on Helen, she was friendly but it stopped there—until I picked up our friendship when I got to Hollywood.

From his first rehearsal, Cobb appeared uncomfortable in the part of Jason and was never really at ease. Mr. and Mrs. Cobb were not on speaking terms, which bemused the rest of the cast. There was an underlying animosity between them, especially in their most tender moments. When some of us gathered at one of the nearby watering holes, after the show, we replayed their lines of affection, laced with arsenic.

As Nick Conte's understudy, I had rehearsed and learned the part of Mike Ambler, but I never got a chance to perform it. Nick was healthy and having too much fun playing the colorful character of Mike Ambler. Several years later I did tour in the play, playing the Mike Ambler part, with Franchot Tone as Jason and Betsy Von Furstenberg as his wife.

After Nick got decent notices from the critics, he became cocky, as a reaction, I imagine, to the terrible criticism he was hit with by Abbott during the rehearsals.

After *Jason* had folded, I toured the Subway Circuit (Brooklyn, Queens, Manhattan, and New Jersey. No subway in Jersey, so what?) with *Jason* and *Native Son*. I then auditioned for the Little Neck Summer Theater on Long Island, was accepted and was cast in several lead roles during the ten-week season.

As a teenager, the girls I went to school with were untouchable, and I mean that literally. The late thirties were not like the nineties. It was more like a century back. Teenagers are horny as hell and the only relief, aside from a hand job, was a whore. A couple of my pals and I tried that. It was a disaster. We were nervous and scared and the lady was no help. She wasn't going to waste much time on three high school kids. We paid the two dollars and left the way we came in—virgins.

On New Year's Eve, 1941, all the apartments in Lady's building were available for the festivities and I wandered from one to another. I finally settled next to Brooke Fleming, could she be the one?

I had turned twenty on Christmas Eve and was eagerly, fervidly ready to dive into deep sexual waters, but I was adrift in ignorance. That night, the last of 1941, I yearned for reality—I simply wanted to get laid. But how? I wanted Brooke but failed to make a move. We talked until eventually she wandered away.

At about three in the morning I went up to the chicken coop. Rarey was visiting his girl, soon to be Mrs. Rarey, so I was alone. It was a beautiful night. The moon shone through a cloudless sky into the large windows. I lay in bed wondering how it all worked. Why wasn't it easier to get laid?

Then the door opened and there she stood in the doorway, her nightgown shining in the moonlight. Minutes went by and Brooke didn't move. I froze.

It took an image to get me to speak: The image of Humphrey Bogart, quietly tough, in *Casablanca*. "Close the door and get into bed or leave," I whispered hoarsely, not as seductive as Bogey, but to my great surprise—and fear—it worked.

She closed the door and slowly moved to the bed, stood for a moment and ghost-like, allowed her nightgown to slip to the floor. In the moonlight her naked body was beautiful. It was the first time I had seen a nude woman and the wonder of her beauty touched the center of my being.

Brooke finally slid under the covers of my narrow bed. Well, we all know when you get what you wish for . . . I wondered, what do I do now?

Believe this: I hopped out of bed, quickly dressed, and said, "I'll be right back, don't leave." I jogged to Penn Station about fifteen blocks away where I found an all-night pharmacy. I bought a packet of condoms and ran back to Brooke, suddenly tormented; what a jackass, what if she's not there?

She was still in bed. Man, was I relieved. Thinking back, I smile, but I'm chagrined at my naiveté when I was twenty.

It was the best of times. As an actor I was working constantly and I had found a mate—Brooke Fleming. Her warmth and affection gave my ego a great lift. One can define "love" as an ache or, on the other hand, the sensation of a soaring heart. Neither applied to me. I did have a sense of well-being, of destiny holding my hand. I valued Brooke's generosity in focusing on me, on fulfilling a young man's seven-year fantasy of exhilarating sex, on making that elusive dream come true—a steady lay.

Rarey was tickled and delighted that I had connected with Brooke. Several months before I was drafted, Uncle Sam sent Rarey greetings and he was off to basic training. He was evaluated and judged to be a good candidate for pilot training. Rarey told them they had to be mistaken, he had never even driven an automobile. But the Army got it right: Rarey became a fighter pilot and was finally shipped off to England.

1943–46 U.S. Army—London—Paris

Drafted. First marriage. Troopship to England

T he U.S. Army called by way of a postcard: I was drafted. The date of my induction was September 5, 1942. Active duty began September 19, 1942. I was sent to Macon, Georgia to train as a medic and was stationed in the States three months, twelve days; overseas, three years four days.

However, before shipping out, I had a three-day pass. Brooke met me in Newark (the troopship was to leave from a Jersey port). She talked me into marrying her before going overseas. I wasn't hot for the idea; I felt it was a mistake while the war was going on. But she persisted and I thought what the hell, she had been a fine companion for the last nine months and I owed her. At least she would receive a small monthly spousal payment from the Army. So we headed for Arlington, Virginia where it took half a day to get hitched. Our parting was not sad at all; Brooke was happy to be a bride and I welcomed the adventure into the unknown.

The troopship I was stuffed into left for England on January 5, 1943. A pleasure cruise it wasn't. A visit to the ship's galley left me hopelessly seasick. The walls were crawling with cockroaches. When I asked one of the Chinese cooks, "What the hell is that?," he pointed to the cockroaches, giggled, and said, "Raisin cake, raisin cake." That was my only visit to the galley, leaving me on a starvation diet for nine days. The ship zigzagged across the Atlantic to avoid Nazi submarine torpedoes, adding three days to the crossing. When the ship docked in England on January 14, I experienced the joy of one being rescued from an angry sea.

I was stationed in London for about a year as a medical assistant in the 7th General Dispensary. When the Army discovered that I was an actor, they ordered me to the Special Service Unit as Entertainment Director.

The officer in charge of the unit told me, "You're not a pill pusher any longer; let's see what you're made of. You are now the host of "A Yank in London," a weekly interview show on the BBC. Are you up to it?" The assignment took me by surprise, but being well-known for my unerring riposte, I said, "Huh?"

Before the army, I had acted on radio with a script in front of me, but on the BBC show there was nothing. Needless to say, I sweated through the first couple of interviews. However, guests like John Huston, Irwin Shaw, and Bill Saroyan were articulate and voluble, making the program interesting and entertaining. John Huston was a fine talker; his timing was excellent, for the most part slow-time, always emphasizing the key word. Irwin was blunt and intelligent; Saroyan had his own peculiar slant, whimsical and amusing.

One evening Shaw, Saroyan, and I went to see *The Merchant of Venice*. The house was sold out so we stood in the back of the theater. Saroyan leaned against the wall under a dim light reading a copy of the play he had brought with him, cackling now and then, commenting when an actor had either missed a passage or got it wrong. He persisted during the whole performance, paying no attention to the people in the back rows hushing him.

The radio program was also beamed to the States. I interviewed officers and G.I.s, concentrating on their feelings about the English, their beefs or opinions on army life and other sporty things like women and pub crawling. I had fun doing it, but I had to drop it because, dumb to the difficulties, I got involved in putting a musical together to entertain the Allied troops. We were given the biggest theater in London, the Queens.

There were a couple of talented guys in my Special Service Unit. One of them wrote the lyrics, the other the music; I wrote the book, which was not very elaborate. The show was called *Three Joes in a Jam.*

I had played a lot of hookey while in a Brooklyn high school, going to Minsky's Burlesque. I loved Minsky's. To me it was heaven, not only watching, bug-eyed, as the silvery tassels twirled fifty times a second around the nipples of the strippers, but the comics, man they fascinated me. I recalled their funniest skits and put them all in the musical.

I found a dozen ladies from the Women's Army Corps (WAC) for the chorus line. As the director, I had first choice and chose the prettiest WAC as my companion: Linda Mae Hunt, from (where else?) Huntsville, Alabama. She was a sweet, shy Southern girl but the logistics of an army at war finally separated us.

Once again, no good deed goes unpunished. The captain assigned to aid us with the musical was, from the beginning, a fat pain in the ass. He rejected everything I requested: props, costumes, simple sets, stagehands. I had to scrounge to get what I needed to put the show on. God only knows why he was in the unit. He had never been inside a theater. Before the army he was a hotel clerk. Now being a hotel clerk ain't a bad job; especially when guests check in, you wink when they claim to be husband and blonde wife and the "husband" drops a twenty in the palm of your hand.

I soon realized he wanted to sabotage the show. He was a prude and thought the lyrics were obscene (they weren't). He was too stupid to realize he would get most of the credit and probably make major.

Opening night, the theater was jammed—it was free to anyone in uniform. And there was a lot of brass, including General Devers, the head honcho of the London area. He came backstage with his aides after the show. The Captain beamed as the general praised his leadership in putting the show on. Like a maddened submarine commander, I launched my torpedo—a tirade of disrespect aimed at the captain for the lack of help I had gotten from him. The general and his aides beat a quick retreat.

The following day the captain, his uniform newly pressed, his shoes shined and a fierce look in his eyes, busted Corporal Knox to private. He had performed his military duty for the day.

Despite the German bombers, the buzz-bombs and the V2s, London was the heart of the war effort to defeat the Nazis and an exciting place to be. Months before the invasion of France, one could sense the acceleration of the city's heartbeat.

I always looked forward, with high good feelings, to seeing George Rarey. We met a few times in London with his fighter pilot friends and once I was invited to visit the 379th Fighter Squadron in the village of Wormingford.

When they got two or three days off, Rarey and his buddies came to London to shed the tension, the stress of fighter missions—two in a day at times. They came to drink, to find a few hours of distraction. They wanted fun, they wanted laughter, anything to ease the darkness of ever-present death and the ever-present ache in their souls.

Since our days in the "chicken coop" in New York, Rarey didn't seem to have changed; his friendship was warm, generous, and against all odds, he was still devoid of cynicism. Yet he had changed, he looked older, worn down.

At dinner one night we were all feeling the good scotch we had drunk and laughing a little too much when a fucking bomb exploded close enough to shake the plaster loose over our heads, rattle the tables and knock the lights out. That brought on gales of high-pitched laughter.

One weekend, I got a two-day pass and took the train to Rarey's airbase in Wormingford. It was early spring but it was cold. The sky was gray and it was damp. The pilots were out on the second mission that day and I watched as they flew back in, roaring as they sped down the landing strip. They were P47s (Thunderbolts), not as graceful as the P38 or the English Mosquito. The P47 was chunky and blunt-nosed, but the men who flew them loved them for their power and reliability.

Watching them taxi in, I thought, "Man, that's what I should be doing." The air smelled of burned fuel, hot landing tires, and adventure. It was a pipe dream; I was nearsighted and in any case would have made a lousy pilot.

Rarey and I corresponded often. He drew P47s flying across the envelopes and the letters. He loved that aircraft and the men he flew with loved Rarey; that was clear to me when I saw them together. He had a kind of stability that was rare among the fighter pilots I got to know.

The last time I saw Rarey, I joined him and the others in their Nissen hut (the Nissen hut, where the men lived, was made of prefabricated corrugated tin, shaped like a cylinder cut in half lengthwise and rested on its flat side). We sat around a potbellied stove. Not a word was said. They stared at the stove, still in their flying suits, their faces showing the form of their goggles. They were too exhausted to wash. I didn't dare ask what had happened during the mission.

I stayed the night on one of the cots and left for London early morning. I never saw Rarey again.

Sometime in July, 1944, I got a visit from Rarey's closest friend in his squadron. His face was gray. He stared at me, then turned his gaze to the ground. A chill streamed down my body and I sensed a dreadful foreboding.

We went for a drink and, tears sliding down his cheeks, he told me that Rarey had been shot down over France about a month earlier, on June 27th.

Although he couldn't drive a car, Rarey told me he loved flying, but he hated strafing. He was shot down strafing German military trucks—decoys to lure fighters to camouflaged antiaircraft artillery hidden a short distance from the trucks.

As the years passed, I often tried to find where Rarey was buried. I had no idea where his wife Betty Lou was, or anyone who might know. I wrote or called all related government agencies in my search for Rarey's grave, but all I had was his name, that he flew

Thunderbolts and was based in England. No one was helpful; more information was needed. I called the military cemetery in Arlington. Rarey wasn't there.

It's a strange way to get a laugh—trying to find where a dead wartime buddy is buried. But bureaucrats can be ludicrous: I wrote a letter to Veterans Affairs, detailing what I knew, emphasizing that Rarey was a fighter pilot who flew Thunderbolts. The letter was returned to me stapled to a form for me to fill out. The form? A request to locate a deceased Civil War soldier.

By chance, the information I sought saw daylight. My friend Gore Vidal told former U.S. senator James Abourezk to look me up in Rome. He did and we became good friends. He introduced me to Karen Heitkotter in 1993; she was the private secretary to the American Ambassador to Italy. She and I had dinner a few times and I invited her to an Italian party or two.

I had recently received the Veterans Affairs form regarding dead Civil War soldiers and mentioned it to Karen. She asked me to give her all the details I knew about Rarey. I wrote down the little I knew and suggested she not lose time, since it would probably be hopeless.

Two days later she asked that I come to her office. She handed me an envelope containing a fax from Colonel Roger King of the Department of Defence 50th Anniversary of World War II Commemoration Committee, dated, 13 January 94:

Karen: Following is the information you are seeking on the Downed Airman: Captain George Rarey, Service number 0-79-3536
379th Fighter Squadron, 362nd Fighter Group.
Died on 27 June 1944
Normandy American (cemetery), St. Laurent-sur-Mer, France,
Plot F, Row 14, Grave #25

A week later I stood over Grave 25 at the American Cemetery in Normandy.

There were acres of white crosses, interrupted by a Jewish star here and there, on the green bluff overlooking the beaches. A cold, wet, wintery wind sprayed a light drizzle on the graves. I was numb. Well, it was cold.

Betty Rarey eventually married Rarey's best friend in his squadron. As a civilian he tested aircraft and was killed when the plane he was flying failed its test.

But Betty had a son, Damon Rarey, who had never seen his father, having been born while Rarey was in England. Damon and I recently met. He's a fine sweet man just like his old man.

1944 London

Life in wartime London. Shipped to France.
War over, I remain in Paris.

I rwin Shaw was a literary hero of mine. He had written a stunning play, *Bury the Dead*, set during World War I, in which dead young soldiers refuse to be buried, having died for no good reason.

Irwin introduced me to the Little French Club. I was billeted nearby, off Green Park and Piccadilly. It was practically around the corner on a short narrow lane off St. James Street. Much too convenient. I became a regular.

In my teens I had read the expatriate American writers living in France. They seduced me. I yearned to one day visit France and experience its beauty. The Little French Club was for me the first step to the real thing.

Alwyn Vaughn, a large, imposing woman, ran the place. She had started the club for the men and women of the Free French Army stationed in London. She loved France and the French. Although it was in back of the Ritz Hotel and in a tony part of London, it was, by far, the cheapest place for booze and a meal in the city. The congenial atmosphere was enough to attract Americans like Irwin Shaw, John Huston, movie director, Anatole Litvak, and William Saroyan. All ardent, instant lovers of the French after paying about fifteen cents for a shot of good Scotch and a dollar for a good French meal.

It wasn't a large place, about a dozen tables covered with red, checkered tablecloths and the air had the pleasant smell of English and Gauloise tobacco. It did have a substantial bar and Alwyn had her own seat at the end of it, hardly ever leaving. And she drank steadily. After a couple of hours her glasses would slip to a forty-five degree angle and they would stay that way until she staggered out at the end of the night.

Elsbeth Grant, a thin, fortyish, not unattractive journalist for the *Express*, a London paper, was a regular at the Little French Club. She was amiable, liked to drink and chat about America, a country she had never visited.

She enjoyed flirting and not so subtly suggested we could have nice fun, given the chance. But her eyes belied that cute idea. She was an avocational teaser.

What bothered but fascinated me was how she felt when she met Hitler before the war. "He's so attractive, so handsome, so sexy, and I must say it, inspiring." She seemed love-struck and I was dumb-struck. Any thought of coupling with the lady vanished.

She had seen me in a play, *The Eve Of St. Mark,* put on by the Red Cross for the troops at the Scala Theater in London. (It had been a successful Broadway play by Maxwell Anderson.) Knowing I was an actor, she asked if I'd like to review John Geilgud's Hamlet, for the *Express*. The play was to open soon and already had her editor's approval.

Once again, before thinking, I dived in. I had read the play, but review it in a London paper? I had more courage than brains. So, I went to the play and was enthralled by Geilgud's performance.

I went back to my billet and spent a couple of hours trying to write the review. It wasn't easy. I didn't understand many of the speeches because of the English accent and the speed of delivery so it was difficult to write a coherent sentence. I must have written about two hundred words and thought that Elsbeth would shape it so it would be acceptable. Well, she or her editor gave it a crew cut because what appeared in the paper was my byline and, "I like the play and thought John Geilgud was wonderful as Hamlet." That was it!

I took a bit of solace in the fact that the *Express*, during wartime, only had four pages and had no room for a two-hundred-word review, good or bad.

In April of 1944 I was transferred to the Signal Corps, sending and receiving coded messages. The volume of traffic increased tenfold until it all stopped a couple of days before D-Day—the invasion of France, June 6, 1944.

Aside from the nightly air raids, London was a fascinating place to be. Although there wasn't a London street that didn't suffer bomb damage, the English were remarkably optimistic. When the expected German invasion of England didn't materialize, morale shot up. Then came the V-Is (buzz bombs), followed by the V-2 rockets. And we lived with them. Except for the times we G.I.s were assigned the grisly task of digging out the dead.

There was a theory, spread no doubt, by G.I.s, that fucking standing up would avoid getting pregnant. The second rumor that logically followed the first rumor was that air raids make men and women horny. Girls serving tea and crumpets in canteens run by civilians for the Allied troops were lovely and willing—as were the girls in uniform.

The genius who created London phone booths deserves a knighthood. The booths are beautiful, roomy, and ideal shelter from rain and falling antiaircraft shrapnel. And perfect for girls and boys to merrily fuck standing up. The nightly blackouts supplied the necessary privacy.

In October, 1944 my Signal Corps unit was assigned to cross the English Channel and join the war in Europe. I was given a truck loaded with signal equipment to drive to Paris.

The truck and I were in the hold of a Landing Ship Tank (LST). I was asleep in the cab when we were accidentally rammed by an Allied ship. The sound was terrifying; the hold was sealed so there was no escape. My heartbeat jumped and I was ready to give up the ghost. But the LSTs were built for war and the only result was a dent in the hull. We hit the beach, the hold opened and its immense ramp slowly lowered. I drove my truck onto French soil and joined a convoy of other Signal Corps trucks on the drive to Paris.

Paris was liberated from the Germans by the Americans, the Free French Army, and the French Partisan Fighters on August 25, 1944. When I got there at the end of October, the French were still ecstatic and in love with Americans. And for me it was love at first sight. The beauty of Paris moved me to a constant state of joy. Hemingway had seeded the yearning to experience Paris, but Paris proved lovelier to the eye than a writer's description.

I explored the city whenever I had free time. I got lucky the day I wandered into a bar on Rue des Petits Champs, a short, narrow street off Avenue de l'Opera. It was an inviting street and an inviting bar. But I must admit, most bars beckoned to me at that time. I'm not copping a plea when I say that it wasn't only the booze that beckoned me, that it was also the action one might find in bars.

I hit the jackpot when an attractive young woman invited me to sit with her. She owned the bar! Georgette was her name and she was a charmer. I knew some simple French and she knew no English, but there was a mutual understanding as there always is when two people are drawn together by . . . a mysterious magnetism. Whatever the hell it was I couldn't resist the ineluctable desire—no, the need—to head right for Georgette whenever I had free time.

I soon invited my best army buddy, Alex Nicol, and other friends to the bar. Georgette would close the joint to the public and the drinks were on the house. Alex hooked up with Georgette's friend, Gilberte, and we became a fun-loving jolly group.

Georgette and I fit well together. We were tuned in to each other and a romance blossomed. Before we could nourish the romance I was transferred out of Paris.

On May 7, 1945, the German Army surrendered unconditionally. I was in London at the time and joined the Brits in jubilantly celebrating the end of the war in Europe.

Eventually, my unit was assigned to Camp Lucky Strike to prepare for the war with Japan. Those camps were all named after cigarette brands. Today, it would be insanity to name an army camp after a brand of cigarettes.

It was a bad day when we were issued mosquito netting, antimalaria pills, and jungle equipment. I had been overseas for thirty months and I was prematurely sick to my stomach at the thought of being sent by ship to the Far East.

But hold on, there was a long shot. I knew about an outfit just outside of Paris called the Soldier Show Company. It was a complicated plan, but the nub is I faked orders transferring me to the Soldier Show Company. It worked and I returned to Paris and Georgette's arms.

The Soldier Show Company was a droll place; it was part actor's stock company and part G.I. outfit. We actors were free from morning reveille or any other kind of formation. We had few restrictions, one being a sticky regulation—officer, G.I relations.

Our quarters were in a large, walled-in area in Chatou, a village a short distance outside Paris. The officer's club was on a path that led directly to the mess hall from the G.I. living quarters, but we had to walk about a mile around the wall for our meals because enlisted men were prohibited from walking by the officer's club.

I had invited Georgette and Gilberte to lunch in our mess hall. Sergeant Bob Ellis, a friend of mine, was Gilberte's blind date. We were late for our meeting with the girls and I talked Bob into taking the shortcut past the officer's club. About twenty yards past the club we heard a booming command: "Sergeant!" Bob, being the ranking G.I., was busted down to private. (A couple of years later I was walking down Hollywood Boulevard when I was grabbed from behind and whirled around. It was Bob Ellis: "You sonofabitch, you owe me three hundred and fifty bucks! That's what I lost when you got me busted.")

Paddy Chayefsky was also in the unit. He was a kid from the Bronx: likeable and unassuming. He wanted to be a writer and had written some material for the Armed Service Radio Network. He was originally in the infantry and was quick to drop his pants to exhibit a scar on his buttock caused by shrapnel from a land mine. We became friends quickly, but we had different assignments and I didn't see much of him.

The warmth between Georgette and me went up several degrees. When we first met, she had two other lovers: A Basque gangster who bought the bar for her, and Andre, a young wine grower. Given the propinquity, I went from third to first place.

Atom bombs were dropped on Hiroshima and Nagasaki on August 6th and 9th and the Japanese surrendered August 14, 1945. G.I.s and the French were out once again parading down the Champs Elysées to celebrate the final end to World War II.

However, the day that is framed forever in my memory is April 12, 1945, when Franklin Delano Roosevelt suddenly died. Men, women, and children, all openly weeping wherever I wandered. It was a day of grieving and loss for a man no one on the streets of Paris had ever met. But Roosevelt had an aura of hope and optimism during the ugly years of Nazi occupation, and the French, not known for being sentimental, loved him for delivering them from the Boche.

The war was over. I requested that I be discharged from the U.S. Army in Paris. It finally came through January 9, 1946. I was a civilian. My mustering-out pay was $255.52.

Georgette and Paris—my two mistresses—kept me in France for a few more months. But after all, I had a wife, Brooke Fleming, and I did love New York. But those last months in Paris, January through mid-April, 1946, were the best antidote for forty months of army discipline.

1946 Paris—Azores

The Azores Adventure.

I t was time to go home. I was running out of money, and some bum had stolen my duffel bag with my change of clothes, leaving me with a shabby uniform and no civilian duds. I was legally a civilian, but still felt and looked like a G.I.

I knew the layout at Orly Airfield, having been there several times. I checked the listed departures and chose the one going to New York. They were all military planes, mostly C-47s, bucket seats, no hostess, not even a cushion to sit on during the long transatlantic flight, broken only by a short fueling stop at the Azores.

I sauntered to the C-47 as it was loading, went up the access ladder and entered the belly of the plane as if I belonged there. I was a stowaway. Easy as pie. I counted twenty passengers: six G.I.s, a couple of chicken colonels studying some military papers, two majors, six captains, and four lieutenants. They nodded to each other, smiled, or merely stared off into space.

The day the war ended everything about the army loosened up, like air slowly escaping from a huge punctured balloon. As long as I wore the uniform of the U.S. Army, I could become a passenger on a military aircraft and no one was there to check me out.

Once in the air I felt a slow creeping regret. After a few hours the regret turned to anxiety. Was I crazy, leaving Georgette? We had talked vaguely about her coming to the States, but there were no set plans. I had to get back to Paris. I went to the cockpit, chatted with the pilot, a captain, then casually asked him if I was on the manifest.

"Sure you are, soldier, or you wouldn't be here," he said and gave me a large, warm smile, showing a terrific set of ivories.

"You know, my orders were cut in a hurry; you oughta check the manifest to make sure my orders got to Orly in time," I suggested, looking concerned.

"Okay," he said, still smiling, and reached for a clipboard. "What's your name?" I told him and he ran his finger down the passenger list.

"Hot damn! Somebody goofed; you're not on the manifest. I'm awful sorry, kid, I got to stop at the Azores to refuel. I'll have to drop you off. I'm really sorry."

It worked. So far. Nonetheless, the Azores could be a major obstacle to getting back to Paree and sweet fucking.

I went from the plane, right after it taxied to a stop, to a cell in the guardhouse. The pilot must have radioed ahead. After an hour's wait, a sergeant told me we were going to see the commanding officer of the Island, a colonel. The sergeant was pleasant enough; he whispered that the colonel was chicken shit and to watch my step. I forgot I was a civilian and felt a blush of shame—I was unshaven, my uniform baggy, my shoes and trousers muddy after the walk from the plane to the guardhouse across a field of puddles.

The door to the colonel's office opened. The sight startled me; it was luxurious. The carpet was a beauty. His desk looked to be antique. There were paintings on the walls, the room softly lit by floor lamps. The colonel's uniform was sharply pressed; the buttons and the silver eagles on his shoulders were polished and he had an impressive set of ribbons on his chest.

I needed a drink of water. My mouth was dry. I didn't know if I could speak. A colonel was more ominous to me than a general. A colonel bucking for general is made mean by his ambition.

The colonel gestured for me to sit in a chair facing his desk. The chair was a graceful antique, or at the least an excellent copy. I hesitated, instinctively brushed the seat of my pants and carefully sat. I was aware of a clock ticking loudly. I glanced to the left corner of the room: goddamn, a huge grandfather clock, its pendulum gliding back and forth.

The colonel finally spoke, his voice pinched by anger. "Soldier, why were you on that C-47?"

"Trying to get home, sir, I . . ."

He cut in. "Did you commit some crime, were you escaping justice?"

"No, sir, I didn't commit any crime or anything like that, I just wanna go home. I been overseas three years," I said, too whiny.

"I'm going to keep you here until I have you thoroughly checked out with the military and French police in Paris, no matter how long that takes." His eyes glinted with satisfaction.

"But, sir, you can't hold me; I didn't do anything."

"I am the commanding officer here. I can do what I think is the right thing to do. If you are a felon, and I believe you are, I'll find that out. You are dismissed. Sergeant!" he shouted. The door opened and the sergeant entered. "Sir?" he snapped out.

"Take this man back to the guardhouse."

"Yes, sir!" he said smartly and stepped aside to allow me through the door.

The sergeant had left the motor running in the jeep. It coughed as he stepped on the gas and spurted away along the muddy road. It was as cold as a witch's tit.

There was little heat in the guardhouse. The sergeant got me an extra blanket. Dinner was a C-ration, cold and tasteless. Sleep escaped me until the early morning.

Four miserable days went by. The weather was rainy, gray, disheartening. Georgette invaded my thoughts and troubled my dreams.

I drank a lot of coffee; I was wired, ready to snap. Finally, the sergeant led me to the jeep and drove me to see the colonel once again.

I felt good when the sergeant told me the reply from Paris was negative. I even felt cocky. And feeling cocky has haunted me all my life. I lost a wife to macho cockiness.

When I was ushered into the colonel's office, I knew he had nothing on me, but what did he have up his sleeve? He kept silent long enough for doubt to nibble at my confidence. Then he spoke:

"At this point, no communications about you, but something will pop, I'm sure of that. In any case, young man, if they find you aren't a felon, you're shipping out with the first supply ship leaving here for the Pacific. That means at least three months working your way back on a freighter. You must pay for stowing away on a military aircraft."

For once I kept my mouth shut. I remembered how sick I was on the troopship sailing to England. Around the world on a filthy freighter? No way, man.

I had my serious look on. "I wrote four letters, sir, to President Truman (pause), General Marshall (pause), Secretary of War Stimson (pause), and General Eisenhower. I gave the letters to one of the men ordered back to the States yesterday. If he doesn't hear from me within three days, he's to mail the letters. Sir, I want to go back home and I'd rather not send those letters."

"What did you say in those letters?" the colonel asked.

"In the letters I stated my case: Served in the army for three and a half years, three of those years overseas. I was honorably discharged in France, ran out of money, and hitched a ride on a C-47 going to New York. Put in jail in the Azores and although the commanding officer was informed by the military police and the French police that I was not wanted, he said he intended to keep me in the guardhouse until he was absolutely sure I was innocent of breaking the law, no matter how long it took. I wrote that I was a civilian and that the military had no authority to hold me, that I couldn't wait to get home to my wife and family. I urged them to rescue me from a colonel exceeding his function of command by punishing me for hitching a ride home."

"You can cable him from here, soldier. Inform your friend not to send those letters," the colonel said quickly, too eagerly.

I had the bastard. "Sir, you know I'm a civilian, you have no authority to keep me here. I believe General Marshall will agree with me."

The colonel dropped his mean look. He held out a box of Cuban cigars and offered me my pick. "Have one, Mr. Knox, they're fine Cuban cigars."

Mr. Knox, the civilian—well, well. "Sir, I don't believe I'll cable from here." There I was, being cocky again, but my instinct told me it was the way to go. I wanted him pissed off at me; if he felt a measure of compassion, I'd be on the next plane to New York and that was not my objective.

And he did get pissed off. "Sergeant," he shouted, "I want to speak to you, then you can take Mr. Knox back to his cell."

I swear, I swaggered out, but not before I turned to the colonel and smiled. I caught the look in his eye; murder.

In the jeep driving back, the sergeant poked me, hard. "You son of a dog, ya'all done it, he's shipping ya back to Paris on a C-47 coming through tonight to refuel. Ya'all sure are one clever Yankee."

I didn't think I was "one clever Yankee." I thought it was a miracle. Where the hell do ideas come from? Necessity? Survival? How the hell did I dream up the letters?

When we took off for Paris, I felt as though I were rising to heaven. I was too thrilled with my "victory" to entertain the idea that, true to form, the colonel might have planned a nasty surprise for my arrival—an armed reception.

The C-47 taxied to a stop, the props fluttered and slowly petered out. Up into the plane came two MPs with sidearms. They escorted me out of the plane, into a jeep and back into the guardhouse.

Once again, a nice-guy sergeant appeared. He told me the colonel on the Azores had cabled with instructions to hold me and investigate me thoroughly, no matter how long it took.

As the first few hours slipped by, I began to lose my bravado to a depressing, sinking feeling. I tried to shake it, but my resolve was dissipating. Thinking of the letters sparked a welcome thought: David Shoenbrun. David was a war correspondent for one of the radio networks in the States. We had become good friends while I was stationed in Paris.

I asked the sergeant if I could make a call. He shook his head, but said, "I gotta take a leak. Grab yourself a coffee in my office, I'll be back soon," and let me out of my cell.

I called David, found him in (lucky break) and quickly told him what had happened and where I was. He told me not to worry, he'd come get me as quickly as possible. He'd also try to reach Georgette.

David got through to me at the guardhouse and told me he was on his way to bring me back to Paris. He had contacted a friend at the American Embassy, who called the ranking MP officer at Orly and insisted he release me, a civilian, immediately.

David was at Orly airfield quicker than I expected; it was still daylight. He was in his olive drab correspondent's uniform with the proper shoulder patch.

When David meant business, he bustled. He bustled into the guardhouse, accompanied by an MP captain. My cell door was opened. David put his arm around my shoulder and led me out; I was a free man.

Across the road in front of the airport entrance, David had a surprise for me. Georgette. She waved when she saw me in David's jeep. He pulled up, I jumped out and, like the end of a B movie, she rushed into my arms. Tears streamed down my face.

1946 Paris—New York—Washington, D.C.—Miami—Hollywood

Back to the States. Divorce Brooke, marry Georgette. Hollywood film contract. First movie, I Walk Alone, *with Burt Lancaster and Kirk Douglas.*

David Shoenbrun proved to be a good friend, but he, like most of the journalist crowd I knew, had a crush on Georgette. The girl was irresistible. David, not being a creepy sneak, begged me to let him make love to her. How do you tell a friend he's a fucking idiot? I didn't want to show my contempt and coolly said, "I don't own the girl, plead your case with her."

He made his case with Georgette and being French, she said, "pourquoi pas?" She later reported to me, and others, that the man was shortchanged. The word spread. It was the price he paid for sleeping with my girl.

I was flat broke. Although it sure was tempting, I couldn't stay and live off Georgette, a sure way to lose her. But how to get home? I could work my way across on a ship and get back with a few bucks in my pocket. I have to admit that I resisted the idea, but I had no choice, and didn't have the guts to go the air route again.

We had arranged for Georgette to come to the States in June. She had booked passage on a ship loaded with civilians and brides-to-be.

She came with me to Le Havre, where I was hoping to sign onto the first ship to New York. In two days I was hired to work in the galley of the *New Amsterdam*, a Dutch ship.

The night before leaving, I thought I could bank orgasms. I made love to Georgette four times, thinking the memory of that night would suffice until she docked in New Jersey. Not true. Distance might make the heart grow fonder, but there's no doubt it also makes you hornier.

The purser of the ship who signed me on was an American and when he saw my name he asked if I was married to Brooke Fleming. I was taken by surprise and after a long pause, I said, "Yeah, who are you?" "Great!" he shouted, "I'm her cousin. I'll wire her from the ship to meet us." I shoulda said "Brooke who?" The last one I wanted to see at the dock was Brooke. I pleaded with him not to send the wire because I wanted to surprise her. He winked, smiled and playfully hit my shoulder. I almost jumped ship.

The trip over was a nightmare. I was seasick most of the time, but there was no respite from work in the stinking galley. The cook could have made a career in Hollywood. He was a big man with a huge torso, bulging belly, heavy arms, and a bullet-bald head, the image of a brutal Nazi. He was relentlessly angry and gave me no time to lie down during the worst spells of seasickness.

He was right. I worked through the stomach turnovers and the weakness in my gut. I got to know how sailors feel when they have to dominate the heaving and the throbbing headaches. It wasn't a major test, but thanks to the bullet-headed Dutchman, I passed it.

When we docked in New York, the purser paid the crew. It felt good picking up my wages for the week; I had earned it. The purser told me a surprise awaited me. Oh, shit, he wired Brooke.

I debarked through the crew exit, which avoided the crowd waiting at the central gangplank. Brooke was there but didn't see me.

I had a sense of dread, but I knew I had to face her; there was no way out. I went directly to the house on Seventh Avenue and 18th Street. A note was stuck on her door: "If I miss you at the dock wait for me, I'll be right back." So I waited. Man, I wanted to fly the coop before she came but I had no stomach for guilt.

She came running up the steps and rushed into my arms. "Let's go in," I said. She sensed my coolness, sat down and asked what was troubling me. I was going to wing it. A mistake. The words I needed would not come to mind. Then I did something shameful. I wanted to hurt her so she would despise me and order me the hell out of her apartment. I showed her a photo of Georgette and mumbled, "She's French and she's coming to join me . . . listen, I have to catch a train, my family is waiting for me." Brooke began tearing up and pleaded with me to stay the night. I left her sitting in her chair, silently crying.

There was no escaping the guilt. It ate at me the moment I walked out of the apartment and continued on the train to Washington, D.C.

I got to 755 Princeton Place in Washington. As I started up the steps to the house, a big guy I didn't recognize came down and hugged me.

Jesus, it was my little brother Carl. He was a kid when I left almost five years earlier. My other little brother, Seymour, was three years younger than Carl and still a little kid. He stared at me, then smiled warmly. It was an awkward evening. I couldn't make connections. I kept seeing Brooke sitting in her chair.

The day came to meet Georgette's ship. Nate, my stepfather, my mother, and I drove up to New York in the family's Dodge. I checked with the shipping line for the time of arrival and location of the dock. I was stung to hear that the ship had arrived earlier than scheduled and the passengers were already disembarking. The dock was just south of Newark in the port of Bayonne.

We were going to be way late. I cursed my bad luck and prodded Nate to speed it up. When we got to the dock the ship was there, but the passengers had all disembarked and were gone. The dock was empty of people, except for the guard. I asked him if he remembered seeing a French girl looking for someone to meet her. Yes, he had . . . actually there were two French girls. They were the last passengers on the dock and they had finally taken a taxi together. What the hell do I do now?

New Jersey taxis could drive passengers to New York, but they had to return to Jersey before they could pick up another fare. We drove back to the New York side of the Holland Tunnel. I got out of the car and stopped every cab with Jersey plates on its way back to Jersey and asked the driver if he had driven a couple of French girls to New York. It seemed hopeless, until about the fifteenth cab: Yes, he had taken two French women to a hotel on 59th street. He couldn't recall its name, but it sounded French.

I ran back to our car and had Nate speed to 59th Street where I spotted the Hotel St. Moritz. Bingo!

Before I hustled into the lobby of the hotel, I knew she'd be there. And there she was, sitting deep in a large armchair, unsmiling, grim. But her eyes lit up in surprise when she saw me.

She was a big hit with my family, especially my kid brothers. Although she knew hardly any English, she seemed to fit right in, especially in the kitchen. She was a good cook.

Georgette and I went to Miami for my divorce; six weeks' residence and you were free. I worked on a construction site hauling buckets of cement up two and three floors. There were no huge construction cranes then. It was plain old hard labor. Georgette got a beauty of a tan sunbathing on South Beach, always surrounded by a gang of young studs.

Getting married in Arlington, Virginia had an advantage; it only took one day—no three-day waiting period and my family lived in Washington, providing us with a place to stay. So in 1964 we were married in Arlington, where I had married Brooke Fleming three years earlier. Georgette was then my second marriage. (The third time, the same clerk was still there. Twenty years had gone by since the first civil ceremony. She looked up, examined me for a moment, then said, "You again?") I don't believe Joan, my third wife, ever forgave me for marrying her in Arlington.

• • •

We found a small apartment in New York on Second Avenue and 59th Street. I had to make do with the "52-20 club": twenty bucks a week for fifty-two weeks for unemployed veterans. However, rents were low in 1946 ($30 a month for us) so we could squeeze through the month without falling too far in debt.

We saw a lot of my old army buddies, Alex Nicol, Paddy Chayefsky, and Mark Blitzstein, a composer and playwright I had met when he was a guest on the interview program I had in London during the war. He wrote *The Cradle Will Rock*, a play with music that caused an upheaval in the theater during the Great Depression. It dramatized the crisis and unrest among the working people in the country at the time. Mark was an articulate force in the fight for social justice and struggle for a leftward turn in politics.

He was also an important influence in my political education. Although I was weaned on Red politics, Mark reinforced those beliefs. He also advanced my career as an actor—he introduced me to Irene Lee, Hal Wallis's New York representative. We had a good meeting and she suggested I see Hal Wallis when he next came to New York.

Hal Wallis had been with Warner Brothers since the mid-twenties. He started in public relations, became a producer, and eventually rose to head of production. He produced *Casablanca* among many other successful films during the thirties and early forties. He then became one of the first important independent producers in Hollywood. He had his offices at Paramount Studios, the film company that financed and distributed his movies.

Wallis came to New York sometime in November, 1946 and I met with him at his hotel. He introduced himself and asked, "Why are you wearing an army trench coat?"

"It's the only coat I have," I replied. Snappy, memorable dialogue. (When I got discharged in Paris, my G.I. issue overcoat was shabby and dirty and I replaced it with an officer's trench coat. I had always admired its dashing look.)

That was the end of the interview, which took place in the doorway of Wallis's suite. But he did call Irene Lee to tell her to sign me to a seven-year contract. I guess the coat impressed him.

I had a Hollywood contract! Celebration time indeed. I was to get $350 a week, not bad at all in 1946. Georgette soon calculated my monthly and yearly salary. A French mind at work—where's the money and how much is it? Practical people.

Hollywood! Mecca for young actors. The first day we arrived, we walked along Hollywood Boulevard. Well, Georgette walked and I floated. She wasn't impressed, but she did admire the weather.

At first we stayed in a small hotel, then a rooming house and finally a small, two-story Spanish-style house on Sarah Street in the San Fernando Valley. It was ideal and idyllic: a large lawn and a lovely oak in front of the house, a two-car garage, a back patio and about a half acre of walled-in ground back of the lawn. The original owner of the house also owned Rin Tin Tin, the first film star dog and apparently buried somewhere behind the wall.

Georgette was a smash hit in Movietown; her French accent, French charm, and French sex appeal were the ticket. Curt Conway, a buddy in the Soldier Show Company was coarsely blunt: "I can tell you now, the first chance I get, I'm going to fuck Georgette."

"Don't hang by your thumbs, Curt, you don't interest her," I said, and it was true; he didn't appeal to her at all. He's one of the players who never got to first base. But there were home-run hitters in the wings.

When I joined Wallis's "stable," the other actors he had under contract were Burt Lancaster, Kirk Douglas, Lisbeth Scott, and Wendall Corey. Wallis later brought Dean Martin, Jerry Lewis, Elvis Presley, and Shirley MacLaine to Hollywood.

Kirk Douglas began his career on the stage and eventually signed on with Wallis. As I got to know Kirk, it was clear that he was frustrated and unhappy. He was looking for that magic film that would rocket him to stardom. And he had that hard confidence in his talent, physical looks and determination that becoming a film star was his destiny.

Wallis didn't understand Kirk's talent, his possibilities. However, Kirk did understand Wallis' lack of enthusiasm. He asked Wallis to release him from his contract. Wallis agreed.

Kirk quickly scored. Wallis's mistake. Kirk appeared in *The Champion,* an enormously successful low-budget fight movie. It was Kirk's magic film; he was on his way to being a major film star for more than fifty years.

I also got to know Burt Lancaster, who told me how he had sat on the steps of a bungalow in Universal Studios waiting long after the appointment time to be interviewed by producer Mark Hellinger for the lead in *The Killers.* He finally got pissed off and was on his way out of the studio, determined to leave Hollywood, when the door to the bungalow opened and Burt was called back. *The Killers,* was Burt's first film and made him a star. It happened that quickly—one stage play, one film, and the brass ring was his.

Burt's second film was *Desert Fury* for Wallis, then *I Walk Alone*—my first film. The whole "mishpucha," Burt, Lisbeth, Kirk, and Wendall, was in that one.

I played a young killer. Not a big part, but showy. I got no sleep the night before my first day on the set, but when I walked onto that sound stage I was wide awake.

Burt was making $750 a week; I was making $350, but Burt was taller and they used to pay by height in those days.

Burt and I became friends the first day I worked on *I Walk Alone.* He approached me, introduced himself, and we compared notes. Where are you from? Were you in the army? How long have you been an actor? We both came from New York and that loosened the awkwardness between us.

In Burt's early films, it wasn't his ability as an actor that made him a leading player. He conveyed threat. The moment he appeared on screen you sensed it. He developed into a strong, convincing actor in the middle years of his career. He was, for a man who started acting in his thirties, the most adventurous actor in his choice of film roles.

Early on he chose *Come Back Little Sheba* in which he played Shirley Booth's husband, a middle-aged unattractive weakling. Other roles followed that not many male stars would have accepted. He played the *Birdman of Alcatraz*, a part Cary Grant or John Wayne never would have accepted. Burt received the Academy Award for best actor in *Elmer Gantry* in 1960. By the time he played the old man in *Atlantic City*, he had reached his peak as an actor.

He had a hunger to learn and he didn't just read novels; he read books on philosophy, biographies, autobiographies. There were countless nights we discussed and argued literature until two or three in the morning.

Burt had a deep appreciation for classical music. He especially dug chamber music. He was knowledgeable about composers, musicians, and opera singers. He knew many arias and, although his voice was untrained, rough actually, he would cut loose. When he sang there was a genuine joy on his face.

FAST FORWARD:

I met with Georgette in Paris many years after she divorced me. She told me then that she had been in love with Burt. That didn't surprise me; she was quite the coquette. We had seen the Lancasters often and the attraction between them was, on looking back, percolating.

The last time I saw Burt, we had lunch at his golf club. He was then in his midseventies and Georgette was seventy. Burt told me she had called him from Paris a few days earlier and asked him to join her for a cozy weekend. Burt chided her, "Georgette, we're in our seventies, for God's sake. Are you kidding?"

I don't think Burt meant to sting me, but he let me know after all those years that he had betrayed our friendship. Was that the reason he had invited me to lunch, to finally unburden himself? It didn't touch me at all.

1947 Hollywood

Burt Lancaster and Shelley Winters.
Arthur Penn double-crossed.

I first met Shelley Winters soon after I came to Hollywood. She was pretty, vivacious, and ambitious. When I worked on *Killer McCoy* at MGM she had a bit part. She and another girl slowly drove through the scene in which I was training for a championship fight. They waved at me and shouted, "Hi, champ!"

In the morning, before shooting started, she told me she had to be at Universal Studios for an important interview that afternoon. She was anxiously hoping they would film her scene in the morning so she could make the long drive to Universal and get there in time. I was pretty friendly with Roy Rowland, the director, and asked him when he planned to shoot the scene with the two girls who drove by as I trained outdoors. "In the afternoon," he said, I asked him if he could schedule it before the lunch break because one of the girls had an important interview in the afternoon. He thought for a moment and said, sure.

She made the interview and got the part—the lead opposite Ronald Coleman in *Double Life*. The film was a hit and she was noticed and talked about. Shelley Winters, the movie star, was born.

I read her autobiography and found that in writing about her lucky day, she completely forgot I was instrumental in arranging for her to be free in the afternoon. She credited the other girl in the car. She also got the name of the director wrong. When I called her on it she said, "So what, let him sue me." Always a bit careless, our Shelley.

Burt Lancaster and Shelley Winters? Yes. And it wasn't a shallow affair. It was a depth bomb.

Shelley, throughout the years, attracted a lot of men. I caught her on a TV talk show and she never missed a beat. Leading men were brought up by the host, who then turned to Shelley and she laughed her own personal merry laugh, and said "yeah, him too," making it obvious it was just a cute game she was playing.

Burt kept me informed. In the beginning he said it was no big deal, however, it soon became a big deal. Love has its devilish ways, and finally hooked Burt but good. Shelley was unpredictable, but her affair with Burt took on its own life.

Norma Lancaster could be a tough bird. She finally laid down the law when she felt she was losing Burt to Shelley. Burt knew the consequences would be dire if he left Norma for Shelley. (He used words like dire.)

So he began the painful business of cutting Shelley out of his life. Hard to believe, but he told me he would sit in his car across from Shelley's home for hours to check her male visitors. I could not visualize Burt slumped in his car, suffering, as he watched Shelley's guests come and go.

Many rumors swirled around Burt, as they do with most movie people. Some were true, some weren't—so what? Sure, he had his preferences, who doesn't, but they never included drugs or booze.

Burt's quick rise to stardom was accompanied by a rise in confrontations and power plays: first with Hal Wallis, then with directors. He learned fast that his movies were bringing in the moolah and he wanted his share. He told me that he and his agent, Harold Hecht, had had a meeting with Wallis, which had turned into a heated argument. Burt had a scary flash of temper and threatened to throw Wallis out the window. Shaken, Wallis agreed to dump the seven-year exclusive contract he had with Burt and write a picture deal, allowing Burt to accept outside films. The deal made Burt rich.

It didn't take long for Burt to flex his muscle. I heard him warn a well-known director that if the scene wasn't done Burt's way, one of them would have to go, and the director knew who that would be. Burt won that encounter.

He used his clout in the industry to give young directors, or would-be directors, the opportunity to prove their talent. He, in effect, hired John Frankenheimer to direct *Birdman of Alcatraz*. Burt had admired Frankenheimer's TV work and he starred in the first film Frankenheimer directed.

Sydney Pollack was a young actor who got a job coaching some kids in *The Young Savages*, a film Burt acted in. Burt got to talking to Sydney about a scene that troubled him. Sydney was intelligent and convincing when he offered his opinion. Burt asked if he had thought about becoming a director. Sydney said no. Burt told him he ought to consider it. In his blunt way, Burt told Sydney he probably could do a hell of a lot better than many of the bums in Hollywood directing movies. He then asked Sydney if he knew of Lew Wasserman, the head of MCA, the most important talent agency in Hollywood. Sydney had never heard of him. Then and there Burt called Wasserman and told him he was with a young fellow he thought had the stuff to make a good director. Would Wasserman meet Pollack and give him a hand?

Wasserman got Pollack a six-month contract at $75 a week. During that period he hung around sound stages, observing filming. Sydney quickly learned the technical requirements of the craft. In due time he was given a TV program to direct. He had proven Burt right.

Eventually Sydney directed a couple of Lancaster's films—*The Scalphunters* in 1968, and *Castle Keep* in 1969. Sydney Pollack then went on to direct some of the most acclaimed films of the last three decades.

But Burt could be ruthless. Arthur Penn, who received a Tony award for directing the play *The Miracle Worker* (he also directed the film), acquired material for a film called *The Train*. It dramatized a Nazi attempt to run a train loaded with stolen art treasures from France to Germany, and the French underground partisans' effort to prevent the Nazi theft. Arthur wouldn't sell the script unless he directed it.

A deal was reached for Penn to direct *The Train*, starring Lancaster, for United Artists. After lunch on the first day's shooting in France, Burt fired Penn and replaced him immediately with John Frankenheimer. John was already in France waiting in the wings. Lancaster had it all arranged beforehand.

1947 Hollywood

Cast in the play Galileo, *with Charles Laughton and Bertolt Brecht.*

While still under contract to Hal Wallis, I got a call from my agent. "We want you to read for Charles Laughton. He's doing a play called *Galileo*, by that German fella, you know, Brecht. They fired an actor and they want you to replace him, okay?"

Okay? I was thrilled. Charles Laughton. Now there was an icon. He fascinated audiences, no matter what character he played. As Captain Bligh of the *Bounty* he left an indelible mark on cinematic history. He was a special kind of actor. He didn't look like an actor. Olivier and Gable looked like actors. But Laughton brought the unexpected, convincingly, to each character he played.

Yes, I was thrilled to have the chance to work with Laughton in a play. But first I had to audition for him at his home. I hesitated before ringing the front doorbell and once again checked the address. Push the damn bell, I said to myself. The ring startled me. The door finally opened. Elsa Lanchester, Laughton's wife, stood in the doorway. It was weird. She didn't say a word, simply turned and led me down a corridor and into a small sitting room.

Laughton was seated on a two-place couch, and gestured for me to sit next to him. After a bit of introductory conversation, we began to read a scene from the play. He put his hand on my knee. I paused and asked if I could sit across from him so I could face him while reading. He said, "Fine, my boy, fine."

I got the part. Hal Wallis was quietly pleased. It couldn't hurt having one of his actors perform in a play by Bertolt Brecht starring Charles Laughton.

Joe Losey was the director, but he did little directing and a lot of grumbling as he sat in the back of the theater during rehearsals. Brecht simply took over.

After the play opened, Brecht left and Joe took charge. He had been frustrated during the month-long period of rehearsals and now that the play was up and running, there was little for him to do except be a pain in the ass. One day he pinned an announcement on the bulletin board requesting the presence of some, but not all of the cast at a meeting to discuss the play. Now that's a good way to keep the company happy.

I played the part of the "Little Monk." Brecht made it difficult for me. What I knew about acting I had learned by reading Stanislavsky, studying the Method with Morris Carnovsky and Michael Chekhov, and having acted in over thirty plays (most in stock companies) before coming to Hollywood.

But Brecht had other thoughts. His plays are called epic. He said theater might arouse emotions in the audience, but emotion is soon forgotten. If you are able to invade the intellect with essential, fundamental ideas, they will not be soon forgotten. Consequently, actors were not to convey emotion in his plays. Brecht spoke softly but one immediately got the sense of a man with a hard center, focused and convinced of his superior intelligence. He was odd looking, with an owl-like face, hair closely cropped to his skull, and a wiry figure that somehow emanated physical strength.

In a key scene, Laughton and I sat on a bench, center stage, discussing Galileo's discovery that the Earth was not the center of the universe, but a small planet rotating around the sun. This opposed the teachings of the time—that the sun and the universe revolved around the Earth.

The monk I played had difficulty accepting that. He spoke to Galileo about his parents, who worked the fields from dawn to sunset, leaving them bent over in later years. Now they were to be told that the Earth is only a grain of sand in God's scheme of things, and not the centerpiece where every human being was special.

I relied on the Method. Brecht told me to forget the Method, I should think mathematically: two and two is four, four and four is eight, etc. He didn't want me to show any emotion when talking about my parents' suffering. I did what I was told, but believing I was betraying my instincts and my training.

I was invited to dinner by Laughton, as was Brecht. The reason? I had a recording of Mark Blitzstein's ringing Airborne Symphony, a paean to the war against Nazism and fascism. Brecht, who knew Mark when he studied composing in Germany, was anxious to hear it. He hated it. Jingoist, glorifying war, he said.

I was silent but attentive during the conversation between Brecht and Laughton. It was, at first, about the music: could it be a weapon in the struggle against capitalism? "Yes, it's a powerful weapon," said Brecht. For Laughton, the talk became too Red and he adroitly turned the subject to Galileo, the man. He admired Galileo's courage in withstanding the Vatican's pressure to recant his findings, but he understood why he had finally recanted.

The political talk interested me—Brecht defended the Soviet Union's efforts to put Marxist-Leninism into play under difficult circumstances. The war against Germany and the West's attempt to undermine the Communist government was a terrible burden on the country and its people. Laughton listened closely but did not express any skepticism. I listened too, but I had heard it all many times before and had my own thoughts on the matter.

I went home that night, my mind captured by the evening's intellectual exercise. Was Brecht right about the style of acting he demanded for his plays? Yes, but it was not achievable. Passion and emotion are what defines an actor. Performing "mathematically" is finally impossible. An actor cannot express or convey a symbol.

Laughton hardly ever opposed Brecht's direction. It was Brecht's play and his right to direct it as he pleased. Brecht wisely did not interfere with Laughton's characterization of Galileo.

We performed the play in the newly dedicated Coronet Theater in a limited run. It was the world premiere of *Galileo*.

Brecht's revolutionary plays and political reputation drew a subpoena for the playwright to appear before the House Un-American Activities Committee, but he slipped back to East Germany before they could get their fangs into him.

1947 Hollywood

Paddy Chayefsky arrives in Hollywood.

I received my first letter from the Bronx; it was Paddy Chayefsky. He was bored hanging out at the neighborhood candy store with his old gang and planned on coming out for a visit. Could I help him land a writing assignment?

I had rented a room in a large white shingled house in the Hollywood Hills owned by a couple of elderly Russian immigrants. They had a spare bedroom they wanted to rent, so Paddy came west.

I got to know Harold Hecht, Burt Lancaster's agent, through Burt. The Lancasters, the Hechts, and the Knoxs saw each other several times a week for dinner. Hecht was a literary agent. Burt was the only actor he handled, having signed him when they were both living in New York. I figured Hecht was Paddy's yellow brick road to fame and riches as a screenwriter.

Paddy moved into the room down the hall from me and Georgette. One evening we sat on the porch with the Russians. Paddy moaned that he was already nostalgic for his friends in the Bronx and wished he was back on the street corner with them (he had been gone from the Bronx for all of a week). The old Russian commiserated, sighed, and softly said in his Russian-Jewish accent: "Oy, (another sigh) me too . . . I miss my shtetl."

Paddy: "Where was your shtetl, Mr. Bilifstein?"

Mr. Bilifstein: "Siberia."

Mr. Bilifstein didn't seem to know why we broke up, but joined us and nearly split a gut laughing.

I taught Paddy to drive an old '35 Dodge sedan. After the war it was almost impossible to buy a new car; the auto companies needed time to retool from making tanks. That old Dodge magically had a modern feature; it shifted without the use of the clutch. No one could figure out how that worked, so Paddy learned to drive without knowing what a clutch was.

I also taught him to drink dry martinis. It was a hell of a first lesson. The Cock and Bull was a fine English-style pub on Sunset Boulevard. Paddy loved his first martini, his second, and his third. I barely got off the stool and mumbled, "We better get our asses out of here, les go." Paddy had a real stupid grin on his face, but he didn't move; he couldn't get off the barstool. The bartender helped me get the stool from under his scarred ass and to the car.

A couple of days later, I made an appointment for Harold Hecht to meet Paddy.

Harold: "Well, Paddy, tell me, what have you done, what credits do you have?"

Paddy: (mumbles) "Credits? What do you mean?"

Harold: "Credits . . . you know, what have you written? Plays, screenplays, books . . . you know."

Paddy: "Oh . . . I wrote radio episodes for Armed Forces Network, during the war."

Harold: "But you got no credits . . . you need credits, without credits there's nothing I can do for you."

Mickey: "Jesus, Harold, that's why we're here, for you to find him a writing job. He's good. He can show things he's written, right Paddy?"

Paddy nodded, too depressed to speak.

Harold: "Get yourself a job, kid, then come back, I'll see what I can do for you."

"So long, fellows."

Outside the office, I was embarrassed. I apologized for Harold's brush-off.

I finally found a house with a guest room and Paddy was invited to stay with us. I knew Roy Huggins, a writer who worked at Universal Studios. I invited him over to meet Paddy. They talked together for quite a while. Roy then asked Paddy to have lunch with him the next day at the studio. He sensed that Paddy had the goods and used his influence to get him a job as a junior writer on his project.

But Paddy wasn't happy. He had been planning to write for the theater and when the job at Universal played out, he went back to his beloved Bronx. He made a name for himself writing teleplays for *Playhouse Ninety*, an hour-and-a-half weekly CBS, live TV play. Several of his teleplays were made into movies: *Marty* (get this: produced by Harold Hecht), *Bachelor Party*, and *The Catered Affair* with Bette Davis. He then wrote some memorable films, among them: *Network*, *Hospital*, and *The Goddess*.

His screenplay credits and Academy Awards are indeed impressive: in 1955 *Marty* won the Oscar for best film and Paddy won the Oscar for best screenplay; in 1971 he won the awards for best screenplay and original story for *Hospital*; in 1976 he got the award for best screenplay for *Network*. He also wrote the screenplays for *Bachelor Party* and *The Catered Affair*. Among his produced plays were, *Middle Of The Night*, *The Tenth Man*, and *Gideon*.

1947 Hollywood

Lightweight Champ in Killer McCoy, *with Mickey Rooney.*

L ife was good. I had made my first film, had a weekly paycheck, a nice home with a fine tree in the middle of the lawn and I was envied by friend and foe for having a French charmer of a wife. And I quickly got a second film. Hal Wallis lent me out to MGM for a boxing movie with Mickey Rooney, *Killer McCoy,* a remake of a film made in the thirties, *The Crowd Roars.* I was moving up in the world: From hit man to lightweight champion of the world.

In the film I discover Rooney boxing in a neighborhood gym. He shows spirit and courage and I help him become a winning fighter. I retire and fall on bad times, forcing me to make a comeback. Predictably, the promoters sign Rooney as my opponent.

In an emotional scene I put aside my pride and suggest to Rooney that he go easy on me, since I'm in lousy condition. In my close-up, Rooney is off-camera, but he's not only speaking his dialogue, he's behaving like an orchestra leader: waving his hands, trying to regulate my tone, the pitch of my voice, the degree of emotion. My concentration scattered. Rooney, I'm sure, felt he was helping an actor new to films.

Roy Rowland, the director, decided to call an early lunch. Rooney was number one at the box office at the time and Roy, being a mild-mannered nice guy, didn't think he should tangle with him.

Sam Levine, a fine actor, played my trainer. He was a blunt-talking man, but a sensitive blunt-talking man. He took me to the commissary and talked to me, calmed me, restored my confidence.

I went back to the set and quietly asked Rooney to just say the lines and lay off trying to direct me. We finished the scene and I came away a little wiser.

I had trained for six weeks before and during the filming for the big fight scene between Rooney and me. He had been married to Ava Gardner when she was about twenty and beautiful. While resting on the roof of the gym I asked him about her. They were divorced, so he either spoke out of malice or just for the hell of it. "Ava? Ava is a red, for Christ's sakes, so I divorced her." I kept my mouth shut and didn't pursue it, but I liked her color.

The studio hired Johnny Indrosano to train us and stage the fight. Indrosano, a former boxer, won seventy-two fights and lost one due to a broken jaw. In a rematch, he beat the fighter who had defeated him.

After he retired from the ring, like many ex-boxers, he drifted to Hollywood hoping to work in films. He proved good at staging fights and worked on many of the marvelous fight pictures of the thirties, forties, and fifties.

He had a house in the Valley and was a warm host. His parents, Italian immigrants, came to America at the turn of the century and ended up in Boston along with thousands of other Italians. Johnny loved to cook. He had huge pots for pasta and he cooked meatballs to soak up the spicy tomato sauce. Sunday was his day to invite a mix of movie stars, featured actors, and extras for a huge midday meal, eaten alfresco.

He was a big, rugged, handsome man with thick black curly hair and dark friendly eyes. However, as I got to know Johnny better, I found there was a veil of melancholy in his eyes. I knew little about his personal life except that he was Catholic and had been

divorced. Coming from a strict Catholic family, he must have suffered hellish guilt.

It hurt to hear in 1960 that he hanged himself.

I never missed a training session for the upcoming fight scene;
Rooney missed all but one. The result: I learned the moves, Rooney
didn't. The day we were to shoot the fight scene, Indrosano tried to
show Rooney the moves as hundreds of extras in the arena looked
on. Rooney gestured Indrosano to lay off. He then turned to me and
said, "Come on Mick, let's just mix it up. We don't need Indrosano."
I looked at Roy Rowland for direction. He appeared unhappy,
shrugged, and remained silent.

The bell rang and Rooney came flying out of his corner. We both
swung wildly and I hit him in the face. (Man, I was a kid back in
Brooklyn again and liking it.) That was the end of a ten-second
round. Rooney was bleeding from the mouth. That's it, I thought,
that's the end of my film career. A doctor was called, cleaned the
blood off Rooney's mouth, and stopped the bleeding.

But Rooney brushed off the doc and the others fretting around
him. Noticing my obvious unease, he smiled and said, "Forget it, kid,
it was an accident." He called Indrosano back into the ring, now
ready to learn the moves.

Roy, out of frustration, had called Sam Zimbalist, the film's producer and one of the most powerful men at MGM. I could see Roy
talking to Zimbalist, who nodded, smiled to Rooney, gave him the
thumbs up sign, and walked off the set.

Rooney was one of the most talented actors in Hollywood. He
could do anything and be convincing. He could sing, dance, play
musical instruments, cry instantly, and had a photographic memory.
He learned the staging of the fight in half an hour. And he was good.
He looked like a professional fighter.

I did have a sense of foreboding about the fourth round, when the
script called for him to knock me out. I had to take the punch. He
hit me hard. It hurt but it felt good to drop to the canvas.

Roy was, through marriage, related to L. B. Mayer, the famous head of MGM Studios. He would go to Mayer's home after work to see the previous day's filming with L. B. One morning, Roy took me aside and told me L. B. was interested in signing me to a long-term contract. Roy knew I was under contract to Hal Wallis, but suggested I talk to my agent to work something out that would be to my benefit.

I was with the most important talent agency at that time, MCA. I told my agent about L. B.'s interest, but he never spoke to Wallis about either releasing me or splitting my contract. It's the code in Hollywood that actors never speak to producers or studio casting people about salary, contracts, or anything related to business. That's a large reason why agents get their ten percent; they face tightfisted producers and it can get raucous trying to get their clients a fat paycheck. So it never occurred to me to speak directly to Wallis. My concern was that Wallis rarely made more than a couple of films a year; MGM made several hundred a year. The possibilities for an actor at a studio that productive were limitless. It was the first of several missed opportunities during my early career in Hollywood. But I say to myself, forget it, keep moving and don't drop your left.

1948 Hollywood

Knock on Any Door, *with Humphrey Bogart and John Derek.*

The year 1948 was my second as a film actor. I had been in five movies when the opportunity for a leading role in a major film was about to knock on my door.

Hal Wallis, the coolest character I got to know in Hollywood, hardly ever spoke to me. It didn't bother me at all. He was the boss and I had an innate distrust of any bossman. Wallis put me off balance. He never said much and when he did, he spoke softly, his voice detached, unreadable.

When I got the call that he wanted to see me, I felt apprehensive. I thought agents only brought good news when they called.

It was good news. He asked if I had read a novel titled, *Knock on Any Door*. Yes, I had. He told me that Humphrey Bogart had bought the film rights but was having a hard time getting a screenplay he could approve. Wallis asked Bogart if he could acquire the film rights from him. If Bogart agreed, Wallis told me, I'd play the lead role.

It was a remarkable book, written by Willard Motley, a noted black writer, about a gang of white kids in Chicago. The protagonist was the leader of the gang, a nifty role; tough, quick-witted, emotional, and finally, tender. A hell of a part, but I didn't dwell on the thought. I had learned while working in the theater that you don't have the job until you're on the stage performing.

But Bogey wasn't a quitter. He got new writers and finally decided to make the movie.

He did call Wallis and ask if he'd loan me out for a part in the film. Wallis said, "Sure, if Mickey agrees." I agreed, not that I had a choice. It wasn't a very big role. At the time, an actor under a seven-year contract did what the studio, or in my case, the boss, wanted him to do. Like everyone else, I admired Bogart's work and felt favored to be in the movie.

I had no scenes with Bogart, but he was on the set often. Bogey was on the wagon, but had a supply of cold beer in his onstage dressing room for the cast and crew. Friendly and available, he took pleasure in the company of actors. He was generous with his time and we spent the work pauses telling theater and movie tales.

Although it was Bogey's independent company, he hired a producer to oversee the day-to-day production activities. However, Bogey was protective of the people working on the set. One afternoon, the assistant director knocked on Bogey's door and told him they were ready for him. When Bogey stepped out and saw the producer on the set, he stepped back into his dressing room and turned to the assistant director. "A producer has no business being on the set. All he does is make the cast and crew nervous. Get him outta here," he growled.

Nick Ray was the director. What a break, a real director, I thought. My previous experience with movie directors had been disappointing.

The first day on the set, Nick put his arm around my shoulder and led me on a tour of the stage. I waited for him to speak, tell me the secret life of the character I was playing, but not a word was said. It was a large stage so we must have walked for a full minute. When we got back to the camera position, he patted me on the back and said, "Okay?" I nodded, not knowing what else to do. Another disappointment.

John Derek got the part I had yearned for. It was his first starring role. But he was a reluctant actor. He was a quiet, unassuming kid.

One day he softly said to me, "I don't know what I'm doing on a movie set. I'd rather be with horses and on a ranch."

He was extremely good looking and was told by Harry Cohn, the head of Columbia Pictures, that if he signed with the studio he'd make him a star and very rich. Tough to turn down. I'm sure John envisioned the ranch he would buy, reason enough to be an actor.

But he didn't fare too well with Nick Ray, who at one point took hold of John by the head. With suppressed annoyance, he turned John's head to the left and told him to keep looking in that direction during the scene. Patience and tact were not in Nick Ray's playbook.

Knowing John Derek's film career, I believe his experience on *Knock On Any Door* soured him on acting. He is the sole male movie actor who starred in all of his films and then dumped his career while still a young man. He never did act again.

1949 Hollywood

I lead a gang of Brooklyn kids in City Across the River.

I loved Universal Studios. It was only a five-minute drive from where we lived on Sarah Street. It was a little shabby, in need of painting, and smaller than the other major studios. There were aging wood bungalows with shingled roofs, the pavement needed repairing, the dressing rooms were quaintly old-fashioned. It was like a small village. I worked in three films at Universal; it felt like a home away from home.

I played Larry Tunafish, the leader of a gang of kids, in the most important film for me at the time, *City Across the River*. It was shot on location—Brooklyn—giving the atmosphere a true feel of authenticity. Coming from that part of the world, I grasped the Tunafish character and played him as hard, constantly angry at the gang members for being jerks.

The film was adapted from the novel *The Amboy Dukes*, by Irving Shulman. Universal changed the title, fearing "Amboy Dukes" sounded like a film about English dukes and knights. (The title refers to Amboy Street in Brooklyn.)

The film was released in 1949 on a low budget, but has remained in the memory of many adults who saw the movie as teenagers. The reason, I believe, is that the movie's gang members seemed to be just ordinary kids, allowing teenagers to identify with them. Over fifty years later, I still get letters related to that film and get stopped on the street by aging fans who call out things like: "Hey, you're Mickey Knox—you were Larry Tunafish, the leader of the Amboy Dukes, ain't ya?"

It was my first film after I had asked Wallis to release me from the contract I had with him. He had agreed. He simply didn't produce enough films.

After the preview of *City*, Universal asked my agency if I would like to sign a term contract with the studio. I had received many favorable audience preview cards, but I wasn't about to sign any long-term contract. I was in demand and figured I would do better on my own.

In 1949, I was in another film with John Derek. I was up for the part of his brother in *Saturday's Hero*, based on the book by Millard Lampell, who also wrote the screenplay. He was a good writer and would later become fair game for the ferrets of the House Un-American Activities Committee. Another gutsy guy, he didn't betray his friends and was blacklisted. The executive producer, Sidney Buchman, a true gentleman and scholar, was also eventually called before the committee and rendered unemployed due to the blacklist.

Buchman and David Miller, the director, wanted me for the part. But the line producer, Buddy Adler, wanted me to audition before a decision was made. In the film our parents were Polish immigrants and John was an outstanding college football hero sought after by the professional teams.

I read a scene with John; Buchman and Miller nodded. Adler had his doubts, "I think Mickey is too Jewish." Miller turned to Derek and asked, "Are you Jewish, John?"

Caught by surprise, John stammered, "Who, me? No, no, I'm not . . ."

"I can't tell who is Jewish and who isn't Jewish," Miller said.

Buchman closed the deal. "Okay, Mickey you got the part."

Sweet words an actor loves to hear.

1949 Hollywood

White Heat, *with James Cagney.*

T he movie, *White Heat* has become a classic of genre gangster films, but for me it was a chance to work with one of my boyhood idols, James Cagney.

Cagney on the set was distant but not unfriendly. He was polite, but rarely engaged in small talk. When he finished a scene, he would disappear into his on-set trailer until the next setup.

When he heard I was Jewish, he opened up. He told me he had learned Yiddish as a kid when he lived on the upper East Side of Manhattan, just south of East Harlem where many Jewish families lived. Some of the kids he had palled around with were Jews.

He was the "Shabbes bucher," a Gentile kid who turned on the gas stove and the electric lights during the Sabbath when religious Jews are restricted to prayer and contemplation. Quaint, but Cagney learned a lot of Yiddish.

During the thirties, he told me, he was politically on the left side of the great divide. However, when I worked with him in 1949, he had already quit reading newspapers or listening to the radio (television wasn't around much then). He had become intensely private and confessed that he had lost all interest in politics and the affairs of nations.

I was part of Cagney's gang in the story. In one of the scenes, we were having a meeting in a farmhouse, plotting a robbery. I was assigned to drive the getaway car. The next shot, outside the farm-house, I was in the car, in the driver's seat. Cagney approached, stuck his head in the open window, and said: *Fages nischt, dafst gayen linkst* . . . He continued speaking Yiddish for the rest of the scene.

Raoul Walsh, a seasoned, well-known director with an eye patch, stared with his unpatched eye at Cagney. After a moment of open-mouthed bewilderment, he shouted, "What the fuck is that you're saying, Jim? I don't understand a fucking word!"

"Mickey understands me, Raoul, that's the only important thing."

If only I had that outtake.

1949 Hollywood

Any Number Can Play, *with Clark Gable.*

C lark Gable! The King! The number one box office star. The charmer who was handy with his fists. The dames loved him, the guys wanted to be him.

The movie, *Any Number Can Play*, was my eighth film, the second for MGM, the most productive studio in Hollywood at that time.

It was about gambling and in it, Gable ran a classy casino. Since it was one of my films that I never saw, I barely remember the plot. (Like many actors, I get edgy watching myself on the screen.) What I recall is that I was a dealer and a loyal Gable friend.

Gable was the only actor in Hollywood who had, in his contract, short working hours: nine to five and he was off the set. No one, including the director, could ask him for one more take. I loved it. I was at his side or near him when shooting for most of the six weeks I was on the film, so his hours were also my hours.

The Naked And The Dead, Norman Mailer's best seller, was the talk of the town, being the first serious World War II novel to be published. While waiting to film a scene, Gable and I talked about the book. He surprised me. "The kid capitalizes on using dirty words. I don't go for that."

That stopped me. He wasn't kidding. He-man Gable offended by

FUG? Finally I found my voice, "You were in the Air Force, you know how we spoke: Fuck dat, shit, piss and corruption, fuck the army, fuck the sergeant. But I didn't see any dirty words in the book, those days he couldn't use any. He had to spell fuck "fug" and fug ain't no dirty word."

The look of outrage on Gable's face ended the conversation. As did my esteem for the man.

A couple of crew members told me Gable was not the Gable he had been in the old days. He used to get a kick out of playing practical jokes and was always in a good humor, quick to laugh. Carole Lombard, his wife, a marvelous actress and a born comedienne was the love of Gable's life. When she died in a plane crash on a tour selling war bonds, Gable never fully recovered. His personality flipped; he became humorless and grave.

Richard Brooks had written the screenplay for *White Heat*. He had previously written a novel I had read about striking workers. At the end of the novel, the strikers fought National Guard tanks, starting a small revolution in the town. A radical writer, I thought, but more on that later.

Brooks wanted to direct movies, so L. B. Mayer told him to hang around the set and watch Mervyn Leroy, the director; he might learn something. During the rehearsal of a complicated scene, Leroy had a problem solving the mechanics. The casino is held up by a couple of gangsters. One of them, about six feet away, holds a gun on Gable and me. The screenplay had me leap at the gunman and try to wrestle the gun out of his hand. A sure way to get killed. The gunman could have yawned and still had time to shoot or pistol-whip me.

I could see that Brooks was itching to get started as a director and, as luck would have it, he chose that scene. He asked Leroy if he could stage it for him. Leroy, relieved, said, "It's all yours." Brooks took the gangster's place and told me to reach out and go for the gun. Actors rarely hurt each other when rehearsing scenes of violence. So I trustingly reached out and made a move for the gun that Brooks was pretending to aim at me.

Suddenly, I was sprawled on the floor. Brooks had grabbed my arm, whirled me around, and flung me away. "Jesus, Richard, are you crazy? You're as strong as an ox, you trying to kill me?" I shouted at him.

"Well," he replied, "I used to play football in college. I guess I don't know my own strength. I'm sorry kid, let's try it again."

"Forget it," I said.

"Please, I'll be careful, I promise," he pleaded.

He was arrogant and I was stupid. He convinced me. "Okay, now take it easy," I said.

I shoulda said fuck you.

Once again I hit the floor. The assistant director helped me up and brushed me off. "That's it, Richard, no more," I snarled.

Richard looked to Mervyn Leroy, who said, "Dick, will you please be careful next time?"

"No more next time." I said.

Leroy took Brooks aside and whispered something to him. Leroy approached and whispered to me, "This means a lot to Richard, give him one more chance, do it for me."

It's tough to say no to a director. I agreed and admonished Richard to just go slow and easy and we'd work it out.

I'm embarrassed at how stupid I can be. Richard was a nut. This time he smashed me against the edge of the craps table. The only luck I had was that the edge of the table hit between my teeth and nose. I was bleeding like a stuck pig. My upper gum was gashed. My mouth quickly swelled so I couldn't speak, but the wild look I gave Richard delivered the message.

I was sent to first aid. When I returned it was after five and the day's work was over. It was odd; Gable was there alongside me during my crashes, yet never said a word to me or Richard or Leroy.

The following morning, Leroy put his arm around my shoulders and said, "I was with Richard last night, he felt terrible."

I stared at him in disbelief. "The poor bastard," I muttered.

Mervyn Leroy was a well-liked director and had many decent

films to his credit. But Hollywood was hit by an epidemic in the forties: gin rummy. Mervyn became a compulsive gin player. Directing a movie is a full-time job. You can't screw around when you should be preparing for the following day's work. Mervyn was up playing cards half the night and came to work in the morning sleepy and not very alert.

After lunch the crew would drift back to the stage and find Mervyn sitting in a chair facing the set, supposedly thinking about the staging of the next shot. The assistant director would keep everyone quiet and in back of where Mervyn was sitting. One day I got close to the chair and found Mervyn softly snoring.

Richard Brooks went on to become a well-known director, but he was peculiar. I heard from a couple of friends of mine who worked in his films that before hiring them he wouldn't allow them to read the whole script, only the scenes they were in. He did play it close to the vest.

Sometime after Brooks started directing, I was with Burt Lancaster in Tijuana, Mexico for the bullfights. Burt and I were sitting in a bar having a drink. We were talking about a petition we had signed—an *amicus curiae*, requesting that the Supreme Court hear the Contempt of Congress case against John Howard Lawson and Dalton Trumbo, two well-known writers of the Hollywood Ten.

Brooks, of all people, wandered into the bar and joined us. When Burt asked him if he had signed the petition for the amicus curiae, Brooks became livid. He told Burt that he was a fool to sign it, he'd only get in trouble, and for what? Defending the Hollywood Ten, a bunch of commies?

Pissed off and agitated, Brooks finally stalked out of the bar. Burt and I later agreed that Brooks wouldn't sign, not out of principle, but out of fear of being tainted pink—or, god forbid, red.

The Hollywood Ten was not a musical group or chorus line—no, they were respected writers and directors in the film industry. They were also "unfriendly" witnesses before the House Un-American Activities Committee (HUAC) in 1947. "Are you now or have you ever been a member of the Communist Party?" They all refused to answer the question, but challenged the Committee on its right to ask that question. Rather than take the Fifth Amendment, the constitutional guarantee against self-incrimination, the Ten chose the First Amendment, guaranteeing free speech.

They were found to be in contempt of Congress and lost the appeal in Federal court. Hence, the amicus curiae, requesting that the Supreme Court hear the case. It was denied.

In 1950 the Ten went to jail—two for six months the others for a year.

1949 Hollywood

Norman Mailer.

The day that began a lifelong friendship and made a difference in my life. A friend brought Norman Mailer to my house.

I had read *The Naked And The Dead* and marveled how a writer of twenty-five could have the insight to write a novel of men at war that had such depth.

In the doorway stood my friend and the author. Mailer and I smiled, read each other briefly. He was slight, with a lot of curly dark hair, alert, very blue eyes, and seemed timid. I knew he had spent some of his childhood in Brooklyn and the gang I hung out with was anything but timid. (I had mistaken cautiousness for timidity.) He said he had seen *City Across The River*. The fact that he mentioned it made him even more welcome.

By the time he left, I sensed a friendship had formed. We exchanged phone numbers and planned on meeting again soon.

I quickly saw the metal core in Mailer. He asked me to come along to hear him speak in an auditorium loaded with lefties. He drove silently, but I could hear the wheels turning in his brain. He faced that crowd and blasted Stalin at a time when many of those present thought of Stalin as the Hero of the Soviet Union.

I knew he had guts, got that from his book, but I never forgot that night. Through the years there were many speeches, encounters, debates, and fights, but his courage never flagged.

Norman came to Hollywood the first time to spread the word for Henry Wallace, a liberal, running for president on the Progressive party ticket in 1948. I didn't know Mailer then, but I had heard about his appearances at the homes of movie stars. He would talk up Wallace before, for the most part, groups of liberals who were inclined to vote for Wallace in any case.

Norman had a close friend, Jean Malaquais, a French writer who had translated *The Naked and the Dead* into French. Malaquais had Stalin measured before most lefties. For those on the left, these were difficult days. The political climate was hot, inflaming a red-scare. The House Un-American Activities Committees in Washington and California were hammering unfriendly witnesses and romancing the friendlies. Politicians love crusades, especially when they result in headlines.

Jean Malaquais had documentary proof of Stalin's slaughter of the early revolutionaries, of his paranoia that led to the imprisonment and death of countless thousands. In my gut I knew it was true, but I hated the rising anti-red tide in America and I thought it was the wrong time to display Stalin's horrors. I secretly wanted Stalin to drop dead to get him out of the conversations. I argued with Jean but he was unrelenting. He was right, of course.

Norman was then married to his first wife, Bea. She was strong-willed, sure of herself. I liked her, liked her humor, her easy laugh. But she was a dominator. Norman also had a cousin, a lawyer, Sy Rembar. He had the hots for Georgette.

One day I got a hunch, a mystic hunch. I drove up one of the canyon roads leading from the Valley to Hollywood. Going up a hill, I saw a car on its way down, containing Georgette and Norman's cousin. I saw them, they saw me. I couldn't make a U-turn, the road was too narrow. Goddamn!

The canyon encounter, followed by other intrigues, led to her final departure for France and our eventual divorce.

• • •

Burt Lancaster and his agent, Harold Hecht, asked me to set up a meeting with Norman Mailer; they were interested in acquiring an option to make a film of *The Naked and the Dead*. I arranged the meeting at my house. I also invited Julie (John) Garfield and he put in his bid to play Sergeant Croft, a major character in the book.

It was a quiet, cautious meeting. Everyone seemed to have due respect for each other. Burt and Harold did option the book, but they couldn't follow through. Whether or not they lost courage, I don't know, but they claimed they had problems with the U.S. Army's willingness to cooperate. *The Naked and the Dead* could not be made as a film without army equipment: armor, uniforms, arms, etc. That wasn't forthcoming. According to Burt and Harold, the army did not want to see the film made.

I didn't buy it. I think they got in over their heads. Making a war picture was expensive and it took considerable producing experience, which they didn't have. When Harold asked Norman to let him off the hook for the next option payment, I was surprised that Norman agreed. That's something rarely done in Hollywood, but Norman was never "Hollywood."

The film rights were bought by Charles Laughton and it was produced in partnership with Warner Bros. The movie was poorly made and not successful at the box office. It was a case of read the book.

After Norman returned to New York, we corresponded fairly often. I missed his presence. I sensed he'd be a loyal friend. He impressed me with his modesty, his perceptiveness, his quick intelligence and, best of all, he laughed at my jokes.

1950 Hollywood
Sam Fuller.

Kirk Douglas called one day to tell me his neighbor, Sam Fuller, a writer, wanted to meet me. Give him my number, I said. A couple of days later, Fuller phoned and I invited him to come to my place.

Sam was short and stocky and loaded with energy. He seemed ready for any kind of action, be it just talk or whatever the situation demanded. But he was cheery and, like most New Yorkers, spoke rapidly. He also had bright, intelligent eyes and chomped on a large cigar. He told me he planned to write a hard-hitting screenplay set in the Korean War, which was then heating up.

He had seen me in *Killer McCoy* and was impressed by my performance. He was going to write the script with me in mind for the lead role, a tough sergeant. I didn't give it much weight, ideas for films rarely reach the silver screen. Hell, he hadn't even written the script.

I liked Sam right off. He probably came from Brooklyn. He was in the same war I was in, except he landed in Normandy on D-Day with the 1st Infantry Division. He was cited for rescuing a wounded buddy from drowning while under fire, he was given the Bronze Star. He was with the 1st Division as they fought their way across Europe. During that tour he earned the Silver Star and the Purple Heart.

The war gave Sam pride in his acts of bravery. Those medals he earned were metaphorically pinned to his chest for eternity.

In 1924 he was thirteen and got a job as a copy boy at the *New York Journal*. Four years later, he became a crime reporter. In 1936, in love with motion pictures, he went to Hollywood and became a screenwriter. What he really wanted was to direct movies and he began that career with a couple of small budget films in 1949.

He believed John Ford's *The Informer* was the best movie ever made. He told me he ran it dozens of times. I don't know where he ran it; there were no VCRs in the late forties. He must have had a sixteen-millimeter copy, a buddy who had access to a projection room, or a Movieola at home. That movie was his schooling on how to make a film—for him it worked, and he became a respected, highly ranked director.

I didn't hear from him for about three months. Kirk had told me he worked quickly so I thought that either he discarded the idea of a war story or he was having problems with it. I was wrong on both counts.

He rang me one day and said, "this is Sam calling."

"Sam who?

"Who? Are you crazy? I'm writing a terrific script for you and you don't know this is Sam Fuller?"

The questions were fired at me so quickly, I had no time to answer cleverly or kiddingly. I muttered, "Oh yeah, Sam Fuller . . . how are you?"

"Forget the niceties, schmuck. I finished the script. When can you come over to my place?"

I hesitated just long enough to irritate him. His voice a pitch higher, he demanded, "I want to read it to you, when are you free?"

I thought, Christ, a three-hour session with this nut reading his damn screenplay. "Sam, can't I read it?"

"No! When can you come over?"

I had never even met the guy, why was he angry? But I said, "Oh, any time."

"Tomorrow at six, okay?" Sam now sounded reasonable.

Trying to be funny, I said, "That's too early for me, schmuck."

He got it. "No, no, the evening, wise guy."

So I went to his place. He led me to a room in the basement where he did his writing. He relit his six-inch cigar, walked to his desk and gestured for me to join him. There it was, under the glass top of his desk: his citation for bravery during the Normandy landings.

I whistled my admiration. He grinned impishly and dragged on his cigar. He had me sit before a low table bearing a bottle of Chivas and a couple of glasses. No water, no ice. A true, tough New York journalist.

He poured a couple of drinks, quickly downed his, picked up his script and began reading. He was good. He clearly loved what he had written and as he went on I realized he loved war. It was his eighty-yard run. His energy never flagged. He read the dialogue loudly, changing his voice for each of his warriors.

He read the descriptive parts softly and slowly. He must have known the energy he gave the dialogue, in contrast to his professorial reading of the descriptive sections, produced the dramatic effect he wanted.

The part he wrote for me (a young Sam Fuller) was a brutally tough sergeant. Those were the days when you couldn't say, "you fucking gooks." He solved that by having the sergeant fire his machine gun to kill gook POWs as he shouted, "You fucking gooks," so the words couldn't be heard, but his lips could be read.

The reading lasted a couple of hours. The bottle of Chivas was three quarters empty. I was loaded. Sam was primed, but not drunk. When he finished he was aglow.

I was appalled, and too drunk to hide it. He loved war! He loved combat, the smell of firing, the rush of killing. I told him all of that, and finished by saying, "I can't be in this movie. I hate war."

He stared at me, outraged, unable to speak for a moment. Then he shouted, "Write your own fucking movie!"

I went home feeling pretty good for being so true to my core beliefs. I quickly forgot Sam Fuller and his war story.

But then the movie *Steel Helmet* came out. I saw it and felt sickened, not by the film but by, once again, my own stupidity. With intelligent foresight, I would have gone home and given the part some thought before turning it down.

Steel Helmet was a critical success and the part of the sergeant was a winner. Gene Evans did a fine job and had a good career. My refusal to be in *Steel Helmet* has at times haunted me and caused more than a few sleepless nights.

Sam Fuller made many successful and critically acclaimed films. In France he's considered a great director and he spent much time in Paris during his last years. He was rarely seen without a huge cigar and smoked them until he died in 1997. He was 86.

1951 Hollywood

Bust up with Georgette—Hello, Lois Andrews.

F ive years into my marriage with Georgette and it was over. I
didn't kid myself about her, she loved intrigue more than any
sex act. Parisian women, as a rule, have lovers as a way of life.
Paris has a civilization within the country's civilization, it's secret is
sexual freedom. Married men have mistresses; their wives, lovers. It
works. "There's no more loving husband than one who returns to his
wife after sleeping with his mistress." We've all heard that one, but
when asked if it's true, the amused Parisian smiles ambiguously.

Many times the lovers and the married families are friends, to wit;
President Mitterand's mistress, his child by her, his wife, and their
children all stood together, grieving, at his funeral. All of France
knew of the affair, yet the media hardly dealt with it. It wasn't news.

Sure, Georgette had lovers, but that didn't bust us up. I knew
about Burt Lancaster and a few others. She had always planned on
returning to France to marry André, the guy she was with when I first
met her. She stayed in Hollywood longer than she expected after all,
she was having a fine time after the ugliness of the German occupation. We had a nice house, amusing friends who adored her, lots of
sunshine, and a more than decent income. Lancaster was probably
another reason she hung in.

Looking for a lost sock one day, I went through her closet and discovered a shoe box full of letters from André, dating from the time we moved to L.A. Soon after, early in 1950, she split for France.

Georgette returned to the States with André, on their way to Mexico. She had a purpose. Her first stop was Washington, D.C. to visit my kid brother, Carl. She knew Carl had a teenage crush on her. He had met her in 1946 when she first arrived from Paris. She spoke no English but had charmed everyone in the family. Carl had been sixteen, but now he was in his twenties and still had a crush on her. He was her target. Georgette and André needed a car and asked Carl to co-sign for them. He was delighted and signed willingly. If they defaulted while in Mexico, Carl was screwed. They never missed a payment.

She divorced me in Mexico. She and André lived in Mexico City for a few years where he represented Hennessy brandy. They then moved to Caracas, Venezuela. Georgette always understood money and craved a lot of it. Through her early years in Caracas she bought up acres of land on the outskirts of the city for a song. She knew or sensed something. Clever lady: land prices shot up, making her a multimillionaire.

She bought a huge estate outside Caracas, an apartment in New York, a home in Paris. Her two daughters studied law at Georgetown University, in Washington, D.C. Some years later, in 1965, she called from Paris and asked if she could come to Rome for a visit. She wanted to meet my wife Joan and my two infant girls. Something was up.

Joan went ballistic. "No former wives in my home!" I told her she'd like Georgette and she wasn't going to stay with us, she was only coming for dinner. "The hell she is, I'm not cooking for any ex-wife."

"Listen," I said, " I pay the rent here and she's coming for dinner. You'll get along with her, you'll see."

Georgette came, charmed Joan, and soon they were friends. After dinner she took a photo album out of her huge purse. The photos were impressive. A group of eight servants (a couple in livery) on a spacious lawn surrounding a huge mansion, all belonging to Georgette.

The purse itself was what is called in French "une baise en ville." It was a roomy bag to store toiletries, spare underwear, or whatever might be needed when going to meet a lover. Then it hit me. I was her *beard*. But who was the lover?

While I was driving Georgette back to her hotel, she told me her happy news: she had an assignation in Rome with an Italian airline pilot; if André called I was to tell him that, yes, I had invited her to visit me in Rome.

1951 Hollywood

Lois Andrews to the Rescue.

The year 1951 began in gloom, but soon brightened. Georgette left for France, our marriage a cinder, and I was left alone in the house on Sarah Street, a house still redolent of the events of the past five years. The melancholy of the moment, however, began to overpower the smell of past love-making, past laughter, and past evening with friends.

The day I left for the apartment I had rented on Doheny Drive in West Hollywood, I sat all morning on the staircase, immersed in self-pity. Georgette was out of my life for good, but not out of my head. Pitying oneself is not all bad. It soothes the wound and allows time to bridge the gap between irrecoverable good times and present loneliness.

The apartment on Doheny was small, but comfortable enough. It had originally been a large, two-story, single-family house, now remodeled into three separate apartments. The largest covered the ground floor; the upper floor was divided into two modest apartments. I had one of them.

The house was owned by a young actress, Lois Andrews. And she was a beauty. She had the height to enhance a fine figure and a face that was appealing and at the same time, lovely. She lived on the ground floor. Before renting the apartment I was ushered into her bedroom by her maid. Lois was in bed with a lunch tray on her lap. She looked me over and said, "The apartment is yours."

At fifteen, Lois had been the focus of George White's *Scandals of 1939*, the last year of the *Scandals*, an elaborate, glamorous Broadway musical, newly staged each year. It featured a long, curved, gleaming staircase with Lois slowly, seductively parading down the wide steps. What sold tickets, however, were the startlingly beautiful dancers and singers.

Lois became the toast of the rich and famous. Georgie Jessel, the chief show biz master of ceremonies, quickly snatched her up and married her. The New York tabloids had a feast featuring her as the "child bride" in photo outlays and articles. She thrived on all the publicity and told in a interview, among other things, that her toilet seat was overlaid with mink. Of course one of the tabloids ran the headline: THE LUCKIEST MINKS IN THE WORLD.

When I moved in, she was divorced from Jessel and had a child by him, a girl named Jeralyn. I was then acting in a film called *Criminal Lawyer*. My second day in the apartment, I arrived home from the studio and found a note from Lois inviting me to come down for a drink. Who knew there was a large party going on downstairs?

I was still in jeans and hadn't showered. When I came through Lois's door and saw the smartly dressed guests, I was about to turn back, but Lois pulled me inside. I told her I'd return, but in Lois's home she did the deciding. She sat me in an armchair and sat on my lap, precluding a quick getaway.

After everyone had left, she made another decision. She led me into her bedroom and from that night on, my upstairs apartment was used almost exclusively as a place to hang my clothes.

There were many dinners and cocktail parties. I brought the gift of dry martinis to Lois and from her first taste, she was hooked.

She was the perfect antidote for my irretrievable marriage. Frequent fucking, partying, and pleasurable drinking together. She was never mean, petty, or argumentative. Her manner with me was intimate and affectionate.

Lois was rich, but not from Jessel. Because of his masterful work as an M.C., he had been given an office and title at 20th Century Fox Studios. He consistently lost his five thousand a week paycheck—a small fortune in 1950—to the gin rummy sharks at his studio and club. He would visit his daughter once a week, have two shots of vodka, tell two jokes, often had to apologize for not having the hundred bucks a week child support, and then split.

No, she was rich because of her ability or instinct to know when to buy real estate. One of the many admirers she had collected in her New York days was the owner of a huge beer company. She borrowed enough money to buy real estate in Palm Springs. The market sky-rocketed and she sold at considerable profit. She paid the beer baron back and proceeded to buy real estate in Los Angeles. The house we lived in was among her acquisitions.

Although she wasn't rabid or too committed to her right-leaning politics, they bothered me. Some of the guests at her parties were Republican politicians and, difficult as it was, I kept my distance—except for one night, when Representative Donald Jackson from California, a loud-mouthed member of the House Un-American Activities Committee, was present. He proudly bragged that he was responsible for having brought down that pinko actor, John Garfield.

He lit the fuse to the Irish Whiskey bomb in my insides. I rushed him, brought him to the floor, and tried to choke the bastard. I was quickly pulled off. When he stood up, he and yelled at Lois, "Who the hell is that nut?"

Lois, cool as a chilled martini, replied, "I suggest you fix your tie and leave."

Jackson, angry and embarrassed, brushed the dust off his jacket and beat a hasty retreat. Lois turned to her guests and called out, "The drinks are on the house!" She got a big laugh and the party continued in a merrier mood.

So did the night-clubbing, the drinking, and the wait for a job. After having worked constantly during the past four years, not a call from my agent, not a whisper of any film coming up for me—what had happened?

THE WIZARD OF WISCONSIN

The year is 1950 and you, Joe McCarthy, are a little known Senator from Wisconsin. Understandably, you yearn for recognition. But how to achieve it?

Then, like a bolt of lightening, an epiphany: Expose the Commie bastards as dangerous subversives! Spread the gospel over the land. Forget truth and fairness. Attack. No one is sacred. Put on the goddamnedest show and finally get the headlines. Your hollow baritone is heard on radio and your dark image appears in the new medium, television, the secret of your success. It works. And the blacklist is born. What a showman!

You gained renown, but sacrificed your name to "McCarthyism" and entered the lexicon of the infamous.

But hold on. I wasn't a Commie bastard. Why was I blacklisted? My FBI file cleared me of any subversive activities. But what did they know?

As a reward for all his efforts, Senator Joe McCarthy was finally censured by his colleagues in the Senate. That shook him up. And he turned to booze as a pain-killer. It not only killed his pain, it laid him to a well-deserved rest in 1957—McCarthy was 49.

So, the last laugh was mine. The blacklisters failed to extinguish my spirit. Despite being on their list, I had a hell of a good life, as these memoirs show. Thank you, Joe McCarthy.

1951 Hollywood
Blacklisted!

THE BLACKLIST!

It was like a sirocco; one could feel the heat of the hot desert wind approaching long before it blew in. A free-floating foreboding, an unnerving instinct, informed me of the coming of the political blast a year before it blew me out of Movieland.

I had acted in fifteen Hollywood films during 1947–51, *Criminal Lawyer* being the last one. (I performed in two independent productions in New York and Florida in the early fifties. One was produced by a German national, the other financed by private sources, and both ignored the blacklist.) I was brought back to Hollywood ten years later by Hal Wallis for *G.I. Blues*, indicating that the heat of the blacklist had become a simmer.

After it was determined that the claims made by McCarthy that the Reds had infiltrated many government agencies and that President Eisenhower was a "pinko," were all false, he was formally censured by his Senate colleagues in 1954 and his influence finally faded away.

The blacklist, begun in the late forties, had paled by 1960. At the height of the red hunt, there were graylists for those of us who had never been called to testify. But for the most part it was just a shade lighter than the blacklist.

What was the blacklist? It was a secret conspiracy among the major film companies to prevent actors, writers, directors, and producers from working in the industry if found by congressional or state committees, red-baiting publications like *Red Channels*, or even a New England supermarket chain, that they were Communists, fellow travelers, or just pinkos. The heads of the studios gathered the names but kept the lists for "their eyes only."

After being unemployed for almost a year, I figured that the iron curtain of the blacklist had slammed down. I tried lifting that curtain off my blacklisted ass, but it was too amorphous.

How did I discover beyond any doubt that I was blacklisted? Chester Erskine, a well-known Hollywood producer and friend of mine, being far-sighted, had bought the television rights to the *Reader's Digest*. He hired me, much to my delight, to play a gangster in one of the segments. But delight soon turned to despair.

Before the start of filming, Chester called: "It's important that I speak to you, come to my office." But we didn't talk in his office, he led me outside. "Studerbaker, the sponsor, informed me that I couldn't use you. I insisted, told them I had already signed you and they said, okay, but just this once. Don't quote me, this is strictly between you and me. I hate to tell you this, my friend. You are blacklisted."

It was true! Blacklisted. The blacklist was like a spreading oil spill, staining the targeted, and once stained, it was hell washing it off.

The Screen Actors Guild was the place to look for a strong detergent, so I met with John Dales, the Guild's administrator.

"I was told I was blacklisted by a reliable source. What can I do about it?" He reached for a couple of red books, evidently found my name listed, and asked, "Did you sign an ad in the *Hollywood Reporter* captioned "The Thomas-Rankin Committee Must Go," contributed by the Actors Division of the Progressive Citizens of America?"

I vaguely remembered the ad, but I had no memory of signing it, although I would have if I had been asked, so I told Dales that, yes, I had signed it. (When I researched that ad I found that my name was listed along with hundreds of others, including many movie stars.)

(Parnell Thomas, a member of HUAC, was convicted of taking bribes while in office and was sent to Danbury Prison, where in one of those quirks of fate, Lester Cole and Ring Lardner Jr., two members of the Hollywood Ten convicted of contempt of Congress, were his prison mates.)

John Dales continued. "Did you sign an *amicus curiae* for the Supreme Court to hear the appeal for John Howard Lawson and Dalton Trumbo?"

"I did."

"Were you involved with the Actors Lab Theater?"

I told him I was, having attended an acting class moderated by Morris Carnovsky. (I later found that the Lab was listed as a communist front by the California State Senate Committee.)

When Dales asked if I would sign a loyalty oath I said, sure, if I could write it.

"Fine," he said, "write it." So, I wrote it, stating in it that I was not a member of the Actors Division of the Progressive Citizens of America (I wasn't), and that I had been in the U.S. Army for three and a half years during World War II, three of those years overseas. That I was not a subversive and had no intentions of overthrowing the government of the United States of America.

It was corny as hell, but I had no idea what a loyalty oath was, I just wanted to convince him I was no threat to this extraordinary country. My one object was to be free to work as an actor again.

Some time before I began working on this book, I received my FBI file. Most of it is blacked out to protect the people the FBI agents questioned about me. However, I will quote the file's final statement:

"No information concerning past or recent Communist Party affiliations in Hollywood on the part of KNOX has been brought to the attention of this office by established confidential sources, and there is no information available indicating that the subject is presently engaged in any Communist party functions.

"Inasmuch as no evidence has been developed reflecting Party membership or activity on the part of the subject, no further investigation is deemed warranted, and this case is being CLOSED."

1951 Hollywood

Anthony Quinn sheds the "graylist" mantle.

I had no intention of languishing in Hollywood without work. I had no recourse. There was no one to open doors unless I visited Ward Bond to convince him that I was not a pinko, or worse, a red. And that I could never do.

I digress to relate what Anthony Quinn told me about his meeting with Ward Bond. (Ward Bond was a burly actor and a solid member of John Wayne's clan. Being a staunch patriot, he declared himself a clearinghouse for repentant Commies and red sympathizers.)

Tony spent a lot of time at the Actors Lab, as did I. The Lab was a place where actors could take classes, exercise their talent, and take part in new plays being tried out on its small stage. Morris Carnofsky, formerly a member of the influential Group Theater in the thirties, moderated the classes. The Actors Studio, I believe, was a spin-off of the Lab.

It was, however, considered a left-wing roost—for the most part it was true and that's what tainted Tony. Sometime in 1949 Tony thought he had a part in a film and was puzzled when it fell through at the last moment. Someone in production quietly suggested he see Ward Bond and if Ward cleared him of being a subversive he would be in the film. Tony made an appointment with Bond and showed up at his office. The door was open but Bond wasn't there. Tony called out, "Hey Ward, it's Tony Quinn, you in?"

A voice from the bathroom shouted, "Yeah, Tony, I wanna talk to you, I'm in the john, come on in."

So Tony joined Ward in the bathroom. He was sitting on the throne taking a dump. He pointed to the edge of the tub and said, "sit there." Tony sat, desperately trying to hide his embarrassment in an effort to smile and be friendly. His career depended on passing the Ward Bond test.

Ward was blunt. "You a Commie, Tony, a red?"

"Hell no. Jesus be my judge, I never been even pink, much less red. Ward, I'm a loyal American, for chrissakes, you gotta believe me."

Ward grunted, squeezed, and finally unloaded. "Okay Tony, you're all right, go to work."

Tony got the part. He was on what was called the graylist; he never signed any political ads or petitions, but he hung out at the Lab. After his meeting with Bond he never returned there. He never was political. His fierce ambition was to be recognized as a great actor—and a movie star.

Tony was only mildly suspect. Even a buffoon like Bond could clear him. It's all so much like a bad Hollywood B movie, except that it's laughable—and chilling.

Tony Quinn's ugly episode with Bond told me I had to get out of Hollywood and back to New York.

1951 New York—Cross Country to Los Angeles

Driving cross-country with Norman Mailer.

Norman and I saw each other regularly. I met Bill Styron through him and later met James Jones at a loud, crowded New York party that Norman took me to. The four of us hung out at times. One night we were walking in the village. Styron, young and enthusiastic, put his arms around Norman's and Jim's shoulders, joyously announcing: "Here we are, the three best young writers in America!" Neither Norman or Jim objected, but let it be noted that they did appear both pleased and embarrassed.

Mailer, Jones, and I did some pub crawling on Eighth Avenue in midtown Manhattan. We played liar's poker between drinks. Jones didn't win a hand, and after each loss (we played for only a dollar) he shook his head, licked his moustache and grunted.

There was a lot of arm wrestling at parties and anywhere a few guys got together. Norman and Jim had avoided arm wrestling on previous occasions. At the last bar one night, the match finally took place. They sat in a booth, facing each other. Their forearms held the middle position for endless seconds. They shifted, barely, back and forth until the back of Jim's hand was a couple of inches above the table.

The look on Jim's face was concentrated determination. He was not going to be put down. He wasn't. He slowly pushed Norman's arm up until they reached the middle position again and it was over: a tie. They unclasped at the same time without a word being said.

I had beaten Jim the few times we matched up. It's not that I was stronger than he, I had to use timing and speed. It might be called cheating, what I did. I would snap his arm back the moment we clasped hands, not giving him a chance to brace himself.

He couldn't understand why I could put him down, but he paid me back by telling the guys at a party they couldn't beat me at arm wrestling. Boy, could they beat me. The experienced wrestlers knew the drill and it puzzled Jim that I couldn't beat everyone I wrestled with. I couldn't beat Norman; he knew the drill too.

Virtually all top-level writers I've known have had a streak of competitiveness, for the most part with each other, but it doesn't exclude friends or even strangers. You would think that a serious writer who has achieved fame and awards would be relaxed self-confident when in touch with the outside world. It doesn't always work that way, conflict seems to be the driving force to crack someone's carapace and discover what's within. That's not to say that writers cannot be polite, understanding, and even gentle. It happens.

Why do I hang out with writers? My biological father, Max Knox, was a poet—in Yiddish, but still a poet. He published regularly in the two New York Jewish newspapers, the *Forward* and *Freiheit*. The first was moderate, the second openly Communist. His brother, Israel Knox, a professor of philosophy, wrote his doctoral thesis on the Aesthetics of Kant, Hegel, and Schopenhauer. (I tried reading it, but it was a struggle.) Sperm plus blood are genealogical travelers, I figure.

My mother, an intellectual manqué (five children, raised during the Great Depression, having to work much of that time) talked me into loving literature from the time I learned to read, and I read any book I could get my hands on.

Norman and Bea, his first wife, had split. He was seriously involved with Adele, soon to be his second wife. It was a rough time and his next book was hatching in his brain. I was planning on returning to L.A. to see Lois and to explore the work atmosphere. Norman decided to join me for two reasons: He was wrestling with his personal life and the book he was contemplating was set in Hollywood and Palm Springs.

Before starting the cross-country trip, my stepfather lent me the money to buy a new Chevy, an inexpensive car at the time. I drove up to Vermont, where Norman was living, to pick him up. He decided he'd like to try out the new Chevy. I sat in the passenger seat while he drove along a rutted country lane bordered by bushes and brambles. He lost no time in playing Fangio, the legendary race-car driver, enjoying it immensely. He must have been doing at least forty, bumping and swerving over the ruts and scraping the sides of the new Chevy against the brambles.

He finally stopped the car, but didn't stop laughing. I grabbed his jacket from the backseat, dropped it on the dirt road and began dancing on it, or more accurately, stamping on it. It pissed me off that he didn't give a shit and kept laughing. *I gotta travel three thousand miles with this nut*, I thought. *Holy cow!*

We spelled each other during the trip. The one who sat in the passenger seat was the navigator and held the map. There were no super highways then. It was mostly state roads through towns and cities, but the driving was a hell of a lot more fun.

Norman wanted to stop off in Arkansas to visit with Fig, his army buddy. As we came within a few miles of where he lived, a terrific rainstorm thundered on us. The night was pitch dark and the headlights weren't much help. Their beams reflected the sheets of rain back to us, hardly illuminating the road. Norman was driving and I kept my door open to signal if we were too close to the shoulder. We finally made it to Fig's house. I was worn out by the last few miles.

I hit the sack quickly. Norman stayed up late talking to Fig. He had the rough part of the last leg and should have collapsed, but he didn't and was up and ready to go the next day.

We were somewhere in the middle of the U.S. and I was holding the map. When we came to a crossroads I said we should turn left. He insisted we had to turn to the right. I argued with him and tried to show him the map, but he won out. Having gone to Harvard and having learned surveying in the army, I had to yield, given those credentials.

One hundred miles later, we had to turn around and backtrack. Two hundred miles of extra driving ain't amusing. He was angry with me and I was angry with him. Then silence. Neither of us spoke that day or night when we stopped at a motel. The next morning it was still silence. After a wordless breakfast it was back on the road. The ice finally melted and the burden of the extra two hundred miles was silently forgotten.

A few hundred miles out of L.A., Norman asked if we could detour to Palm Springs. He was polite, asking if it didn't take us too far out of our way. The lost two hundred miles earlier lay somewhere in the innards of the Chevy. I readily agreed, noting that the detour would not add too much mileage.

I slowly drove through Palm Springs without stopping. When *The Deer Park* came out I had to admire the accuracy off Norman's observations. The architecture, the flora of the place and the town's character were stored in his memory after no more than twenty minutes in "The Springs."

In L.A., Norman checked into a hotel. I checked into Lois Andrews at her home on Doheny Drive. I introduced Lois to Norman. He was impressed and eventually used her as a model for Dorothea O'Faye in his play of *The Deer Park*, as he imagined Lois would be in later years.

One day Norman and I were on the Malibu beach horsing around. We were sparring as we usually did, without actually hitting each other. Before starting, he tossed his shirt over my head, leaving me vulnerable for a few seconds. He didn't take advantage of the moment, though, just laughed at the fun of it. Where did this guy I believed was so pure and so gentle when we first met learn street smarts? It was a small thing, but Norm was not always predictable.

Norman returned to New York and I stayed with Lois. Then Max Nosseck came into my life and caused an unexpected but welcome turn of events.

Max Nosseck, a short 5'4" movie director, befriended me. He was a Jew who had escaped Hitler's Germany, come to America, and directed a couple of hit movies: *Black Stallion* and *Dillinger*. He had a pronounced German accent that he would use for laughs at the drop of a vowel. He was always in good humor and he adored Lois.

He had come back from Italy to announce to me and Lois that he had made a deal with an Italian producer to film *Othello*. He had spoken to Canada Lee, a black former ranked boxer turned actor, and a good one, about playing Othello. Canada had the lead in *Native Son*, a play directed by Orson Welles, and had gotten good reviews for his acting. I was in a road company with Canada. Like most boxers, he had a cool, modest manner.

Max wanted me for Iago. Since an Italian actress was to play Desdemona, he'd find something for Lois. It all sounded glorious, especially since my movie career had taken a nosedive.

1952 S.S. *Independence*—Naples

Lois and I sail to Naples. Lunch and dinner with the notorious Mafia godfather, Lucky Luciano.

I was ready to kiss Hollywood good-bye and get going to Italy. *Othello* was the impetus, but I would have made the trip in any case. Italy seemed poised on the threshold of becoming the film center of Europe. A few Italian films had been released in main U.S. city art houses. Critics were in awe of *Open City* and *Bicycle Thief*. The Italians called their film movement Neo-Realism. It was inspired by the defeat of Fascism and the post-war poverty of the country.

I wanted to fly, but when Lois insisted we sail to Italy there was no way I could win that battle. When she flatly declared first class or she would stop packing her steamer trunk, I lost that battle too. Now, I can't argue with first class. It's the way to go, but I had a problem dealing with the cost: triple, at least, of steerage. And steerage would have been fine, since I get seasick no matter what class.

So I boarded the S.S. *Independence* as a gentleman, his lady on his arm. It was a true luxury liner, filled with elegant lounges, bars, and restaurants. Lois managed to get us seated at the captain's table. But the captain wasn't honored with my presence often after the first day out; I was in our first-class cabin, throwing my guts up in a bucket or just lying there moaning. Lois, the sailor girl, was the hit of the night owls, singing and dancing until sunrise. Lois drank, but I didn't believe that was the reason she didn't get sick, hell no, the more the ship rocked, the more she loved it.

What a waste. A beautiful ship, great food, and me miserable. Lois, out of pity, got the ship's doc to visit. He was sympathetic and helpful. "I've never known a drinking man to get seasick and I've been a ship's doctor over twenty years. See you at the bar, son."

I was always fearless in pursuit of getting value for my money; in this case, first-class fare. I dressed on shaky legs, repressing the need to heave, and made my way to the closest bar. What to order? The idea of booze caused my empty stomach to rebel. Maybe a crème de menthe, that might do it—nice and smooth on the way down.

After the second menthe I felt better. The good doc joined me half an hour later and I had a third one. I then went looking for Lois and found her on the dance floor. I cut in; she laughed, saying her *caballero* had finally showed up.

I sensed I shouldn't get drunk, just keep a little buzz going. So for the last three days of the eight-day trip, I had a mild drink every couple of hours or so. I did vomit most mornings, but what the hell.

After the ship docked at Naples, I was on Italian soil for the first time. We had booked a suite (of course) at the Hotel Excelsior, an old ornate building.

Lois was a friend of Joey Adonis, a handsome Mafioso who took time off from family business to be a Hollywood playboy. He told Lois to contact Lucky Luciano when in Naples; the desk clerk at the Exselsior would know how to reach him. (Lucky Luciano was the most famous and powerful Mafia boss of bosses during the 1930s. In the forties he was exiled to Italy.)

When we checked in at the hotel, I asked the desk clerk to get a message to Lucky Luciano. He looked blankly at me and said he never heard of him. "If you hear from him, tell him we got a message from Joey Adonis, okay," I whispered. And I winked like an asshole wise guy.

As we entered the suite, the phone rang. Lucky already? I glanced to Lois to answer it, I tipped the bellhop and pushed him out.

"Lucky! How nice to talk to you. This is Lois Andrews. A dear friend of ours, Joey Adonis—oh, just fine. He sends his best regards. Sure, we'd love to, I'm here with a friend. . . . Oh good. See you then," Lois trilled. She hung up and twirled a quick dance.

Lucky picked us up an hour later and we walked to Zia Maria, an outdoor restaurant overlooking the harbor, a short distance from the hotel.

Lucky Luciano spoke so softly one had to lean forward and concentrate on what he was saying—a clue to his success. He wore rimless glasses; his eyes were brown, almost black, penetrating. It felt as though he were seeking any sign of betrayal. I tried to appear as innocent as I really was. Not easy when those black eyes seemed to read my whole life. I might be trying to be too friendly, I thought, that would alert him. Fuck it, I wasn't there to plug him.

He must have bodyguards somewhere nearby; I didn't think he'd meet total strangers without protection. I glanced at the nearby tables searching for Mafiosi, but, shit, all the men looked to be from the Mafia, even the waiters.

Lucky took a fountain pen out of his jacket pocket and held it up, "This is a Parker 51, authentic, from America." He smiled. The Parker 51 was the newest creation and went on sale that year.

I wondered why he was so proud of it. Authentic? I later found out the "authentic" pens were not then available in Italy, but in Naples, that was no problem. They made them illegally, but they were phony. They had no innards; they were only shells. Lucky, however, had the real article.

"I miss America. They won't let me back. It makes me sad, know what I mean?" Lucky said wistfully. He had a slight but not unpleasant Sicilian accent.

After reading me during the first few minutes he turned his quiet magnetic charm on Lois, asking about Joey Adonis and her connection to him. She told Lucky she had a wide circle of friends, from millionaires to businessmen to politicians and Joey Adonis fit right in.

After lunch he asked if we'd like to have dinner at a Neapolitan nightclub.

That evening he once again came to get us. The club had a small group playing mostly Neapolitan music. When Lois said she'd like to dance, Lucky approached the leader of the band and whispered to him. The music changed to an American dance number. Lucky was somewhat stiff as he led Lois in an old-fashioned two-step.

Shortly after they returned to the table, Lois went to the powder room. Lucky leaned toward me and asked, "Is Lois your girl?" I nodded. He raised his hands in surrender and said, "Okay, that's good." Lucky was taken by Lois, but Mafia honor prevailed.

Mafia. Cosa Nostra. Family. Capo. Omerta. Words, like long-burning sparklers, spark the imagination to any number of scenarios. It's the underbelly of the American dream. Literature and movies have glorified the mafiosi's loyalty, their daring, their intense lives. I can't deny that I anticipated meeting Lucky with a degree of excitement.

I was struck by the thought that Lucky Luciano and I were soul mates. Soul mates? Okay, he was a mafioso, a killer, exiled to Italy by the U.S. Government. I, a blacklisted actor, in effect, was also exiled; I had come to Italy to keep working, just as Lucky was forced to do. Because, have no doubt, he still ran his Mafia operations from Italy. Know what I mean?

1952 Rome

Rome: I work with Jean Renoir and Anna Magnani.
Shelley Winters in Rome. I take a dive off a moving train.

R ome was a lovely revelation. My first love was Paris, but
Rome seduced me. The blacklist faded to Roman pink.
The city had a serene beauty. There were not many cars
on the streets. Trolley bells (and there were miles of trolley lines)
rang pleasingly; there were motorbikes, but not nearly in the numbers that came later as an antidote to slow-moving traffic.

The "trattoria" was a grand discovery. They were all over Rome:
small, family-run restaurants, much like the Paris bistro. Many a
pleasant hour was spent either at an outdoor table or inside a homey
"trattoria."

"The Snake Pit"—the bar at the Excelsior Hotel on the Via
Veneto, we soon discovered, was a meeting place, frequented by
barons, princes, counts, no-accounts, well-dressed Italians without
a lira in their pockets, and girls, plain to gorgeous. They hoped to
get into movies, while the men were hoping to get into the girls.
And of course there were the ever-present wannabe directors and
producers.

Lois was always the main attraction: seductively dressed, flirting,
enjoying all of the attention. I knew she was playing her game and I
was amused watching her, knowing we would invariably come back
to our hotel room together at the end of the night. Max Nosseck was

always with us, beaming as he was fawned over by Casanovas who hoped he was Lois's agent or uncle.

Othello quickly faded out of the picture. Max was conned by a couple of Italian producers who were hoping he would bring financing from the "golden streets" of America. All the producers had was a bare office and Italian suits. A Roman might not have a pot to piss in, but he maintained "faccia"—a wealthy, successful appearance.

Lois was having an extravagant time and gave it no thought. She had never believed she would be in a movie called *Othello*. She had little acting experience, having worked mainly as a nightclub singer.

The day came for her to return to the States. I had previously decided to stay in Rome and look for work, having been denied that choice back home. What the hell, it didn't bother me; I was young, enchanted by Rome and the Romans. Movies were being made in Italy and they were desperate for actors, for, as Orson Welles remarked, the best Italian actors are on the city streets.

We returned to Naples. Lois boarded the S.S. *Independence* once again and I watched her sail away. She left an ache, but I was also happy to be on my own.

• • •

Anna Magnani. Her passion, her power to move an audience, was seen in *Open City*, a drama of the Nazi occupation of Rome and the first Italian film after World War II to hit American screens and it did so with electrifying force. It was the beginning of Italian "Neo-Realism."

Open City was the harbinger of a nascent film industry, and I wanted to be there as it developed. I had used the G.I. Bill to study Italian for a few months. I already knew French fairly well. Knowing languages was the key to my first film job in Italy.

Magnani was starring in *The Golden Coach*, a movie being shot in Rome, directed by Jean Renoir. It followed a troupe of Italian *commedia dell'arte* actors performing in South America in the seventeenth century. Since it was being shot in English, I was hired to coach the Italian actors along with another coach.

Renoir knew little English. His wife, Dido, told me she insisted that he study English when he was in Hollywood, a refugee from the Nazis. Although he was internationally known, when directing films in America, he was obliged to speak English. Renoir resisted. Like many of his compatriots, he claimed French was the only civilized language and he couldn't clutter his mind with English.

Dido, a strong Portuguese woman fluent in several languages, including English, finally engaged an English teacher for Renoir. A few months later, the Renoirs, while exploring downtown Los Angeles, came to a Salvation Army meeting hall and decided to go in. They sat on a bench in back of a large room, partly filled with the homeless, listening to a Salvation Army speaker. After a few minutes, Renoir turned to Dido and whispered, "You see, I learned English, I understand what he is saying."

Dido smiled scornfully and said, "Jean, you are a cretin. The gentleman is speaking Spanish."

Jean Renoir was the son of the famous French painter Auguste Renoir, and was in many of his father's paintings as a sweet-looking child. When I met him he must have been in his sixties. He was a large, heavy man, gentle, and, for a Frenchman, warm and amiable. He liked Hollywood, its informality, its sunny climate. Anyone who has spent time in Paris during the winter months can understand how inviting Californian weather is to the French.

Renoir always wore a hat, probably to protect his balding head from the sun when shooting outside. However, before calling action on a sound stage, he would remove the hat. I asked why. His answer was short. "Out of respect for the actors."

My first day on the set, I watched as the other dialogue coach badgered Magnani over her pronunciation. She not only knew no English, she was an actress of great emotion and had a difficult and frustrating time dealing with a language not her own.

Renoir was also frustrated, not knowing what the hell was going on. "Lay off her, fercrissakes, you're fucking her up," I called out. I have a big New York mouth, but I, too, was frustrated watching her frustration. (Ten years later, Magnani told me she was grateful that I tried to protect her performance that day, and so got me the job on the film, *Rose Tattoo*.)

Magnani knew she had made a mistake when she agreed to try acting in English. It was decided that she could speak her dialogue in Italian, except for close-ups, at which time she would have to learn the lines in English, where her lip movements would be critical for the dubbing. There she asked for me for help. We had a good working rapport, but nothing more than that, no socializing or taking meals together. It was not until we worked on *Rose Tattoo* that we became close, though never intimate, friends.

There were several English actors in the film. Renoir wanted to visually convey the clear difference between the nobility and the peasants. The romantic lead opposite Magnani was an American actor who could pass as English. Magnani was never happy with the choice. She didn't find him masculine enough. After the first day's shooting a love scene, she insisted that he be replaced.

Renoir and Magnani ran the tests they had shot of English actors when casting. They chose Duncan Lamont, a handsome, rugged actor, to replace the American. He had originally been hired to play a small role. Upon his arrival on the set, Lamont was told he was to play the leading role opposite Magnani. He was as cool as only the English can be. "Very nice, thank you," he said softly.

During the shooting, I asked him, as he had shown hardly any emotion when told he was to star in the film, how he really felt that day. He laughed. "Are you pulling my leg? My heart plummeted to my stomach. I felt as though I was about to drop through the floor."

Lamont was a very good actor and I felt he would score big when the film came out. But *The Golden Coach*, for reasons I never understood, was hardly distributed in the States. A brilliant film, it sunk out of sight. Magnani's performance alone was worth the price of admission.

Stan Swinton, the Bureau Chief for the Associated Press in Rome, was a hotshot journalist. Before coming to Italy, he had been the youngest bureau chief at any American news organizations with offices abroad. In his case, the Far East.

We met in Rome. Actors intrigued him. It was good enough reason to become friends. He had a large apartment and asked me to be his guest. It was timely; I was running out of cash.

He had, what in Yiddish is called "shpilkes," meaning pins and needles; a metaphor for restive. In describing Stan, I'd add fidgety. He also had to prove he was always on the ball.

Our bedrooms were separated by French doors, allowing me to clearly hear when he was on the phone. Often he would be called by the New York AP office in the middle of the night. Stan would clear his throat and shout, "Stan, you're up and ready. You're awake, right? Right! So answer the goddamn phone! Hello! Of course I'm awake fer chrissakes!" His girlfriend was a screamer and when she stayed the night it was either her screaming or Stan shouting. What a character. He was always good for a laugh, even in the middle of the night.

I fell out of a moving train on my lucky day. It was lucky because I survived without serious injury. It was a weird accident. Or was it an accident? I was returning from a trip to a rugged little island north of Rome, Isola del Giglio. As the train approached Civitavecchia, an hour or so from Rome, it started to slow. It was a hot day and the train was jammed.

I was standing at the end of the car next to the exit, hoping to get a breath of cool air. Facing me was a man who caught my eye. He had a full head of wild jet-black hair and dark intense eyes staring at me.

I was spooked. If there was a devil, this was him. He suddenly pushed me aside and, in gruff Italian, said, "Let me get to the door. I have to get out. I have no ticket."

I said, "You want to get out, be my guest," I opened the door. That was the last thing I remembered.

I landed on my head on the railroad's bed of rocks. I came to in a hospital bed. My head was shaved and bandaged. Trying to remember what had happened, I had a sinking feeling. The train was moving fairly fast. I could have fallen under the wheels. And was that really the devil? What lunacy gripped me when I mindlessly pulled that door open?

They x-rayed my head and informed me that what had saved my ass was a double-thick skull. Embarrassing, but what the hell.

It's still a mystery to me how Stan got the news so quickly. It was on the wire to the States that same day. The headline read FILM ACTOR HURT IN ITALY (April 15, 1952). The next day, he wrote a follow-up account stating that a double-thick skull saved my life. Now the whole world knew.

The three railroad workers who carried me to the hospital came to visit. I knew they were earning the equivalent of a buck a day at that time. I beseeched them to accept some cash as a token of my appreciation. They flat-out refused. Their sweetness and genuine concern marked the moment when I fell in love with Italians.

By definition, journalists are heralds of disasters. Stan Swinton, being a journalist in his blood, tried his best to contain the thrill when he called from his office to report the rotten news—John Garfield had died. He was thirty-nine. Stan was aware that Garfield was a friend of mine, that he was blacklisted, and that he was having a rough time dealing with it.

Garfield was born Jacob Julius Garfinkle. As a young actor in New York he changed his name to Julie Garfield. When Warner Brothers brought him to Hollywood he became John Garfield, but he was always Julie to his friends.

He was in the Group Theater during much of the thirties and made his mark in a Clifford Odets play, *Awake and Sing*.

Odets wrote his hit play, *Golden Boy*, with Garfield in mind as the boxer, the leading character. But Luther Adler, a more experienced actor, was given the part. The group needed a commercial success and I supposed they felt safer with Adler.

Adler was reported to be good in the part, but knowing the emotional power Garfield had, he might have set the stage on fire with his passion. A pity he didn't play the golden boy in the film. William Holden had the honor.

Julie's first film role was in *Four Daughters*. He played a bitter piano-playing wanderer, and a star was born. Garfield was a superb, instinctive actor. He was often cast as a hard-luck, tough but honest bloke, a gangster, or a revolutionary and once a lovesick Mexican in John Steinbeck's *Tortilla Flats*. He was loved by working stiffs, the poor, and the marginal. They identified with his gritty resistance to injustice, to authority.

Harold Clurman, one of the founders of the Group Theater and noted stage director, wrote an autobiography, whimsically titled, *All People Are Famous* and subtitled, "instead of an autobiography." The following is a quote from that book:

"Theater folk are generally innocents: unpretentious, sentimental, credulous, enthusiastic, and where their immediate professional interests are not threatened, generous, and kindhearted. They are usually glad to help the unfortunate, as the record of wartime charities, and of contributions in time and money to those caught in natural or social disasters, amply testifies.

"This was especially true of Garfield, who was a thoroughly sweet boy. Orphaned young, he became a problem child. A wise educator, Angelo Patri, the principal of a Bronx high school, took him in hand, so successfully that Jules Garfinkel endeared himself to everyone in the theater: first to Eva Le Gallienne and later to all of us in the Group.

"The total absence of malice in him, his love of laughter and his capacity for friendship won him the confidence of all sorts of people everywhere. Even his constant malapropisms charmed everyone."

For those who remember Garfield, admired his talent, and were moved by his troubles and death, the Clurman quote will give his life some definition.

Garfield was blacklisted in the film industry because he refused to name friends who were communists, but he was anything but political. He loved the Group Theater for accepting him and training him to fully use his talent as an actor.

He listened to the talk of the time; the politics of the Great Depression. Most of the people in the Group were on the left and some were members of the Communist Party, but Garfield was not a member. The House Un-American Committee knew that, but they were convinced that he knew those in the Group who were or had been communists.

He appeared twice before the Committee and was willing to aid them in any way except naming names, but that didn't satisfy his interrogators, although they already knew who the communists were. Garfield suffered terribly. No one in Hollywood would defy the blacklist and put him to work. But Garfield couldn't violate his personal code and betry his friends, and he paid dearly. Acting was his lifeblood. When Hollywood completely shut him out, he withered and died.

We saw each other for the last time when Robbie, his wife, invited me to dinner. Julie was in a nervous, tortured mood. After diner he asked me to go for a walk in Central Park.

He was agitated, angry. He kept repeating the lament, "What do they want from me? What did I do?" He was inconsolable. The blacklist had destroyed him.

There were lurid stories in the tabloids of Garfield having died in bed and in the saddle. It was untrue. He had played poker late that night, didn't feel well, and asked a girl he knew to put him up for the night. (He had argued with his wife, Robbie, and wasn't living at home.) I knew the girl and she told me he was in no condition for any activity, much less sex. Julie felt rotten, finally fell asleep in his underwear, and never woke up. His heart stopped pumping in the dead of night.

FLASH FORWARD:

Within a few years, Stan Swinton had reached a high position at the Associated Press. He was married and lived in New York, enjoying a rich, full life. I was in New York in 1982 when I got word he had cancer.

I was invited to a party at a friend's loft. The lights were low and it was crowded. I was standing near a dark corner of the loft when I heard a feeble, unrecognizable voice calling me. I turned and approached to see a skeleton wrapped in skin sitting in the semidark. His eyes were bright and angry.

I had no idea who he was. "You don't know me, do ya?" he said. I didn't answer. "Jesus, it's me, Stan Swinton."

I then said something stupid: "Stan! How the hell are you?" And Stan confirmed my stupidity: "How am I? Always the kidder. I'm dying, okay?"

He died later that year.

• • •

The Via Veneto was the center of Rome's social life. It was only two long blocks featuring outdoor cafés along both sides of the street. At first, movie people gathered to meet each other and enjoy some conversation while having an espresso, but movie stars attract the citizenry and in due time everyone flocked to Veneto.

Man, to sit and "people-watch" for hours on end was the greatest show in town. Each day the same crowd would gather to join the growing number of tourists strolling up and down the Veneto, checking out those seated, as they themselves were being stared at. I was part of a gang that table-hopped and after several days I got to know most of the regulars.

My days in Rome were sweet and fun. One had to experience life on the Veneto and the streets of Rome to sense the underlying humor of it all. Half the people on the Veneto were on the make—for a girl, for any job in movies, for a loan, even a cappuccino. Movie stars came to be fawned over, to display their wardrobes, and just to bask in all the attention. Via Veneto became known around the world and was the inspiration for *La Dolce Vita*, Fellini's acclaimed film.

Tom Shaw was one of the best assistant directors in the business. He eventually worked most of John Huston's films. I got to know him on a film I was in at Universal Studios. He had the face of an ex-boxer and it fit his personality. He was tough and blunt-talking, but he had a tender soul.

I ran into Tom in the Snake Pit, in fact, he hung that name on the joint. He had graduated to production manager and was in Rome to back up an inexperienced American producer's film, *Raw is the Wind* to be shot completely in Italy. (In the early years after World War II, American film companies that distributed films in Europe could not exchange the local currency they had earned for dollars, simply because those countries didn't have much hard currency. So the U.S. companies made films with the local currency they had accumulated. They then distributed those films in the U.S. and the rest of the world to earn dollars.)

Aside from Jeff Chandler and Esther Williams, the other actors were Italian, but had to speak their dialogue in English. Tom hired me on the spot to be the dialogue director, coaching the Italian actors to learn the English dialogue and memorize it. When Tom said, "Mickey, this is your big chance. Name your price and you got it. We're making this film with frozen assets so you'll be paid in lire," I knew I had tread on horseshit.

Richard Wilson, the writer-director of the film, was an admirer of the playwright-actor, Edoardo De Filippo (known as simply Edoardo to all of Italy.) Among others, Anna Magnani had praised his humorous, profound and superb plays about the poor of Naples, where Edoardo came from. He was also considered a unique stage actor, never flamboyant, always subtle.

I believe Wilson wanted to get to know Edoardo, so he wrote a part for him. But Edoardo spoke not a word of English and it was torture for him to learn any of the dialogue. He gave it a try, but it was useless. He also had a drab, uninteresting role, which didn't compel him to suffer the hard work. I convinced Wilson to let him speak in Italian and dub him in English later. That obvious suggestion was the basis for a longtime friendship between Edoardo and me.

Edoardo, many years later, was made an honorary member of the Italian Senate—a rare privilege.

Rome was full of surprises. Seeing Shelley Winters on the Veneto was one of them. She was working on a film and, like all of us, fell in love with Rome. We saw each other from time to time. Shelley didn't believe in wasting a moment of her life by not being involved—with men, but most of all, her work.

We arranged to meet at the Snake Pit to talk about her latest dilemma. She was being wooed by two handsome Italian actors. She was flattered, amused, and jittery; which actor to choose? I had met them both.

In the normal course of pursuing pussy, Roman men are relentless. Either the woman succumbs or, after the flattery fades to annoyance, the chick shout angrily and, with luck, the stud will shake his head in wonder and turn away.

Shelley's dilemma was between Vittorio Gassman and Raf Valone. Both actors had class, after all. They had recently become movie stars, having worked on the same film, *Bitter Rice*, the first international smash hit that Dino De Laurentis produced.

Unlike most pursuers, they had some cash to spend. Gassman had grandly offered to take her to romantic Venice; Valone had invited her for an exciting tour of sunny Sicily. They were both spectacularly handsome and they appealed to her equally. What to do?

Life is chock full of choices I told her, so flip a coin. She did. Vittorio Gassman was the coin's choice and beautiful Venice it was.

Shelley came back from Venice where the romance had flourished, and she moved in with Vittorio. Venice had been idyllic; Rome—reality. Several days later she called me in tears. She had had a serious argument with her Italian lover. It had gotten so bad she had packed her bags. Would I meet her? She had to talk to me (Dr. Knox). Back to the Snake Pit.

She cried some and told me the inevitable. She had expected Vittorio to be faithful, but he, a proud Italian male, said it was his right to screw around. She howled, "What about me, what if I get laid? That ought to be okay too." He hovered over her, furious, and said, "I kill you if you fucked another man!"

His rage scared her and she decided to get her ass out of the danger zone. It was bad judgment, she said, she should have chosen Raf Valone. Little did she know the coin had two tails.

Ambition and love won out. Shelley and Vittorio reassembled and voyaged to Hollywood. He got his lead role in a major MGM film and flunked. It wasn't his fault. He was a good actor, but it's tough for a foreigner with an accent to find stardom in Movieland.

Vittorio returned to Rome without Shelley and became one of Italy's leading actors on stage and screen for almost fifty years.

1952 Rome—Monte Carlo—Paris

Robert Capa.

Robert Capa was known internationally as a superb photo-journalist and an envied playboy. Women adored him and flocked to him, and he adored them. Capa was Hungarian. He never lost his accent, which enhanced his appeal. His skin was darkened by long hours in the sun and by the elements. His hair was thick and black and fell over his forehead. His eyes were magnets that attracted both men and women; men for his companionship, women for more intimate connections.

A Rome nightclub, Pappagallo, was hot during the fifties. I was there with Capa and my date one night: When he left, he left with her. It didn't bother me, it amused me. She was just a date, a new acquaintance, and he knew that. I admired his ease and his casual, gentle way with women.

Capa had taken a photograph during the Spanish Civil War of a Loyalist soldier in the instant he was shot in the forehead. His arms are outflung as if trying to prevent himself from falling backward. That photo circled the globe and made Capa famous.

He covered World War II and somehow managed to survive despite his crazy demand that he be dropped with Allied paratroopers behind the German lines in Yugoslavia. He insisted on landing with the first waves on D-Day and survived. He took hundreds of photos of the invasion and sent them to London to be developed. It was unbelievably lousy luck that almost all of the negatives were ruined in the developing process. The loss still nags at one.

He remained in Rome for a couple of weeks and we saw each other often. Funny, we never talked about women or the girl that came with me and left with him. He met my friends, I met the people he knew. He had that special talent for bringing people together, stirring them up and making the time spent together fun. I don't think he had any enemies, but he did hate the Germans.

I told him I was planning on a trip to Paris, his base. He had a green convertible Ford that he had driven down to Rome, but he didn't have the time for the trip back and asked if I would mind driving his Ford to Paris. I didn't mind at all. The drive appealed to me.

Capa and a few other well-known photographers, including Henri Cartier-Bresson, formed their own agency, called Magnum. He asked me if I had a camera; I did. He told me to take pictures of anything that looked interesting on my way to Paris. I might get lucky and sell one or two. I was an amateur and knew nothing technically about shooting professional photos. He gave me one quick lesson: Keep snapping, never rest your finger, and when you see what you want to photograph, shoot a hundred pictures. You get one good one, you're a professional.

He reminded me of the day I took him to the set of a film Anna Magnani was making at the Rome film studio, Cinecittà. He annoyed the cast and director by constantly snapping away. He got one good picture of Magnani and was happy. Capa was a steady contributor to *Life* magazine. They published that photo of Magnani.

Ingrid, a Swedish girl I barely knew, heard that I was driving to Paris and asked if she could hitch a ride with me. How could I refuse? She was gorgeous.

When the day came to leave Rome, the ache and remorse I felt was relieved by my blonde passenger, Ingrid.

Off we drove, up the coast to Monte Carlo. At the border we had to show our passports to French customs. She gave me her passport.

Of course I sneaked a look and saw: Profession: Countess. What the hell is a professional countess? Do you need a college degree? A license? Or just a father who counts?

I wanted to continue on to Cannes but she asked if we could stay the night in Monte Carlo. What the hell, why not a night at the Hotel de Paris; elegant, exclusive and expensive? The countess, dressed for the night in an evening gown. Yes, the nobility travel with dress-up clothes always at the ready.

After dinner we went to the casino. Once inside I was no more than a vaguely known acquaintance. She sat at the baccarat table as though she were queen of Sweden, treated her cards with controlled scorn, and looked at none of the other players. I got heartburn watching the size of the tips she would toss at the croupier when she won. Cold, classy, detached, that was my countess.

Monte Carlo behind us, she was once again just a simple Swedish girl. That suited me fine. As a gambling countess, she was too aloof and a pain in the ass. Surprisingly, she traveled with a heap of cash. She was a modest winner and offered to pay the hotel bill. I was mad enough and cheap enough to split the cost.

The night in Monte Carlo was "white," as they say in Italy: no sex. I was asleep when she got in, as first light came up in the east. But the next night I discovered she was a sexual adventurer. It was a memorable night and it wiped out any misgivings I felt about taking the trip with her.

Upon arrival in Paris, the Ford, possibly unhappy being among Parisian cars, conked out. The amazing place it chose to quit was alongside Longchamps, the Paris racetrack. Capa loved the ponies and Longchamps was his field of joy. (His green convertible Ford, needed to find his boss and knew "this is the place.")

Capa laughed happily when I called to tell him where to find his wounded Ford. The following day, the countess and I joined him at the track. I knew zero about horses or betting on them. The first three races Capa would not give me a horse to bet on. He covered his card with a cupped hand so I couldn't see his choice.

The equivalent of two bits was the smallest amount one could bet. I bought a two-bit ticket, win, place, and show on every horse in the race. I fanned the winning tickets under Capa's nose.

He was puzzled, genuinely surprised. "You didn't tell me you can handicap. What do you have in the next race?"

I faked weighing the possibilities, then sagely said, "You'll find out when the race is over."

I had the winning tickets, of course. His eyes bugged out. I didn't press it and passed a couple of races. I was sure he'd get it. He never did. It cost me a few bucks, but they were well spent.

I took a lot of useless photos during the drive north to Paris. I knew they were lousy. I had no eye for composition or what to shoot. It was just a lot of wasted film, except for one shot. After the races were over, Capa aimed his ever-present Nikon at me, proclaiming me the champ of the day. I aimed my camera and shot him as he was shooting me, proclaiming him chump of the day. That was the only photo Capa kept for his personal use. I had contributed to Magnum.

Years later, on a *Life* assignment in Japan, Capa was informed by his editor to wrap it and get his ass to Vietnam, where the French were fighting to hold on to their colony. He was in a field in Vietnam, his weapon, a Nikon, at the ready, when he stepped on a land mine.

The year was 1954. He was 41 years old.

1952 Paris

Sidney Chaplin.

The Lancaster Hotel in Paris on the Rue de Berri, off the Champs Elysées, was the place to stay in the early fifties. American actors, taking advantage of the new tax law allowing a total exemption of earnings in a foreign country by U.S. citizens, probably stopped at the Lancaster. (I wasn't flush enough.)

I walked into the lobby one early evening and ran into Sidney Chaplin, Charlie's second son. We had met in Hollywood shortly before I left for Italy, while I was living with Lois Andrews. She had been in a play at the Circle Theater with Sidney.

He was laid back, very funny, a true original. All who knew Sidney were attracted to him and wanted to be his companion. His charm was easy and natural, his attitudes weren't sharp or disagreeable. Yet he wasn't quick to get close to anyone or engage in more than just a passing friendship. That, too, attracted men and women to him (oh yes, the women). Many wanted a deeper friendship than he was willing to give.

Although we didn't know each other too well, he was happy to see a familiar face. He had just arrived from London to test for a part in a film Anatole Litvak was preparing, based on a novel about wartime Rome: *The Girl On the Via Flaminia*, by John Horne Burns.

Sidney was pleased to be in Paris. He suggested we go up to his room and order champagne and strawberries. Litvak was picking up the tab.

That sounded fine to me. We had two bottles of champagne poured over ripe, sweet strawberries, a happy combination. We were then in an exhuberant mood to hit the town. We were joined by a mutual acquaintance we had met in the lobby.

The journey through the clubs and bars of Paris lasted three days. We were on a constant alcohol high, but not high enough to stumble along the way. I don't remember too much of those three days, but there was a lot of laughter, bonhomie, and little introspection.

I do remember in fairly good detail the final night: we ended up playing strip poker with three girls. A fine game for fit young bodies. If you play strip poker long enough everyone ends up nude. Our friend was delirious with joy. "Isn't this the greatest thing, Sid?" he said.

"This happens to me all the time," Sidney bellowed in his baritone voice. It's surprising how timely that simple phrase can be—"This happens to me all the time," and it's always good for a laugh.

When we finally got back to the Lancaster, we found an unfriendly note from Litvak: "The hotel bill is yours to pay, goodbye." The strawberries and champagne, added to the price of the room were beyond Sidney's resources. But he had a fallback position: United Artists offices were around the corner. Sidney's father was one of the founders of the film company, along with Douglas Fairbanks and Gloria Swanson. But Charlie Chaplin still had some control.

Sidney decisively went to the accounting department, handed the hotel bill to the girl behind the counter and said, absolutely sure of himself, "Take care of this, I'm Sidney Chaplin, put it on my father's account. Thank you." He smiled at the girl and walked out.

I ran into Litvak a couple of days later. He was even less friendly than his note to Sidney. "You led Sidney astray, you got him drunk.

He disappeared for three days. Well, he lost his chance, I'm not testing him."

Kirk Douglas got the part, although Sidney did play a different role in *Act of Love*. It was not a bad movie.

1952 Paris—London

Gregg Sherwood and Horace Dodge.

P aris during 1952 was too exciting for me to leave. The truth is, Paris is always difficult to leave. Paris is a "walking city." It was always pleasing to discover a neighborhood I didn't know. Away from the wide avenues, the side streets had the appealing smell of garlic and black tobacco. It was pleasant for the eye to scan the gray, age-old buildings and see the locals lifting a glass of wine in the bars.

One evening I walked the streets I knew, the 8th Arrondissement, ending up at the upper end of the Champs Elysées. I walked down the avenue George Cinq and wandered into the Hotel George Cinq bar. I was dry and tired and envisioned a frosted martini glass sitting on the bar. It brought me a happy grin of anticipation. For a decent dry martini, the one bar that delivered was the Hotel George Cinq.

The bartender knew me. He nodded, I nodded, and in a couple of minutes there it was: a graceful iced martini glass, brimming with clear, fine English gin. No olive, no onion, just gin and a drop of dry vermouth, stirred in a cold steel shaker.

(A devotée of the dry martini doesn't immediately reach for the glass, no matter how thirsty. He contemplates it for a moment, anticipating the cold taste and the liquid making its way down into one's center, then further delays its delight by taking a deep breath and carefully lifting the glass by its stem, never the body of the glass, heedful not to lose a drop while bringing it to his lips, he breathes the aroma of the good gin, nods a silent "thank you" to the bartender, and sips to clear the brim. The cold gin lights a spark of silent bliss as it washes over the taste buds.)

I drank slowly, allowing the gin to gradually spread its warmth. Before I emptied the glass, the bartender surprised me by setting another dry martini in front of me.

He looked beyond me and moved his eyes to a nearby table. An attractive blonde woman, sitting with a middle-aged gentleman, smiled and waved for me to join them. I turned back to the bartender. He gave me a pursed smile and a Gallic shrug.

I left the dry martini on the bar, expecting to return. That's how I met Gregg Sherwood and Horace Dodge. Her smile was too inviting not to join them. I went back to the bar to claim the martini they had ordered for me.

Gregg Sherwood? The name jogged my memory. Yes, she had been in the tabloids a year or two before. Her husband, Mr. Sherwin, was an executive with the New York Yankees (treasurer?). There was some disagreement between him and Yankee brass. Greg divorced him soon afterwards.

A few moments after I joined them, Gregg Sherwood said, "I want to show you something." She opened her alligator-skin purse, took out a lizard-skin wallet, found a folded magazine clipping, and handed it to me. It was a photo of me cut from a movie magazine. She knew the films I had been in and said she liked my looks. Well, I sure liked her looks.

Gregg chatted and smiled often as she touched my arm. I finished my martini, stood up, and thanked them for the drink. Gregg turned to Horace, "Hon, we want Mickey to have dinner with us, don't we?"

"Sure, baby, sure, the three of us will have dinner."

"Thanks, but . . . "

Gregg, on hearing "but," cut in. "No buts. We want you to join us." She looked into my eyes, trying to transmit a message. I accepted the dinner invite.

We went to a ritzy expensive Right Bank restaurant, not my normal eatery. My hangout was the Left Bank and the bistro.

After dinner it was off to a nightclub to dance. If one is on the make, dancing is critical. Horace sat and drank champagne while Gregg and I danced. She whispered in my ear, "It's you and me tonight, you know that, don't you?" I didn't know that, but I discarded any idea of arguing.

Naturally, they had a chauffeured limo. Gregg, an experienced intriguer, had Horace dropped off first, insisting he needed his rest and should go right to bed. Horace agreed and even apologized to me for not taking me to my hotel first.

When we arrived at my hotel, Gregg slipped out of the limo, said something to the driver, and came up to my room. She got undressed and jumped into bed. Not a word was said until I asked if the chauffeur could be trusted. "Have no fear, I control the purse strings," she giggled.

Horace Dodge was the son of the founder of the Dodge Automobile Company. The family was rich, filthy rich is what I mean. Horace did no work. His mother was the boss of the company and planned it so that Horace would be on the road most of the time. Gregg fit the bill. She kept him away from Detroit and for the most part, out of the country.

They were leaving in a few days for a castle in England that the Dodge family had bought. Gregg invited me to join them. I didn't think it was a good idea. Gregg said, "My dear, there are a hundred and one rooms in the old castle, he'll never find us."

I accepted the invite on condition that I come along with a friend, Sidney Chaplin. "Charlie's son? Of course he can come along, silly," she said. And that's how Sidney and I got to an ancient, recon-structed, huge castle, not far from Westminster, which the English kings and queens called their home away from home.

Gregg sent a driver to pick us up in London in an open Rolls. It was a warm sunny day. As we drove through the streets of Westminster, lined with sightseers, Sidney stood up and waved royally to the people. Thinking they were seeing a prince of the realm, they shouted, hooray, and applauded. His performance was right on.

The castle was indeed impressive, right off the pages of an illustrated history of England; a moat, battlements, a drawbridge, and a hundred and one rooms. Sidney had a large bedroom with a canopied bed, as did I.

A bishop of the Church of England and a local English gentleman were invited to dinner the first night. Horace was accompanied by his "bodyguard." That's what Horace called him, but he was in reality a male nurse, hired to look after Horace and make sure he didn't drink himself to death.

After dinner we retired to one of the salons for coffee and brandy. I imagined myself on the set of an English murder mystery movie. Horace carried a loaded leather briefcase to dinner and then to the afterdinner salon, where he set it down next to his armchair and told his bodyguard-nurse to protect it with his life.

"What's in it?" I had the audacity to ask.

"Oh, can't tell you, but I will say they are state secrets."

Looking for a laugh, which I didn't get, I asked, "What state, or is it the state of what?" Horace looked up at his bodyguard: "Tell him, will you?"

"*State* secrets, right sir?"

Horace just grinned.

He then went on to regale us with tales of his heroics during World War II; his exploits as a spy taken to the coast of France in a sub to make contact with the French underground, how he demolished bridges and blew up German garrisons, and so on. (Gregg later told me his briefcase was full of comic books, and that his wartime exploits came straight out of comics.)

Suddenly, Horace asked his man to help him up. He half stood while holding on to the arms of his chair. "I think I can get rid of it here," he said hoarsely. He held his breath, grunted, puffed out his cheeks, and generally exerted himself.

"Not here, sir," his man whispered. Then he did it: blasted a windbreaker and sighed happily. The bishop and the English gentleman glanced at each other but showed no further reaction.

Sidney and I returned to Paris, Gregg to New York. I promised to call her when next in the Big Apple. In New York, we made a date for lunch. She had the look of someone who had big news to tell, but was holding on to it, as though it were an orgasm held to the last moment. Her eyes were slits as she smiled in anticipation.

After the coffee was served, she held up her cup to toast something unknown; I obliged her by lifting my cup and touching hers. And out it came: "Okay, my honey, the time has come. Let's get married. I have over three hundred thousand dollars in cash and jewelry. We can have a fabulous time for a year."

Three hundred big ones—over a million in today's market. "You must be kidding, Gregg. Marriage just ain't a good idea . . . nope, not a good idea," I said. For the first time since we met, she lost her merry look and turned puzzled. Then came the tears. I was silent and reached for her hand, but she stood up and walked out of the restaurant.

I never saw her again, but I read about her. She married Horace Dodge. He soon passed to where the idle rich end up, but his mother lived well into her nineties. Gregg got an allowance and the use of a credit card in a couple swank department stores. Finally, mother joined son and a fortune fell into Gregg's lap. She moved to Palm Beach, Florida, and after serving an apprenticeship, became the chairwoman of the Board of the Palm Beach Society for the Very Rich.

1952 New York
Lois Andrews.

merica for me is New York. The city feeds my energy. I was accepted as a member of the Actors Studio, found a small flat, and worked on scenes at the Studio. I watched a tiny TV screen, fascinated, as Senator Joe McCarthy succeeded in tearing up the country.

Lois and I kept in touch by phone and mail. Lois used the phone and I wrote letters. Putting aside the cost of long distance calls, I enjoyed the intimacy and freedom to write whatever came to mind.

One day I got a serious call from Lois. "I have something real important to ask you so sit down and listen. I was in Mexico and met this Italian prince, so he said . . . anyway, I'm knocked up, and . . ."

I finished her thought. "And you want me to marry you, right?"

A long, pregnant, pause, "Right."

Oh, man, what do I do. I did feel I owed her; she had always been generous in spirit and coin (wouldn't accept any rent). I hesitated, then: "Okay, Lois, you're on."

"Listen, Mick, I swear, if you want a divorce after the baby is born, or even before, we go to Tijuana and get a quickie divorce."

What the hell . . . but I didn't have money for the trip back to L.A. "Okay Lois, when do you want me in L.A.?"

She knew, all right. "I'll send you a plane ticket today, you should have it in a couple of days, come out as soon as you can."

The letter with the plane ticket, including a thank-you note, arrived. A couple of days later, I called to tell her what time I'd be arriving. Her maid answered and I could hear her embarrassed tone when I asked to speak to Lois. "She's out."

"Did she say what time she's be back?"

"No, she didn't . . . "

"Didn't she tell you anything, in case I called?"

"Yes, she did, she said she'd be back . . ." The maid didn't want to continue.

"Is she out of town?"

"Yes, sir, she was seeing a friend off on the boat going to Hawaii and she never came off that boat."

I had a giddy feeling of relief; it was a load off my mind. I was the groom left at the altar. I knew my darling Lois; she bought the champagne, drank most of it, got loaded and suddenly fell in love with another long boat trip. She adored sailing, never got seasick, sang with the band, and danced and flirted with the ship's officers.

She had little to fear; if she were married to me, her baby would be legitimate. Given the life she led, it was funny how proper she could be. Having a child out of wedlock was not in her book of etiquette.

I sent the plane ticket back with a short note saying, in effect, that she didn't give a damn about me or her unborn baby, so the deal was off. I did feel resentment and diminished by her whims, even if, at the same time, I was pleased the half-assed wedding was off.

She called me when she returned from Hawaii, saying she thought I'd be in L.A. by then. She had gotten my letter with the plane ticket and was unhappy with my decision not to marry her.

Soon after, she had a miscarriage. At least, that's what she said. I believed her; she didn't go to the alternative, she was oddly old-fashioned.

FLASH FORWARD:

Her close girlfriend kept me informed about Lois. She married an army captain and followed him to his post in Maryland, just outside Washington. I was visiting my family in D.C. and called her. I didn't intend to see her, I was just curious to know how she liked life away from the action. I knew she wasn't well, but to what extent, I was ignorant. She was pleased to hear from me and insisted she drive in so we could have dinner together.

It was difficult hiding my astonishment at the way she looked. She was only in her midthirties, but she had shrunk. She was as thin as a razor blade (she was so nicely zaftig the time I lived with her). Her makeup, always discreet in the past, was a thick mask.

It was clear she had a serious illness. It was the most difficult meal to get through. It was unreal, the chatter about our past: the good times, the fun, the sex, the trips, the parties. The conversation was eerily hollow. Not a word was said about her illness.

I gotta confess, I was relieved when the dinner was finally over. At the door to her car we embraced and she held on tightly for a long, long moment. I was assailed, as I drove home, by a kaleidoscope of past images with Lois. I was in a deepening funk.

At four in the morning my mother woke me; a phone call: Lois urged me to come to her place, her husband was on an assignment out of the state. It was painful, but I refused. Her image lingered on my inner screen for days. She was tough, a fighter, and hung on for several years before lung cancer finally won the battle.

1953 Hollywood—Key West

The making of The Rose Tattoo. *Tennessee Williams,*
Anna Magnani, Burt Lancaster, Ingrid Bergman,
and Roberto Rossellini.

T ennessee Williams was in Rome soon after the World War
II ended. He had seen *Open City*. Anna Magnani's intensity and great talent made a deep impression on him and
he sought to meet her. Magnani knew about his importance as a playwright and agreed to talk to him. It was pure love, uncomplicated by
sex. Anna, I later discovered, had an innate sense of people moments
after meeting them. She knew that Tennessee was rare, a man she
could trust. They had a lifelong friendship.

Tennessee convinced Hal Wallis, who had bought the film rights
to his play *Rose Tattoo* to cast Anna as the Italian woman. It didn't
take much convincing; Anna was perfect for the part. Burt Lancaster
agreed to play opposite her and Danny Mann, who had directed the
play, was signed to direct the film. Anna, whom I had worked with
on *The Golden Coach*, told Wallis she wanted me as her dialogue
coach and he readily agreed.

Long before Magnani came to Hollywood, she had a crush on Burt
Lancaster. She had seen his films in Italy and he impressed her as a
virile, handsome hunk.

They got along fine during the shooting. One evening, after
seeing the dailies and finding them beautiful, Burt invited Anna and
me for champagne in his studio bungalow. After a couple of glasses

of bubbly, Anna leaped onto Burt's back. He galloped around and sang out, "Tonight, I drive you to your hotel."

Anna burst into laughter and shouted, "Si, si, Burt, yes!"

The next morning I was working with her while she was making up (she was one of the few actresses in Hollywood who made herself up.) I didn't ask about her adventures the night before. I knew she'd tell me and she did. Nothing had happened. Burt was probably intimidated by her; he took her to her suite at the Beverly Hills Hotel, made a feeble attempt, and quickly retreated. She pulled her earlobe, the Roman sign that he was gay. Being Italian, she didn't let him off the hook easily: Anna could not believe that a real man was incapable of erecting when offered the great Magnani.

Anna knew exactly how to light her face. She showed Jimmy Wong Howe, the well-known director of photography, where to place her key-light, how to shade her neck, how to get her best angles. He was impressed.

She never studied acting formally. She had begun in Italian music halls, singing Roman songs. She was instinctive. She had the ability to call up emotions at will, to move an audience, to convince them the life on the stage was as real and natural as life in their own kitchen.

I had worked with Eduardo de Filippo, widely known in Europe as a playwright and actor, though unknown in the U.S. Anna, in an interview, was asked who she considered to be the best actor presently working in film or onstage. She named two: Marlon Brando and Eduardo de Filippo.

Eduardo had his own theater in Naples, that produced, for the most part, plays that he had written. (He had several hits in London. Five of his plays ran in Moscow at the same time.) I went to Naples to see him act in a comedy he had authored. His theater was charming. Its box seats had the names of actors, not numbers.

Eduardo made his entrance. He fooled me the first few minutes. He's not doing anything, I thought. Then it hit me. It was the best kind of acting. He had the look of a guy just passing by. He made acting look easy. Try walking across a stage without appearing awkward and feeling silly. (Rumor strongly suggested that Eduardo was the illegitimate son of Pirandello, the greatest Italian playwright of modern times. Pirandello was awarded the Nobel Prize for literature in 1934.)

We shot much of *Rose Tattoo* in Key West, Florida. Tennessee Williams lived there much of the year. He had a modest house and a small bungalow in back where he worked. When we shot around his house, we could hear Tennessee typing away every morning. Now Tennessee wasn't an early-to-bed writer. He was out until the early morning hours at his favorite bars, cruising, and he did like the sauce. But there he was at nine every morning at the typewriter. In the afternoons he would visit a pool and swim forty laps, the key to his physical good health.

He invited the cast and crew to dinner at his house one evening after work. He was in the kitchen cooking and I was at the far end of the living room when I and everyone else heard him call out in his soft southern accent, "Ah think Mickey Knox is the most attractive man in the company."

All in the room turned to look at me, pleased as punch. I faked a laugh, playing it as a joke. The dinner was finally over, Hal Wallis had hired a couple of limos to drive us back to the hotel. They quickly were filled to capacity, leaving me and Nan Grey, an actress, to wait for one of them to return for us.

While waiting for the ride to the hotel, Tennessee approached me.

Tennessee: "Why don't you stay the night, Mickey?"

Mickey: "I don't think so, Tenn. I haven't been to the hotel since this morning. I gotta go back, take a shower, and hit the sack."

Tennessee: "Oh, you can take a shower here."

Mickey: "Nope, I gotta go back to the hotel."

He turned and slowly went up the stairs. The limo finally came. Tennessee ignored my presence for the rest of the shoot.

Soon after returning to Los Angeles, the press agent for Hal Willis organized a pres conference for Magnani. She objected, knowing that journalists could twist and turn whatever she said into sensational copy. She was reassured that she would be treated with respect. Reluctantly, she agreed to face the reporters.

It was a disaster.

Question: "Do you shave your armpits? Do you wear underwear? If so, what color do you prefer?"

Oh shit! Anna looked to me for the translation. I told her to pass, but she insisted. She looked at me in disbelief and anger. She told me, in Italian, to tell the turd to go fuck himself. My translation: "Next question, please."

Question: "How many lovers have you had?"

Answer in Italian: Fuck you! Translation: "Not an acceptable question."

Question: "Was Rossellini good in bed?"

Anna got up. Her last words for the press were, "You are all a bunch of cretins!" That, I translated. End of press conference.

When we finished the filming, Anna went to New York and did some serious shopping. Aside from her Rome apartment, she had a marvelous villa on a spit of land called San Felice Circeo. She was enthralled by American refrigerators, washing machines, stoves, vacuum cleaners, and gardening equipment. (Bear in mind that this was 1953, a few years after the war, and American products looked marvelous to Anna.)

She spent a small fortune and had it all loaded on the ship she was taking back to Italy. She wasn't about to allow all the beautiful appliances and equipment to travel without her. When she got to Naples, the customs officers calculated the import duty she owed. She confronted them as only she could. "I am Anna Magnani the actress. I do not pay any tax, do you understand me?"

They hesitated, looked at each other, each wondering who was to confront her. Finally one of the officers meekly started to speak. "But, Signora . . ."

That was as far as he got. "Enough!" Anna said sternly. "I am taking my things back with me to Rome. Bring me a truck and have it loaded with my precious belongings. Italy does not tax my things, understand?"

They hustled up a truck, loaded it, and off it drove to Rome, with Anna in the front seat riding shotgun.

As coach and actress, Anna and I were tuned into each other. This film, she knew, was the high point of her career and her animal instinct informed her that she could trust me. The key was patience. I discovered at the outset that after fifteen or twenty minutes of concentrating on her English dialogue, she would get mentally weary. She knew she had to master this new language or her performance would suffer. Being an actor, I had the ability to make the dialogue her own, as though speaking the words for the first time. She had to grasp the meaning of each word, each phrase. Only then could she use her own pace, her own emphasis.

Patience: We would stop to gossip, have an espresso, then back to work. The result of the coaching was dramatic when she performed. Her will to succeed was powerful, more so than any of the many foreign actors I had coached.

She did enjoy gossiping about other actors and about her life. Her love, which later turned to hatred, for Roberto Rossellini fascinated me, as it did much of America once it involved Ingrid Bergman.

Anna and Rossellini lived together in Rome. After he directed *Open City*, and it was released to acclaim in America in 1947, Ingrid wrote to Roberto, praising his film and vowing someday to work with him.

Roberto was no fool. A top Swedish-American female star holding her hand out to him was not to be dismissed. He answered her letter, saying he greatly admired her as an actress and that they would certainly work together in the near future.

Roberto soon voyaged to Los Angeles at Ingrid's invitation. She insisted he stay with her and her husband. He objected politely, but caved when asked the second time. Something happened during their first encounter that was about more than making a movie together. Was it instant attraction or just two people meeting at a mutual point in their lives, yearning to excite some lost passion? Whatever it was, the mixture was flammable.

Roberto returned to Rome, his mind bubbling with ideas for a film project that would bring Ingrid to Italy.

Anna, the great animal lover, sniffed the air and it smelled Swedish. Did she control her urge to hit Roberto in the chops or did she fight tooth and nail to hold on to her man? The one decision she didn't entertain was to meekly turn her back.

Roberto made a second trip to L.A. Anna had a large dog, half German shepard, half wolf. He was a beauty and Roberto used him as his ticket to the city of dreams. He told Anna he was taking the dog for a walk. He left the dog with the *portieri* (concierge) and went to the airport. Good-bye Anna. Hello, Ingrid.

Ingrid and her husband split and she came to Rome with Roberto. The scandal in America echoed around the world. In Congress, our outraged representatives stood up and decried that hussy's behavior, blaming it all on corrupt Hollywood morals. Preachers and priests had a ball. A gorgeous movie star, living out of wedlock with a swarthy Eyetalian? Have they no shame? Get this—Congress was talking of banning Ingrid's reentry to the United States of America.

Rossellini was a born charmer. At a dinner table with ten people, I sat next to him. When we talked he never glanced around the table to see if he had missed something. He had the good looks that appealed to both men and women, not pretty, not Hollywood handsome, but, allow me to say, European handsome.

Magnani, given the opportunity for a bit of payback, didn't hesitate. A Roman restaurant: Magnani at the table, across the room, Rossellini and Bergman dining together. Magnini strides across the restaurant, an avenging Circe, heading directly for her ex-lover. The diners ceased eating, their eyes follow Anna to Roberto's table, watch as she decisively lifts his bowl of spaghetti and dumps it on his head.

That evening, Anna's mind was cleared of any lingering regrets.

When she told me of the scene, she roared her unique laugh of delight.

Rose Tattoo was filmed in 1953. Magnani was given the Academy Award for best actress the following year. I was then in Los Angeles, she in Rome. She wired me the day she won, thanking me for the Oscar. Of course, she was being way too generous. Her talent and will won her the Oscar. I may have helped her make Tennessee's dialogue her own but it was Anna's show all the way.

1953 Hollywood

Anthony Quinn.

nthony Quinn and I first met in 1953. It was at a party given by Danny Mann to welcome Anna Magnani when she arrived in Hollywood to begin filming *Rose Tattoo*. Tony was a creative, striking actor with a commanding screen presence. He would have been the ideal casting for the male lead opposite Magnani, but since it was a Hal Wallis production, Burt Lancaster was the man.

Anna was more than a bit paranoid. But it still came as a surprise when she tested me. Just as I arrived at the party, she hid behind a large armchair and listened to me talk for about five minutes before she suddenly appeared from behind the armchair. When I asked her why the hell she was hiding, she laughed and said, "I wanted to hear if you said anything bad about me."

Tony and I talked shop, told a couple of jokes, and made plans to meet again. Our friendship lasted almost half a century until he died in 2001. During the years I was blacklisted as an actor, Tony got me hired as a dialogue coach on several of his films.

He was born in Mexico and moved to Los Angeles as an infant. When he was growing up it wasn't easy being a Mexican kid. It did two things: It spurred his ambition to be "the best" and it fed his arrogance when he began his acting career. "Yes, I'm Mexican, you bastards. So what?" That sense of himself was so deeply felt that it worked: When Cecil B. De Mille sent out a casting call for *Indians who spoke their language*, Tony showed up and proudly spoke a homemade gibberish that fooled De Mille into believing Tony was the real article. He hired him on the spot.

Arrogance, pride, whatever it was, he always delivered. Winning two Academy Awards for best supporting actor is no easy accomplishment. Tony was mentally quick, and he either developed or inherited a reliable instinct for recognizing ill will aimed at him. When he felt comfortable with someone he was open, funny, and a good friend.

But Tony could be ruthless and unfeeling, to wit; I was on a small budget film with him when, early in the shooting, he humiliated the inexperienced movie director and had him in tears. The director had done his homework the night before, planning each camera move, but Tony refused to accommodate the camera's position. The director pleaded with him, but Tony told him, in front of the crew and cast, that he was incompetent and ignorant to boot and if he insisted on having his way, Tony would cease talking to him for the rest of the film. The director weakly backed off.

I received a phone call from Rome offering me a film job. I was quick to accept. A few days before my departure, Tony came to tell me, in no uncertain terms, that I was going to Mexico with him to work on a film. When I said I had already agreed to go to Italy for work (he knew that) he pulled his stone-face, stared at me, then walked away.

All his life he wanted to be considered cultured. He read a lot and as he couldn't read all the books he thought he should, he had a large volume of abbreviated outlines of the greatest books through the ages on his bedside table.

He had a love of painting and sculpture. He worshipped the work of the renowned Mexican painters: Rivera, Orozco, and especially Siqueiros. His friendship with Frank Lloyd Wright also led him to love architecture.

Tony developed into an interesting painter. He was a good draftsman, all his paintings, especially his early ones, have the power to hold a viewer's attention. But while his pictures were overly influenced by Picasso and the Mexican painters, his sculptures were another story. They had originality, mass, and controlled anarchy.

From 1953 to the end of 1956 we got together often. We went to Tijuana to see the bullfights and to Las Vegas to see the shows and gamble a bit. I discovered that if you're with a known film actor you can't lose. I brought five hundred bucks to play with and after two hours I blew it all on the craps table. I sat, dejected, having a drink with Tony in one of the lounges when a dealer approached and asked Tony for his autograph. He chatted for a minute or so and asked how we were doing on the tables. I was in a bitter mood and told him we had recently arrived at the hotel and I had immediately lost the five hundred I came with. He asked if I'd like to win it back. Win it back? Hell, yes! "Okay, I'm dealing blackjack," he said, "come to my table but promise you'll quit when you get your five hundred back. Deal?" Yeah.

Within half an hour I had chips worth five hundred in front of me. I had watched the dealer's eyes and he had subtly indicated when to hold and when to hit. How he knew is still a mystery to me. I cashed in the chips and skipped the tables for the remainder for the weekend.

Tony and I played tennis two or three times a week. He usually beat me. He was steady and I was erratic. One day, to liven up the day, I said, "Okay Tony, this is for the championship. You're Gonzales and I'm Kramer." At the time Gonzales was the top dog in the tennis world, but Kramer was not far behind. To this day I don't know how he did it, Tony turned absolutely white. He tried to control his anger, "I'm Gonzales? Why? Why can't I be Kramer, huh? Because I'm Mexican?"

He had flipped, gone loco. I said, "Tony you always want to be number one, well Gonzales is number one. But I'll tell you what, be fucking Kramer, I don't give a shit."

He declined and beat the hell out of me, playing the hardest tennis of his life.

In 1960 he was on Broadway costarring with Laurence Olivier in *Becket*. I saw the play and went backstage to see Tony. He shut his dressing room door and faced me. "Well, who was number one, me or Olivier?"

I stared at him, trying to see if he was kidding. He wasn't. "Tony," I said, "you and Olivier were both number one. It was a tie." He peered into my eyes, grunted, and seemed to accept the decision. Kid stuff, but Tony was a man of many parts, one part being kid.

Actors choose different means to stimulate their search for "character." No matter what the part, no two actors will play it the same way. In one of his most memorable film roles, Zampano the strongman in *La Strada*, Tony used the image of an ape very effectively to imbue his character. Animals are a great help to actors. Think of the metaphors: weasel out of it, foxy, a snake in the grass, the grace of a leopard, king of the jungle. A lion overlooking its territory appears to know it is king. An actor can use the animal's intent, its attitude, how it moves, to shape the character he's playing.

Tony had a collection of African and primitive masks that also aided him in developing character. He had the special ability to absorb what he needed to create a role from any relevant source.

A resident of Italy for about a quarter of a century, he had a magnificent villa in the country about a forty-five minute drive south of Rome. It was situated on the highest point of a hill. When the air was clear, the sharp-sighted could glimpse the sea about ten miles to the west.

Anthony Quinn was like a prince of past centuries, lording it over his domain, which included his wife and three sons. They had a tennis court, a large swimming pool with ample poolside quarters, and acres of lawn with a clear view of the countryside. His studio where he painted and sculpted was separate from the villa. It was a large estate and Tony's sculptures sat or lay at various points around the villa as witness to the talent and vision of the in-house artist.

Although Tony was already a recognized and successful actor, Fellini's *La Strada* brought him to a high level of international fame. The Italians considered him one of their own.

I only saw Tony a few times during the last five years of his life. He had left his wife Yolanda and was living with Kathy, a young woman who had been his secretary. His attitude with women had been Mediterranean: you are my woman; I am a free soul. Get it? But he matured with Kathy; he no longer behaved like the lord and master, and when I was around, showed her respect and affection.

He was intrigued, like many actors, by the Mafia and he attended several court sessions during John Gotti's trial. Like Gotti, Tony at times was a clothes horse and had a closet full of expensive tailored Italian suits. As an actor he was a giant. He never stopped working, no matter how challenging the role, whether it was on Broadway, touring in *Zorba*, or going to the Arctic or the Sahara Desert to film. And he was in his eighties when he did his last film.

He was a hell of a companion to be on the town with, ready for any adventure that might arise, always open to fun and laughter, especially when, in the presence of the women we were with, we often spoke Italian to each other. The women sensed we were speaking about them. And they loved it.

1953 Hollywood

James Dean.

N ow dead almost fifty years, Jimmy Dean remains a legend. And he only appeared in major roles in three films: *Rebel Without a Cause*, *East of Eden*, and *Giant*. Somehow his quirky personality captured the imagination of the world's movie-goers. He embodied the outsider, the loner, the misfit, yet he had a movie star's good looks. Half a century after his death, people still know and talk about him. That's a legend.

Before going to Hollywood, Jimmy Dean was in the Actors Studio for a short time. He made the mistake of crossing Lee Strasberg by criticizing one of Lee's pet actors. I was there that day.

At the Studio, an actor prepares a scene, performs it in front of the class, then explains what he or she worked on. For example, the heat of fear, anger, or hate. Anyone in the class can comment on the scene, but only about the specific choice—did the actor achieve his objective?

Jimmy went overboard in his criticism. Lee turned to him from his front-row seat and let him have it. His sharp voice told Jimmy his criticism was too general, useless to an actor working on only one aspect of the character, or just working on sense memory. He then added the stinger: he had seen Jimmy onstage and felt he had much to learn before criticizing others. Jimmy never returned to the Studio.

I barely knew him in New York, mainly through a mutual girl-friend. I did see him in a couple of plays on Broadway, *The Immoralist* by Andre Gide and *The Jaguar*. He was impressive in two difficult parts.

In Hollywood, when I worked on *Rose Tattoo*, we got together. Jimmy and Pier Angeli, a lovely Italian actress who had lead roles in a few films, were seeing each other. To me, they were in love. Pier Angeli's sister, Marisa Pavan, was in *Rose Tattoo*, and we double dated with Jimmy and Pier a couple of times.

Pier Angeli's mother detested Jimmy. I was okay because I could speak Italian. When asked why she disliked him and wouldn't allow him in the house, she answered, "I don't like the way he dresses, I don't like his attitude, and he has a small talent compared to my daughter." I disagreed with her on all counts, telling her Jimmy had a rare talent. "I don't care, he doesn't come into my home." Italian mothers are not shy.

So we'd meet at Schwab's, the drug store and counter on Sunset Boulevard. It was a popular hangout for young actors and has-beens alike. Legend has it that Lana Turner was discovered sitting at the counter. Schwab's had the usual eats: soup and an assortment of sandwiches. Jimmy at times was like a little kid; he wanted attention and would slurp his soup loudly; or make sounds while eating a sand-wich. "What the hell are you doing?" I asked him.

"Just havin' fun," he said, and smiled his shy smile.

Pier Angeli's mother finally succeeded in closing down the romance. Jimmy hurt for some time, maybe never got over her. She had a sweet, adorable nature and her face radiated loveliness. Her mother took her back to Italy where she married a musician who composed music for films. Pier died young, rumored to have com-mitted suicide.

Jimmy, too, died young, in a two-car crash. He was twenty-four.

1953 Hollywood
Willy Shoemaker.

Race tracks have enjoyed my presence a dozen or so times during my lifetime. I never caught the fever and I only bet on a race, generally out of courtesy for the name of the horse. Eye-catching inventive names will always get my two-dollar bet.

Being a jockey is a real, albeit small, man's job. There were very few black jockeys and hardly any females. How about Jewish jockeys? Zero. But I did get to know Willy Shoemaker, one of the most victorious jockeys ever to sit atop a race horse.

Gene Kelly, and his wife, Betsy Blair, the best friend a charades player ever had, had held an open house most every night for their inner circle. The Kellys were Francophiles—the reason, I imagined, that Georgette and I were included in the outer circumference of the inner circle.

At the Kellys' one evening, Willy Shoemaker sat next to me, I suspect because I wasn't one of those tall actors he would have liked to hang out with if they were shorter. As it was, I was seven inches taller than Shoemaker, who was 4'11. He had seen me in a boxing film and we talked about that.

Before leaving, he invited me to his home in Pasadena for lunch and then to his place of work: the Santa Anita racetrack. I told him

I was an ignoramus about horses. He suggested I visit the paddock before the race. Being a track-moron, it puzzled me.

The day came for lunch in Pasadena. The first thing I noticed about his home was that all the chairs and tables were shortened. It seemed strange, given that his gracious, pretty wife was a head taller than he. There wasn't too much conversation. I recognized the anticipation of his workday, the unspoken thoughts, the concentration of a man preparing for a serious workday ahead.

The drive to the track was silent. His only words when we parted were, "See you at the paddock." So I waited at the paddock until he appeared on his horse, a beautiful looking animal. Willy circled the paddock, caught my eye, and nodded ever so subtly. It happened so quickly, I felt foolishly unsure.

Did he mean to bet his horse or did he nod in greeting? There's nothing dumber than an amateur. To cover my doubts, I bet five bucks rather than two. I watched the race and as Willy's horse crossed the finish line to win it, I felt like a schmuck.

Cashing in my ticket, I ran into Richard Conte, the actor. I had worked with him, but he was no friend. I told him how I had goofed. He lost his cool, looked up to heaven and asked God why he wasn't with me at the paddock.

Shoemaker had one more race and Conte stuck to me like glue when I hustled over to get the high sign. I zoomed in on Willy as he rode into the paddock, while Conte had his glasses trained on him. But Willy, maddeningly, ignored my presence. He didn't win the race.

1954 New York
James Jones, William Styron, James Baldwin.

James Jones, the author of *From Here to Eternity,* and I hooked up at a party in New York City. When he arrived, the mood changed. His presence was felt. He was someone you were drawn to. Later we had time to talk, to get acquainted, to become friends.

Norman Mailer, in his book *Advertisements For Myself* describes Jim: "The only one of my contemporaries who I felt had more talent than myself was James Jones. And he has also been the one writer of my time for whom I felt any love. We saw each other only six or eight times over the years, but it always gave me a boost to know that Jim was in town. He carried his charge with him, he had the talent to turn a night of heavy drinking into a great time. . . . What was unique about Jones was that he had come out of nowhere, self-taught, a clunk in his lacks, the only one of us who had the beer-guts of a broken-glass brawl."

For a couple of months during 1954, while Jim was in New York, we saw each other almost daily. There were many conversations about books and authors—and women. He spoke fondly about Lowney Handy, who had helped him become a writer, and said that without her guidance he might not have been able to write *From Here To Eternity*. He was passionate in describing his camp for budding writers. I promised to visit him in Marshall, Illinois, one day.

We ate together, there were parties, and much drinking. To Jim, drinking was a ritual. When he lived on the Quai d'Orleans in Paris he bought a pulpit at a flea market or antique shop and set it up as his bar. He would stand behind it while friends would stand or sit around it drinking. The pulpit gave comfort to us boozers.

New York wore him down. He called one day to tell me he was returning to Marshall. He wasn't able to work that morning. Missing one day's work was enough of a message for Jim to get his ass back home.

I returned to work in Hollywood on two films with Tony Quinn. I was blacklisted as an actor but no one bothered me about working as a dialogue director. Actors are up-front; dialogue directors are just part of the crew.

Toward the end of 1956 I got a call from Rome to work on a film Dino De Laurentiis was producing in Italy. I bought a cheap second-hand car and decided to drive East, across the country, the main reason being that I wanted to visit Jim at his home and camp for writers.

Lowney had sent me a couple of long letters, beseeching me to come to the camp and think about becoming a writer. Jones had told her about my love of literature and writing. Well, I wasn't doing much acting, and writing had always interested me, but Italy was calling and that call I would take.

I got to Marshall in the evening. It truly was a camp. There was the main house where Jim and Lowney lived and at the far end of the yard, what appeared to be a barrack for the "recruits." There was even a bulletin board in the large yard with duties to be performed: policing the area, K.P., cleaning the barracks and latrine, etc.

I asked a young fellow who had come to check the bulletin

board where I could find Jones. He and Lowney went to see a movie. What movie? He didn't know. I got directions into town, parked at the first movie house I saw, and asked the girl in the ticket office what was playing around town. She mentioned two or three films including *War and Peace*. No doubt that was the one.

When I got inside the theater I stood for a bit until my eyes were accustomed to the darkness. The place was almost empty. I walked down the aisle and there was Jimbo, sitting with Lowney. He didn't notice as I sat next to him. A few seconds later I poked him in the ribs with my elbow, hard enough to have him whirl around. He quickly recognized me and he loudly said to Lowney, "Hey, Lowney, It's ole Mick, I can't believe it. Let's get outta here and have a martini to celebrate."

"But you're on the wagon, Jim," she said, a bit annoyed.

We went to a bar and had a couple of drinks. Jim wanted to know why I didn't call to tell him I was coming. A surprise, Jim, everyone loves a surprise.

We drove back to his camp. His house was a beaut, all wood outside and inside. Comfortable, lived in, lots of books, a fireplace. For me a dream house.

The games quickly began: chess, darts, arm wrestling, even pinball. Either I brought out his competitiveness or it just came naturally.

Jim and his wife, Gloria, made a smart move to Paris in 1958 and remained residents until 1974. They were relaxed hosts to many gatherings of the famous: acquaintances, visiting writers, painters, and good friends. The time vanished and the evenings became the early morning hours. The conversations, discussions, and arguments never flagged. Neither did the booze.

One night it was Jim, Bill Styron, Jim Baldwin, and myself. We were drinking at the pulpit. It wasn't a fun evening for me. The conversation always turned to Norman Mailer because of the section called "Evaluations—Quick Expensive Comments on the Talent in the Room," from his book, *Advertisements for Myself*.

Jones and Styron were offended by two of the evaluations and never missed the opportunity, when we were together, of using me, Norman's friend, as a surrogate for Mailer. That evening I was surprised that Jim Baldwin joined them in the attack. Baldwin and Mailer had been comfortable with each other, if not close buddies.

Finally, in order to convince me of Mailer's injury to Styron's vanity, Jones left the pulpit and quickly returned with his copy of *Advertisements* It was bookmarked at "Evaluations." He chose a phrase that hurt: "Styron wrote the prettiest novel of our generation." He repeated it several times, causing Styron great discomfort. He didn't read the phrase that followed: *"Lie Down In Darkness* has beauty at its best, is almost never sentimental, even has whispers of near-genius as the work of a twenty-three-year-old . . ."

Actors are often accused of having outsized egos, but they're pussycats compared to writers, and I mean all writers. They have granite-hard egos. Their vanity might be hurt, but never the ego.

Jim and Gloria visited me in Rome a couple of times and the last time I saw Jim was in the early 1970s. I was in Paris when Mailer was there. He and Jim had been on the outs for some time due to the evaluation. He wanted to talk to Jones and asked me where he hung out at night. I knew the place, a quiet club on the Left Bank. Gloria and Jim were at the bar having a drink. Norman and I sat at a table. Jim saw us, but made no move.

I did a stupid thing, as I'm wont to do. I got up, went to the bar, and before I opened my mouth, Gloria, irate as a rattlesnake, hissed a stream of insults at me. It unnerved Jim. He told her to keep quiet. She was fearful Norman had come to fight Jim. That was not true. Norman wanted a conversation, not a fistfight.

There was no conversation or fistfight. It only took the presence of Norman to hit her red button. She was blinded to other possibilities.

Jim gave life as good as he got. He died in 1977, from congestive heart failure.

1954 New York—Florida

Garden of Eden *and* Singing in the Dark.

M ax Nosseck came back into my life just when I needed him. He had a part for me. It was the lead in a small budget movie, financed by an independent German producer, so there was no blacklist to cut me down.

I loved Max Nosseck. He was wonderfully entertaining without trying to be an entertainer. He looked like a mad German composer or musical maestro. His hair was graying and wild all over a head too large for his small frame, but his eyes were always merry, his gestures punctuating his Berlin-accented speech.

In the past we had gone to Rome for a film project that melted away like a Popsicle lying in the sun. But Max saved the day with his humor. Give him a word like *lavanderia* or *cameriere*, (Italian for laundry and waiter) and his accent would twist it to sound funny enough to inspire laughter.

When he came to me in New York, I was attending the Actors Studio and close to my last dollar. There wasn't that much money in Max's offer. He was offering Screen Actors Guild minimum, at the time $250 a week, (not bad in '54) and a percentage of the profit. I knew the last part of the offer would amount to a big zero and so it did.

The film, *Garden of Eden*, took place in a nudist colony in Florida. Cast and crew flew down and moved into the colony. Weird? Oh, boy! We arrived in time for lunch in the communal mess hall to be served by nude waiters and waitresses. The cooks were also nude except for tall white toques. Get the picture? We intruders tried our damndest to convey a cool lack of concern, but that night every one of us had nightmares.

The crew was the first to follow the colony's rules that everyone, visitors and members, (no pun intended) must be nude on the colony grounds. The crew nonchalantly went about their work wearing nothing but a hammer, a screwdriver, pliers, and a pouch of nails hanging from a leather tool belt. The tools swung along in rhythm with the crew's private tools as they walked about. The rest of us were given time to adjust to the rules.

The film's plot was simple: "Girl in trouble, running away from an overbearing father. Hero (me) to the rescue." I was the colony's handyman and for the most part walked around bare-chested wearing jeans. But then I fell into the mood, took off the jeans and jockey shorts, and swung along with the other nude men. Except I began carrying a towel as protection after I once fell asleep against a tree and awoke to see a young woman, her back to me, bending over to diaper a baby (about ten yards away). When I became aware that I was visibly aroused, I panicked. Panic is a fine antidote for just that kind of situation and my nude member subsided. Hence the ever-present towel.

Max was an experienced film director. He had made movies in Germany before Hitler hardened his power over the country. Being Jewish, Max feared for his future and made his way to Hollywood where he directed a couple of hit films *Black Stallion* and *Dillinger*. On *Garden of Eden*, he did the best he could with a dull script. Walter Bibo, the German producer, financed the movie, hoping that exploiting a film about a nudist colony would bring in the big bucks.

The male nudists were for the most part obese or scrawny, but man, were they hung! Reason enough to be a nudist. The women were, in the main, middle-aged or mothers with little kids and not exactly Vogue models. However, they were all, men and women, polite and friendly.

The scene I enjoyed watching most during the filming was a volleyball game between men and women. Think of it—bouncing tits and asses on one side of the net, swinging dicks and swaying balls on the other side. It was the mother of all volleyball games.

The decision was made to juice up the film with attractive, young bodies, so they imported half a dozen beauties from New York. The girls had no problem undressing and cavorting in front of the camera. The pity of it was that dancing was prohibited. But, hey, there were other ways to dance. I was young, handsome, and free—and the star of the film. Pretty girls always attracted me, especially when nude.

There was a lovely grove of orange trees on the colony grounds and they were in bloom. No one should miss making love, at least once, under the powerful, luxuriant smell of orange blossoms. One of the girls promised me a special thrill if I called her when I returned to New York—she would lick my toes. It didn't especially excite me, but as Voltaire said when he declined an invitation to a second orgy: "Once a philosopher; twice a pervert." I decided to be a philosopher and called her when I got back to New York. I scrubbed my feet; the girl did her best, but I felt not a thrill in any of my ten toes—only a slight tickle and a small disappointment.

The film, when ready for distribution, could not get released. Nudity in 1954? No way. Yet, in spite of all the nudity, it was a sexless picture. It was all sweetness and light with no hint that men lusted for women or women seduced men. Just nice clean family fare. The fact is the nudity was half-frontal; tits were okay but nothing below that, except for longshots or scenes photographed from the rear.

But Walter Bibo and Max Nosseck were no dummies. They released the film in a movie house in a southern state. Down came the law—"Are you furriners kiddin'?" and the locals got a writ to bar the showing of Satan's work.

Walter Bibo's plan worked. He needed to publicize his film in a way that would grab the attention of the press. He brought suit against the state on First Amendment grounds. Vocal journalists in the state got a chunk of red meat and chewed the juice out of it. National newspapers picked up the story and ran with it. Bibo's investment in his lawyers paid off. He won the case.

I have no idea how many tickets were sold, but the movie got a lot of play in the agrarian states, always advertised as a family picture. I never saw or heard from Bibo again and my percentage, by contract, of the profit never materialized.

Max called on me again in 1956 to act in *Singing in the Dark,* an indie flick shot in New York that was also below the blacklist radar. Independent productions were just that—independent, financed by individuals and not banks, thus untouchable.

The main attraction of *Singing in the Dark* was that it featured the best known cantor of the time, Moishe Oishe. I was the bad guy trying to steal money from the synagogue and its bingo game. The picture, in truth, was a showcase for Moishe's singing. It played to full houses in Jewish neighborhoods.

After *Singing in the Dark,* Max returned to his beloved Berlin, the city of his birth. I saw him there when working on *For the First Time* in 1958. Some of Max's old Jewish buddies had returned from exile and Max contacted them to re-create the kaffee-klatch they had before the war. Max was once again the chairman of the board, seated at the head of the table.

He asked me to join him one evening at the nightly meeting of the kaffee-klatch. There was more laughter than serious conversation. I understood little German and Max filled me in on the laugh lines. Laughter is a most delicious dish and I stayed for the whole meal. There's a reason that the funniest American comics were born at the turn of the last century. They were the children of Jewish immigrants. The Yiddish language is replete with hilarious descriptions, words, and phrases. And Jewish nascent funnymen were breast-fed biting but funny chatter.

Cheers to jolly Max Nosseck who is long gone.

1956–57 Rome—Thailand

This Angry Age. *Dino De Laurentiis and Silvana Mangano.*
Tony Perkins.

T hat day I loved my phone. It was better than fireworks. Los
Angeles was created to nourish boredom. I was fed up with
that diet and yearned to haul ass.

Toward the end of 1956, the goddamn phone rang. It was a call
from the Dino De Laurentiis office in Rome, at the time the most
important movie producer in Italy. He was soon to start a film in
Thailand and Italy and wanted to hire me as dialogue director. I
kissed my beloved phone.

The film was to be shot in English, but the director, René
Clement, was French and spoke no English or Italian. Speaking
those languages was a requirement for the job and I fit the bill. The
cast included Silvana Mangano (Dino's wife), Tony Perkins, Jo Van
Fleet, and Richard Conte. The crew was Italian.

René Clement was a leading French director. He made a number
of excellent films, including the magnificent *Forbidden Games*, about
how French children were affected by the Second World War.

The film script, written by Irwin Shaw, was adapted from a book
by Marguerite Duras, called *Un Barrage Contre Le Pacifique* ("The
Sea Wall"). Duras wrote about her life as a young girl living on a farm
in Cambodia with her family. Columbia Pictures financed the film
and released it as *This Angry Age*.

A couple of days after I arrived in Rome I went to work coaching Silvana Mangano. She was beautiful, spoke quietly, moved gracefully, and her hands were eloquent in motion. We became good friends but I never really got to know her, to penetrate that small breath of mystery she projected.

It was four years since I'd been in Rome and it felt like I had come back home. It was 1956 and the beauty of the streets was not yet marred by the countless vehicles yet to come.

I was in Rome for about a month before leaving for Bangkok. The shooting wouldn't begin until then, so I had all that time to work with Mangano and meet with René Clement. He was the quintessential urban Frenchman, hair always trimmed and combed to perfection, always close-shaven. He was polite but detached. He conveyed an air of being intellectually superior. He wore that peculiar French-cut suit with padded shoulders, more form-fitting than the looser, more stylish Italian or English cut. But he was a hell of a movie director.

Whereas Monsieur Clement was handsome, Madame Clement was, plainly said, ugly, the classic five by five in height and width. But after one became aware of her sharp intelligence and humor, her ugliness took on a simpatico aspect. The Italian crew referred to her as "the gorilla," not without some affection.

Dino de Laurentiis was a compact, gravel-voiced, shrewd Neapolitan. He could be tough or a softer version of tough, and on rare occasions allowed his charm to sneak out. The Italian crew left for Bangkok a week before the rest of the crew and I found myself on a plane sitting next to Dino. No one else from the company was on the flight.

Within the first hour of the flight, Dino, wasting no time on subtlety, flat out told me what he expected from me. He needed a pair of eyes and ears on the set to keep him informed of any disagreements, any friction between the actors or the director or whatever else I thought he might need to know. I was in the ideal position to keep him informed. I'd be on the set at all times and understood what was said in three languages. (Many producers have someone, usually the assistant director, report back from the set.) I told him I expected to be too busy working with actors and interpreting for the director to be able to hear and see all that went on during the filming, so I begged off. He didn't press the matter, but that was the end of our conversation.

Our first location was a village called Phet Buri, on the Gulf of Siam side of the peninsula. Dino hung around a few days, then returned to Rome. He did fly back a load of pasta for the crew. Italians can't function without their pasta fix. On every location I've been on with Italians there's usually someone in the crew who is the designated cook.

The first shot in the film was of a convertible Mercedes speeding along a narrow country road, filmed from a helicopter. But there was a problem—the actor who was supposed to drive the car, Nick Persoff, hadn't arrived in Thailand in time. Since it was a long shot, I was asked to fill in. I thought it would be difficult to keep up with the hel-icopter. Who knew a Mercedes could out-speed a small helicopter?

As soon as the helicopter rose and attained some height, I stepped on the gas as though my life depended on it. We didn't have wireless phones, so I had no communication with the director flying above me. About five minutes after hitting the gas, I looked up and the sky was cloudless blue, but there was no sight or sound of the chopper. I pulled up alongside the road and waited until it appeared and came down in a nearby field.

René Clement jumped to the ground and ran screaming in my direction. His French was fast and furious. "In the name of God, why the devil were you racing? You must know we can only fly a hundred and ten kilometers an hour, you were driving a hundred and fifty. Are you crazy?"

No, but I was flabbergasted by René's fury and how slow the chopper flew. But I had the solution. Since I couldn't keep looking up and not avoid an accident, I turned the car's side-view mirror to a position which framed the chopper on my left side. It worked. I kept the speed at about a hundred kilometers and never lost sight of the big bird above me.

It was a long drive and miraculously I didn't hit a farmer, a cow, or a two-wheel wagon pulled by a water buffalo. I only had momentary glances at the narrow road, since my eyes were glued to the side-view mirror. Rather than slow down when passing a moving obstacle, I would swerve to avoid it. The stupidest way to drive, I know, but I couldn't face René's wrath.

However, and this is the kicker, when René got what he wanted, the chopper gracefully made a wide turn and went back to where it came from. I was lost. I was so concentrated on that goddamn whirlybird, I had paid no attention to the roads I was taking. I stopped at a couple of villages, but no one knew English and they couldn't understand my pronunciation of the name of the village I wanted to return to.

It was getting dark and I had lost whatever sense of direction I had had to begin with. I hadn't eaten since breakfast but I wasn't hungry. I was pissed off at René for leaving me to wander around the countryside all day.

Finally, by sheer luck, I found our village. The crew was peacefully eating a spicy-smelling dinner and no one was at all concerned that I had been gone in the wilderness all day long. I was puzzled and annoyed that the person I thought would have had a moment of concern, Silvana Mangano, was oblivious to my absence.

The company spent New Year's 1957 and the month of January in the Thai countryside, filming, among other scenes, the construction of the dam on the coast of the Gulf of Siam. It was a charming place to work, once I got used to the heat. The local farmers, especially the kids, were friendly. They laughed easily, in spite of the language difficulties. I tried to learn enough for rudimentary communication, but it was frustrating. I just couldn't get the music of the language.

A couple of the crew members were so taken with the people, the easy, laid-back pace of the days, and the peaceful lack of any violence that they bought small, very rustic homes. They would spend most of the wintertime there.

Bangkok was a city I could live in. Once again it was surprising how mild-mannered and friendly the people were.

In time I learned of the pervasive sexual activity in the city. Married men generally had both a mistress and a favorite prostitute, and many had a gay companion.

When we arrived, the publicity people organized a dinner for the crew and cast to meet the local press. The journalists—about eight of them, all male—were lined up just inside the entrance to the restaurant to greet us. As I was introduced to each of them we shook hands. When the first journalist tickled my palm I thought it was a local joke, but when all eight of them sent me an invitation I thought, holy cow, are they kidding? They weren't kidding at all. In fact, the handshakes were so firm, I had difficulty freeing my hand. But it wasn't only me. All the male crew members had their palms tickled.

Thailand is the only country in that part of the world not to have been colonized by European empire builders. They had clever, resourceful rulers who played one would-be colonizer against another. The Japanese, during World War II, were the only country to ever occupy Thailand.

Bangkok in 1957 had its own kind of beauty. Unlike Rome, Paris, or London, it had no outstanding or breathtaking architecture. Instead there was an undertow of activity that pulled one along. There were over four hundred legal opium dens (since made illegal) that had, for the visiting observer, a ghostly, hypnotic effect. Although I refused to smoke a pipeful when I was told that I would probably suffer nausea. I was with a local, my driver, who must have had some pull in the place, for I was permitted to check the joint out.

It was squalid: gray, dirty cement floors, narrow, stained stalls with a slab of what appeared to be cement where each smoker lay—as if dead. Gaunt men, their eyes closed, they hardly seemed to be breathing. The urinals were open and the acrid smell was difficult to take. One visit was enough to chill any further interest.

I had an enterprising driver. He had a daily surprise for me. A few days after he started driving me, he appeared in a strange outfit: a bandanna around his head, a shirt unbuttoned to his navel, and what looked like a pair of ancient knickers. I stared at him. He smiled and said, "Me pirate, okay?"

"Okay," I replied. Nothing else was said, but he wore his pirate attire without behaving at all like a pirate. Another day he dressed like a cowboy, then he was a dignitary with almost the appropriate clothes.

One night he took me to a couple of whorehouses. I went as a sightseer, not as a mark. The first one was the pits—a plank over a muddy path led to a shack in the middle of a dark, fetid field. Inside were a number of bunk beds, each with filthy sheet and a pillow I wouldn't let a dog lay his head on. The women were skinny, visibly used up, a lot of baggage under the eyes, faces thickly painted, and eyes blank—the last stop.

We quickly got out of there and went to a rich man's whorehouse, a villa enclosed in a high stone wall. We sat on the veranda. I could have been on an antebellum plantation sipping a mint julep in place of a gin and tonic. The madam was solicitous, gracious, and had a young, pretty girl of about thirteen serve me the gin and tonic, then climb up on my lap. She had a trained coyness. She remarked that my tie was pretty and asked did I like her, would I like to play with her? Soon a parade of girls, from thirteen to sixteen, appeared and slowly performed their enticement act.

I thanked the madam for the hospitality, paid a wad for the drink, probably what a girl would cost, and we split.

Most of the company stayed at the Erawan Hotel, a shiny, newly constructed high rise. It had about fifteen floors, high for Bangkok at the time. It was designed for tourists and had all the conveniences and comfort of a western hotel.

But the hotel that I wanted to visit was the Oriental, immortalized by Joseph Conrad who had stayed there in 1900. The old establishment was still open for business and had the sort of charm aging hotels acquire after many years of service.

The bar at the Oriental was as close to perfection as I could want. Silvana and I would usually visit in the evening before dinner. The lighting was warm, not too dim to limit your vision, and not too bright to illuminate the blemishes on your companion's hands or face. The bar itself was made of good hard wood which not only endured the passage of time but added to its fine workmanship and exquisite surface texture; it was indeed a pleasure to run your hand over the dark, bruised grain.

It was called the Bamboo Bar and had a pleasant smell, a mixture of booze, pungent dishes of finger food, cigar and cigarette smoke, and the Gulf of Siam's not unpleasant odor. In contrast, the bar at the Erawan Hotel was to be avoided. The few customers were businessmen in suits and ties having whispered conversations. Now that's an uninviting bar.

The Gulf of Siam was populated by hundreds of anchored sampans that served as living quarters and as markets. The city had a system of klongs (canals) that added to its appeal. There were always groups of Buddhist priests, their heads shaved, in flowing saffron robes aimlessly walking the streets.

The bright saffron was in sharp contrast to the thousands of colorless, uninspiring stone statues of Buddha, many housed in gloomy temples throughout the country. The statutes came in all sizes and positions and the most remarkable was the reclining gold Buddha housed in a temple that had little room for anything else. The Buddha, stone cold, lying on its back, must have been eighty feet long.

Buddha was undoubtedly a genius, by anyone's measure, who dedicated his life to contemplating truth, grasping its deepest meaning, setting about teaching it to the world. That was twenty-five centuries ago and Buddha's teachings are still alive. But his stone images are lifeless, unlike the sublime Renaissance paintings of Christ.

• • •

The Thailand episode isn't complete without writing of a romantic interlude that developed soon after arriving in Bangkok from Phet Buri.

A young Thai woman was hired as Clement's interpreter. She spoke Thai of course, but her English was perfect, as was her French and Italian. She was smart, well-educated and pretty, with lovely walnut-brown skin. I had the luck, or that elusive sixth sense, to be in the production office the morning she was introduced to René. Man, he oozed charm.

He got busy for a few minutes and that's all I needed. I made a date with the sweet beauty for dinner that night. I couldn't allow old René to get his foot in her doorway. I knew he'd make me pay later for ignoring his priority as the director of the film.

She was a delight at dinner: witty, intelligent, and no airs. I suggested we go dancing or to a club after the meal, but she said she couldn't do that. She was married to the French Consul and it wasn't proper to be seen dancing with another man without the Consul being present. How about dinner with another man, tête-a-tête, was that okay? Well, yes and no. Tonight it was okay because the French Consul had worked hard all day and was too weary to be concerned.

I drove up a driveway that led to the grounds of her walled-in-villa. She asked me in for a nightcap. I accepted, thinking it was an innocent request. Boy, was I mistaken. It was dark inside the villa except for the timid moonlight, but it was enough to see her slip out of her Chinese shift. And there she was in all her nude splendor.

"Your husband?"

"Oh, he's sleeping upstairs. He'll never hear us; the air conditioner is on and it is loud."

Well, I was in no mood to turn my unprotected ass to an irate husband intent on stabbing me in the back. I weakly begged off. And, like the coward I am, slunk away.

But "tomorrow is another day" and a sleepless night replaying the previous evening was forgotten when the Thai beauty asked if she could join me at my hotel for a drink.

From that day on we met for about an hour at my hotel room three or four evenings a week. At that point I decided I could live in Bangkok. Of course, my life was pleasantly full, the work was going well, and the weather was right. I was single, free as a bird, and just loved my Thai companion.

About twenty-five years later, she wrote a book called *Emanuelle* in French, a novel revealing the love affairs of a young Thai woman. I heard about the book when the movie version hit the French cinemas and caused a sensation. Was the author my dear Thai? I wondered.

Several years later I was having an espresso at the most elegant coffee bar in Rome, the Café Greco, on the chicest street, Via Condotti. I noticed a middle-aged Thai woman sitting at a table with two other women. Was she my young friend from my time in Bangkok so long ago? I sat at the table next to her and cleverly asked, "Do we know each other?"

She didn't remember me! I hadn't read the book or seen the film, but I had assumed our lovely affair was inscribed in literary history. I was dead wrong. She had little memory of who I was or of the delicious time we had together.

My self-esteem as a lover dropped a dozen points and, once again, I slunk away.

René Clement did try to make my life difficult for preempting his pretty secretary. He barely talked to me, giving me little time to interpret as he spoke rapidly to the actors. He was not only brusque, but when he caught my eye he'd glare daggers.

Jo Van Fleet, cast as Silvana's mother, arrived after we began filming in Phet Buri. I had known her in the Actors Studio and knew her to be a fine actress. There are actresses who need the affection of a personal relationship with the director. A few will seek his approval by keeping him happy after the day's work. Jo wasted no time in fulfilling their mutual needs. But she fell in love with René, and therein lies the danger.

René's wife feared flying, but there was no other way to get to

Thailand unless she was willing to spend a month or so on a cargo ship, hardly her style. He was smarting from the loss of his secretary and was more than eager to shack up with Jo. Once again he had a thin smile for me and allowed me space to interpret his directions.

It all worked out just fine until we returned to Rome to complete the filming. René's wife was on the set all day, every day, shouting her directions to René from the back of the stage. "René, she should laugh at this point, she looks too grim."

"In the name of God, will you please keep quiet!" René would shout back, but she generally had it right and René never failed to transmit her advice to the actors.

But the drama began and didn't end until Jo Van Fleet left for home. Once in Rome, René showed up on the set, for the first time, in a suit, tie and breast pocket handkerchief, all business and addressing Jo as Madame Van Fleet. Jo looked at me, confused and miserable.

Early the following morning, she called me at home. She threatened to end her life because René called her Madame, because he was cold, distant, and formal. How could that be? He had caressed her so lovingly and his wife was so ugly, how could he be so beastly? Jo had to talk and begged me to drive to work with her. In the car she cried and was seriously unhappy.

Her part in the film over, Jo left for home. Rene remained formal and distant to the very end and didn't even have the class to kiss her hand before she slipped away.

Early on, I was called to meet with De Laurentiis and Clement to suggest American actors with some name value for a part in the film. I was reluctant to add Richard Conte to the list since he had given me the shiv in the past, but I owed Dino my best choice. Conte got the part.

He only shot at the studio in Rome and at one point had ten days off before completing his work on the film. He was getting a grand a week for expenses (1957 money). I suggested he could use the cash and free time to go to Paris (my favorite choice) or any other place in Europe either to sightsee or just have himself a jolly time. He said something like, "Yeah, not a bad idea," but the next day he flew back to Los Angeles to rejoin the gin rummy game at his club.

I probably could have had tenure with Dino if I had played my cards right and kept my big mouth shut. I spoke the languages and I was knowledgeable about movie making, but I unintentionally nailed that door shut.

We were at Cinecittà in Rome and the filming was almost complete. Like most films shot in Italy, there was some dubbing to do, due mostly to poor sound. (Dubbing is revoicing the actor's dialogue to get a clean sound track.) I was supervising the dubbing being done by Tony Perkins. After we finished, the assistant in the sound booth cued up the scene where Tony sings a few phrases of a song. The assistant wanted Tony to record the whole song. Tony questioned the necessity of recording the whole song when he only sang a bit of it in the film. The assistant said those were the orders she had received from the production department.

Tony turned to me and asked what he should do. I told him he had to dub the little he did sing, but there was no reason to record the complete song.

Tony refused to record more of the song than he did in the film. I was fired. The assistant told Dino that I had advised Tony not to record the song. Tony had me come with him to see Dino. He told Dino it wasn't my fault, that he himself had decided not to record the song and that if I wasn't rehired he'd pack up and go home. I was back on the film, but to Dino I had betrayed him. Needless to say, I never worked for him again.

1958 Capri—Berlin

For the First Time *with Mario Lanza and Zsa Zsa Gabor.*

I t was to be Mario Lanza's last film. The screenplay was weak and forgettable. And so was the movie, *For the First Time.* (No, it wasn't about virginity or forever losing it.)

I was asked to be the dialogue director. It was produced by Corona, a German company, and distributed by MGM. They insisted that six months before the film was to begin, Lanza, who had a serious drinking problem, had to check into a clinic in Bavaria to dry out. After the cure and his graduation from that institution, all alcoholic drinks were prohibited for the following three months—one drink and the film deal was off. Mario passed the finals and came to Italy to start the movie.

Mario Lanzo had a natural, magnificent operatic voice, but he only performed twice in an opera house. L.B. Mayer saw him sing his second opera and signed him to a movie contract. That was the end of his operatic career. However, he hadn't worked in films for some time and he was in poor physical shape.

Shooting began on Capri, an island everyone should visit. And for one very good reason: sex. On my first visit to Capri in 1952, me and my lady friend at the time discovered that just breathing the air seemed to bring on lust.

My theory?—the island is solid lava underneath its vegetation and the lava emits radiation that excites the pertinent capillaries in men and women. There you have it, right from the author's fantasy.

We were put up at the Hotel Quisissana, the kind of place that cheers one's mood. It's an old hotel with spacious lounges, wide corridors, and large, bright guest rooms.

Zsa Zsa Gabor was in the movie. She was a fun lady with a funny accent. One evening, when the filming was done for the day, I was sitting at the hotel bar, anticipating a cold dry martini. Zsa Zsa came to the bar and sat next to me. I bought her a drink and we chatted for about ten minutes. The lava began working its charms. "Come up to my room with me, dahling," she said.

I choked on my martini, spilling half of it. "What?" I blurted out, "Are you kidding?"

Zsa Zsa's eyebrows shot up, held for a moment, then dropped as she smiled her "you foolish boy" smile. She said, "I am the greatest lay in the vorld!"

I gulped down the remainder of the martini and bravely said, "The vorld is a big place, you know." Bravely because she could have thrown her drink in my face.

But I have to admit, she was classy. "Your loss, dahling." And she nicely bid me goodnight, stood up, and shashayed out of the bar.

It was hard for me to remember ever refusing such an enticing invitation. She was attractive and had appeal. Was I scared of the challenge? Could be. To this day it escapes me. Maybe my lava theory had holes in it.

The beauty and charm of the main piazza on Capri was sullied one sunny Sunday afternoon. I was sitting in the piazza with Kurt Kaznar, an actor in the film, and Franz, an assistant producer with the German film company.

Kurt was a well-known featured actor at the time. He was a jolly fellow, large and chubby, with a slight Austrian accent. His parents, Austrian Jews, had converted to Christianity and raised him as a Christian.

Franz had been a fighter pilot during World War II. Thirteen years after the war had ended, he was still so typically the German fighter pilot that it was laughable. He tended to swagger (he usually carried a swagger stick), wore well-tailored jackets and always a snow-white silk scarf knotted around his neck as if he had just climbed out of the cockpit of his Messerschmitt fighter. Franz was tall, slender, blond, and, sho nuf, blue-eyed. But he was affable and pleasant to be with. His English was studied but fluent and his German accent was perceptible only in certain words.

He was so friendly, I fell into the trap. I felt if I was polite enough, he would answer questions about wartime Germany. He did. I asked if he knew about German Jews being mistreated and rounded up to be sent to concentration camps. He calmly denied any knowledge of mistreatment or the existence of concentration camps. He was a fighter pilot and isolated from the civilian life. "Didn't you ever fly over any of the camps?" I asked. No, he had maps with areas circled in red, which meant, "no overflight" zones. After the war, he understood these were camps for undesirables.

Up to this point the conversation had been quiet and without rancor on either side. Kurt looked off in the distance, seemingly disinterested—until he exploded. He accused me of hounding the poor fellow.

"Did I hound you?" I asked Franz.

"No," he answered, with a thin smile.

Needless to say, Kurt and I had few words to say to each other from that day on.

A couple of weeks into the film, Mario Lanza and I were in a bar having an espresso. As in most coffee bars, the shelves in back of the bartender were lined with bottles of booze. Mario stared at the shelves dreamily. I knew what he was dreaming about, but I thought he would wake up. He didn't. He said to the bartender, " I would like to have several drinks from those bottles on the left, the top shelf." The bartender, without comment, did as he was told.

"Mario," I said, "You're not going to drink those. It's just a game you're playing, right?"

He smiled coyly and sweetly and said, "Yes and no." Of course, he drank the whole mixture. From that moment on, he was at least half drunk until the day we finished shooting the film.

We went to West Berlin to complete the filming. I hadn't been in Berlin since the war, when it was mostly endless piles of rubble. But in 1958, only thirteen years since the end of the war, West Berlin—unlike East Berlin—was almost all rebuilt. Industrious buggers, the Boche.

East Berlin was like another country rather than just the Eastern part of the city. Many of the buildings were bombed-out shells and one had the feeling, walking along some of those streets, that they were haunted. The reconstruction since the war was all Stalinist architecture. Probably the ugliest, most dispiriting style in the western world.

While in Berlin, I got a nonspecific sickness. No aches or pain. I just felt crappy, as if I had some low-level infection that was eating at me. I was sent to a young doctor who spoke excellent English. After hearing me out, he knew what was wrong. His advice—leave Germany. He was right. The day I left Berlin, after the shooting was completed, a deep sense of relief cured me.

I rarely worked with an actor who drank during the day while making a film. Mario had put on about thirty pounds. That and the booze meant every scene he was in had to be staged to fit his condition, the inability to walk straight or maneuver from one point to another. As a result, he was seated throughout much of the film. Mario, like many drinkers; became exaggeratedly generous. One night, after the day's shooting, we trooped into the Kapinsky, our fancy hotel. Mario stopped to survey the lounge. There were about twenty people present. Mario called out, "Champagne for everyone! Waiter! Champagne for all these lounge people!" Within minutes, a platoon of waiters hurried in, pushing serving carts with bottles of champagne and proper glasses.

After work one evening Mario invited the crew and actors to dinner at a Chinese restaurant. The long table was loaded with dishes heaped with food. We left a lot of food uneaten—until Mario took it upon himself to clean the dishes. When he got through there wasn't a scrap left.

The word, at the end of the shooting, was that Mario had spent all of the fee he got for the movie. But he had fun, or so I thought at the time. Several months after we completed the film, rumor had it that Mario had committed suicide. Grief-stricken, Mario's wife, Betty, became addicted to sleeping pills and began drinking heavily. Several months after Mario died she joined him, leaving their four young children orphans.

In the cinematic world, the film barely created a ripple. Mario was not at his best, and the script wasn't exactly Academy Award material.

1958 Rome—Capri

The Naked Maja *with Ava Gardner and Anthony Franciosa. Shelley Winters joins the fun.*

Thanks to joint ventures, many movies are made that most likely would not otherwise have been made. A coproduction between American and Italian film companies facilitated the making of one such film *The Naked Maja*.

Goya, the Spanish artist, is considered by many to be the greatest painter of his time. One of his masterpieces is of the Duchess of Alba reclining nude, titled *La Maja Desnuda*. It caused a scandal in Spain's Royal Court and Goya was compelled to keep the painting hidden. He then painted an exact copy of the Maja in a translucent slip of a dress, making it respectable enough to exhibit. The film was about the passionate love-affair between Goya and the duchess.

It was well-cast; Anthony (Tony) Franciosa was the fiercely independent Goya, and Ava Gardner played the luscious Duchess of Alba.

Irene Lee, in New York, suggested Tony give me a ring when he got to Rome. Tony and I were in the Actors Studio at that time, so we had a passing acquaintance. We saw each other a couple of times and we hit it off. He spoke to the producer about using me on the film and he agreed to hire me as the dialogue director.

Tony, an exciting actor, had the energy of a young man who had had quick success, loved it, and wanted the payoff fast. He was willing to live on the edge to feel the thrill of maintaining his balance without tumbling down the precipice.

Until the shooting started, we had a great time closing the clubs, night after night, then striding down the silent Roman streets singing, happily loaded.

Soon Tony was unhappy. Henry Koster, the film's director, was an old-time studio director and never doubted his job was to shoot to schedule and bring the flick in on time. Like most studio directors, he knew the tricks of the trade—how to save time and money. The most efficient way was not to rehearse the scene with the actors before the lights and camera moves were set and marked. Koster would then briefly rehearse the scene, showing the actors their positions. Those positions couldn't be changed because the scene was technically fixed. That saved a hell of a lot of time, above all with actors like Tony who had been on the stage. A dedicated actor could eat up enough time trying to find the best way to play a scene to turn a pedestrian director glassy-eyed and production manager's hair gray.

Many New York theater actors brought to Hollywood insist on rehearsing before their moves and positions are marked. They want the freedom to explore a scene before their feet are set in concrete. Tony told Koster not to set the scene until he rehearsed it. How could Koster place the lights until he knew where Tony wanted to be in the scene? For Tony, rehearsing meant just that: to rehearse, to be free to move around the set and discover the dynamics of a scene.

Koster quickly assured Tony that of course he would rehearse before setting the lights and camera. And that's the way it went. Until one day Tony came to the set ready to rehearse. The scene was simple; Tony was to stand at the easel and paint. That was it, there was no one else in the scene and no dialogue. But the lights and camera were already in place. Koster was certain that if Tony was alone in the scene, standing at his easel, he'd have no cause to complain.

Complain? Tony erupted. He didn't want Koster to sneak in through the back door.

Tony: "How could you do that? Why is the camera ready to shoot? I told you I wanted to rehearse first."

Koster: "But Tony, you just have to stand at the easel and paint, it's only a short shot."

Tony: "FUCK YOU!"

Koster: "Fuck me?"

Tony: "FUCK YOU!"

Koster took his jacket from the back of a chair and started to walk out. Tony was seething. He stared at Koster as he walked across the stage. I felt Tony was about to rush him, but he restrained himself. I said softly, "Let's go, Tony." He hesitated for a moment. I wasn't sure what inner decision he would make. After a beat, he strode to the exit.

In his dressing room Tony's rage didn't subside. In due time, however, he did quiet down. Then a knock on the door. It was the assistant director asking Tony to apologize to Koster.

Tony looked at him as though he was crazy. "He should apologize to me, that sonofabitch."

"Koster won't come back to work unless you apologize," the assistant said.

That was the dilemma; to apologize or not to apologize. Tony and I sat around discussing the situation. The assistant returned to tell Tony the producer thought he should apologize.

Tony was adamant, no apology. I asked the assistant, what if Tony wrote an apology, would that suffice? He checked with Koster, returned, and said, okay.

Tony still resisted, but he agreed to let me compose the note. Then he'd decide. In the note I blurred the edges of the "fuck you" insult by explaining that Tony, in the heat of anger at feeling betrayed, shouted the first words that came to mind but didn't intend for "fuck you" to be a personal insult. Rather, it was an expression of frustration. That was the substance of the apology.

Tony signed the "apology," Koster accepted it, and we returned to work the next day. And Koster was his old smiling self from then on.

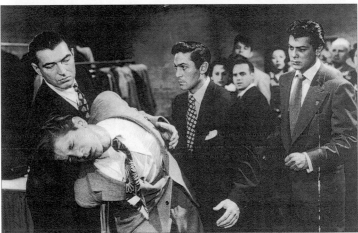

top: *I Walk Alone*—My first movie while under contract with Hal Wallis at Paramount. That's me being threatened by Burt Lancaster. **center:** I'm the leader of the Amboy Dukes, a Brooklyn gang of kids, standing in front of Tony Curtis in *City Across the River*. **bottom:** Getting heat from Cagney sitting across from me in *White Heat*.

Loading artillery with Elvis Presley in G. I. Blues.

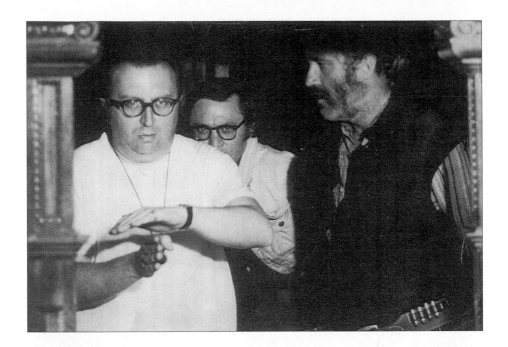

top: I'm next to Jason Robards as Sergio Leone aims his trusty six shooter in *Once Upon a Time in the West*. **bottom:** I'm the Admiral of the fleet as Laurence Olivier orders the attack on Inchon.

top: Myself, Adele Mailer, James Jones, and Norman Mailer at lunch together. **bottom:** My French wife, Georgette, points to my billing in the play *Of Mice and Men*.

top: My third wife, Joan. **bottom:** A corner of the living room in my apartment in Rome.

above: My daughter Valentina.
right: My daughter Melissa.

Ava Gardner had God-given beauty. Being next to her, I felt a slight vertiginous sensation. It's not easy to find words that could accurately describe her allure, her desirability. Her screen image does not convey her true beauty. She had to be seen in the flesh, so to speak.

After the first week, Ava and I were friends. Why? We played a word game, Jotto, to pass the dull time between setups. The name Ava easily lends itself to Jewish lilting—Avala. The first time I called her Avala she seemed pleased, smiled and shared a bit of intimate knowledge: Artie Shaw, a former husband, had called her Avala and she loved him. (By extention I fantasized . . . would she . . . will she . . . A man would be a lunatic not to fervently wish being enmeshed in her web.)

She also deeply loved Frank Sinatra, another former husband. In Rome, Ava had a magnificent upper floor apartment with a terrace overlooking Piazza di Spagna. At times I would be returning home after dinner, late at night, walking through the Piazza. Sometimes Sinatra's voice could be heard reverberating from Ava's terrace.

She had a dance sequence in the film and I sat in during one of her dance rehearsals. She was alone, dancing to recorded music. She was graceful; her body seemed to absorb the rhythms, the essence of the Spanish music. I watched her, enraptured.

The rehearsal ended and she plopped onto the chair next to mine, complaining that her feet hurt. I offered to massage her aching feet. Ava didn't hesitate; she turned her chair to face me and offered her bare feet. She leaned back and relaxed as I massaged each foot, hard, then caressed it softly. I listened to her sounds of pleasure, pleased as punch with myself. She then suggested we continue the massage in her dressing room. So up we went. I fell in love with Ava, and I had no illusions.

I wondered when Tony would make his move. He had good instincts, or was Ms. Gardner wickedly indiscreet? Because he made his move the following day. Sooner rather than later, costars fuck. It makes life much easier working together, rubs the rough edges off ego clashes, and together they have the power to protect themselves against the vagaries of the director or producer.

Tony's wife at the time, Shelley Winters, had decided to fly to Rome to visit her husband. I told Tony he must alert Ava that Shelley was arriving. That kind of surprise was unfair.

We met Shelley at the airport. She was genuinely happy to be in Rome. On the drive to the hotel, she was as effusive as ever and was delighted to be back in Tony's arms. The next morning, she came on set. I was at the Jotto game with Ava when we heard Shelley's high-pitched greeting: "Ava!"

Holy cow! Tony hadn't told Ava that Shelley was coming. Ava looked at me and froze. Shelley was soon upon her, embracing her, telling her how good it was to see her again. Ava unfroze long enough to mutter how surprised she was to see Shelley in Rome. Surprised? Oh, boy!

We had a few days off due to a holiday. Tony, Shelley, and I drove to Naples, then took the *vaporetto* (ferry) to Capri. Everything was jaunty jolly (thanks, Mel) until we arrived there. Shelley was near-sighted, but rarely wore glasses. When we were seated in the crowded piazza on Capri, she couldn't see the full page paparazzo photo of Tony and Ava embracing on the back cover of a scandal magazine that a woman at a nearby table was reading.

After dinner we took a walk. As we passed the Quissana Hotel, a bellhop ran out and told Shelley there was a call for her from Los Angeles. It was odd. We weren't even staying at that hotel. Tony and I had been waiting outside for about ten minutes when Shelley came charging out, shouting, "You're fucking Ava Gardner and you're going to marry her!" Her mother had read in a gossip column that Tony was having an affair with Ava and was planning on marrying her. Tony denied that he was going to marry Ava. They argued and it continued until we got back to the hotel.

I was in the room next to them and they both had the kind of stage voices one can hear not only in the back row of the balcony, but through thick hotel walls.

Shelley called Lovella Parsons, then Hedda Hopper, two top gossip column writers. She put Tony on the phone and he denied any truth to the rumors to each one of them. But the argument didn't stop there. No, siree. It continued on the way back to Rome and into the Excelsior Hotel where Tony and Shelley had a suite.

Tony insisted I not abandon him; he didn't relish being alone with Shelley, given the state she was in. I believe they both wanted an audience, even an audience of one. Finally, the war of words got too heated and I said, "I'm going." Tony said, "Wait, I'm going with you," and out we went.

Tony and Shelley eventually divorced. Ava went on to her life with bullfighter friends in Spain, ever the desirable, gorgeous lady.

1959 Paris

Terror in the streets of Paris.

P aris during wintertime can and does have dreary, wet weather,
but no matter how miserable it gets it rarely subdues my
feeling of awe and joy for this most beautiful, enticing city.

But there was one night in January of terror. A dark, sinister night,
that to this day I cannot shake out of my mind's cache of painful
memories.

A cable had arrived for me at my hotel from my brother Carl in
Washington, D.C. Our mother had suffered a massive heart attack,
putting me into a deep gloom. That night, I walked out of the hotel
and wandered up the Champs Elysées. It was past midnight, cold and
drizzling. The avenue was empty of people. I heard boots clattering
on the pavement and turned to find myself surrounded by a gang of
young skinheads in black leather pants and jackets and metal-tipped
heavy boots.

Their faces were mean, hard, they knew immediately I was an
American. They assailed me in French. "What is a dirty American
doing here? Answer, you dirty American. Don't worry, you won't be
here long." The gang leader faced me. I knew I had to get away
quickly. There was the smell of blood-lust coming off him.

The training I had done for a boxing film surfaced. I hit him hard
in the solar plexus and raced down the avenue to a lone taxi in the

middle island of the Champs Elysées where the taxis wait for fares. It was about a block away and I heard the gang running after me. I got into the taxi and shouted for the driver to get the hell out of there. He had seen the gang approaching in his rear-view mirror and needed no further urging.

I was trembling. Fear, rage, and, yes, panic threatened to overcome me. By the time the taxi had sped through the streets, then cut back to my hotel, I felt empty. I could barely speak.

The following morning I booked a seat on the first trans-Atlantic flight of the jumbo jet, the 747. I called Jones. His advice to me was get a bottle of booze. I did.

I waited in the airport for hours while they went over the 747 with meticulous care. Being its first trip, the airline had to avoid at all costs the possibility of an accident, which would have condemned the jet to the trash heap.

The loudspeakers squawked; the news was hard to understand, and once understood, hard to believe. The flight would be delayed until the following day. That night I took Jim's advice; I got drunk. By the time I landed in New York, took a commuter to Washington, my mother had died.

1959 New York

The Fugitive Kind *with Marlon Brando, Anna Magnani, Joanne Woodward. Sidney Lumet.*

Marlon Brando and Anna Magnani, both Academy Award winners, both actors of profound talent, both in the same film? Yes. But that wasn't all; the screenplay was adapted from a play by Tennessee Williams.

The title of the play, written many years earlier, was *Orpheus Descending*. The film was to be called, *The Fugitive Kind*. An odd title, but any title would do with all that box office power. Joanne Woodward and Maureen Stapleton were added to the cast and Sidney Lumet was signed to direct the film. Magnani got me as her coach.

It all added up to a sure winner, but the math was inaccurate, the deduction flawed.

I got a whiff of failed possibilities when meeting with Lumet before the shooting began. We were in his office talking about Magnani, who had respect for Lumet and high hopes for the film. The talk turned to Tennessee and his play. Lumet: "I'm going to take the kinks out of Tennessee on this one."

For one of the few times in my life I kept my mouth shut. I knew Tennessee wrote superb dialogue that was at times poetic, but if the "kinks" were taken out, what was left would not be Tennessee Williams.

Lumet, on virtually every movie he directs, rehearses for two weeks before filming begins. It's a good idea. It gives the actors a sense of the continuity of the piece, since most, if not all films are shot out of sequence. It also helps the director plan the staging without the stress of the time limitations of actual shooting. For those two weeks it's very much like rehearsing a play.

The first day, the actors sit around a table and read through the screenplay. The director is there and, in the case of *The Fugitive Kind*, Tennessee was also present. I was seated next to Magnani and Tennessee was to my right.

Before we started, Anna wanted to know how it would proceed, since this was her first such experience. She pointedly wanted to know how Brando would handle the reading. I told her, "He will mumble, and will be difficult to hear or understand."

The reading began. Marlon—and Anna—could barely be heard. She fooled me. I thought she would be loud and clear to get one up Marlon before we even started shooting.

Tennessee kept poking me in the ribs and whispering in my ear, "Ah can't hear a thing. What are they saying?" I tried to shush him. After all, he wrote the play, he ought to know the words. Sidney said nothing. Joanne Woodward had a small naughty smile.

Half an hour into the reading, Joanne made her entrance. At that point, the other actors were a bit uneasy. They tried to keep their voices low. Not Joanne Woodward. She blasted her first line of dialogue. Her voice reverberated off the walls of the room. It startled the group into laughter, dissipating the gloomy atmosphere.

After the shooting began, Anna was soon disillusioned; "taking the kinks out" also took away her freedom to invest the part with the full range of her talent and emotions. She was the most intelligent actor I ever worked with and she knew, early on, that the film lacked the spark to ignite it.

It was not easy listening to her laments. She had hopes, after *Rose Tattoo*, that this version of a Tennessee play would add to and affirm her reputation as a great actress.

Before the filming began, Brando invited Anna to join him on the Staten Island Ferry. Anna was thrilled. The romance of being on a boat, even a ferry boat, the New York City lights, the anticipation of starting a movie with Brando, his close presence at the rail of the ferry, sharpened Anna's senses. It was her idea of paradise.

Brando was sweet and attentive. He made Anna feel he was her protector, her admirer. His affection for her that night, in her eager mind, was more than just admiration for her talent. It was open to possibilities of future intimacies. But Brando was just being gracious to his leading lady. Those first weeks, he was always respectful of Anna, worked well with her, and deferred to her on the set. Off the set he became invisible.

But Marlon must have an adventurous soul. One midmorning, I was working with Magnani in her dressing room. She was preparing her makeup, wearing a dressing gown. Brando made an entrance. Anna, not one to miss an opportunity, ordered me out of the room. It was the first time Brando had made an appearance in her quarters. I started out, but Marlon blocked the door. "Don't go. I just came to say hello."

Anna: "I say go, Mickey, go out!" But Brando firmly stood in the doorway. Anna: "Marlon, what kind of man are you?"

Marlon waved good-bye—or was it a gesture of scorn?—and left. Anna, frustrated, looked up and appealed to God in Italian. "Is he a man or what?" And I responded for God, "He's a man, all right, Anna."

The door opened and I did a true double take: Marlon was back in the doorway. "I'm a man, Anna!" he whispered, as only he could. And he dropped his pants; they fell around his ankles.

Anna, standing next to her makeup table about a dozen feet from Marlon, half-shouted: "Go out, Mickey!" But Marlon, in the doorway, didn't budge. "All right, Marlon," Anna said, and, facing him, she opened her dressing gown, displaying her zaftig body. Her black bush triangle was a magnet, drawing two pairs of eyes.

Marlon, forgetting his entrapped ankles, turned to leave, stumbled, and fell on his ass. He slowly got to his feet, pulled his pants up, saluted Anna, and left, closing the door behind him.

Anna's desire for Marlon cooled, but she remained cordial. She had to work with him and her work was more important to her than a romance with Brando.

Despite all the talent and name power put into the project, the film was not a box office blockbuster. Why? Only the recently born muse of film understands.

1959–60 New York
The Party.

T he first time I laid eyes on Joan, Adele Mailer's sister, was
in 1951. Norman had asked me to join him and Adele at
her parents' home in Brooklyn for a Thanksgiving meal.
Joan was sixteen and a silent vision of beauty. She said not a word
during or after the meal. Her exquisite face, the creation of the union
between a Peruvian Indian father and a Spanish mother, needed no
voice. (I later found she was shy about revealing her pronounced
Brooklyn accent.)

When I returned to New York in 1959, after filming, Norman and
I saw each other often. He had an apartment in the Village where
Joan would baby-sit from time to time. I was there one night when
Joan was present. She was a successful fashion model and had
become a mature, stunning revelation. The Mailers left and I
remained to keep Joan company. When she offered to cook me a
hamburger, I was hooked. It's either instinct or intelligence for a
woman, when interested in a man she has recently met, to cook for
him. Even a lowly hamburger will do. It rarely fails to intrigue.

Mailer officially became a member of the Actors Studio in 1958.
He was in the writer's group, but like many of the writers, he often
observed the actors' sessions. Almost ten years later it served him
well when his play, *The Deer Park*, went into rehearsal.

For the first years of my friendship with Norman, I admired his insight into politics and politicians. I admired his perception of events and his seemingly smooth ability to articulate his thoughts. And I admired his talent as a writer Not since Hemingway has a writer so influenced other writers of his generation. But Hemingway influenced Norman more as a macho adventurer than as a writer. John Dos Passos, author of the superb trilogy *U.S.A.*, Norman has said was the writer who influenced him the most.

Norman's behavior was as complex and contradictory as the rest of us, only, at times, more flamboyant. The party Norman gave on November 19, 1960, was called spooky, mayhem, a debacle: violent, out of control. But for all that, it was historic. Somehow Norman managed to shake up his high-powered guests, unnerve them, anger them, and break everyone's belief in "party rules." Rule number one: no fistfights. Norman took care of that one; he was ready to throw punches with any takers. Fights went out on the street.

I had seen Norman in most of his moods, light to dark, but that night he was in a strange zone. The few conversations he had were inexplicably detached. The reason for the party was to announce that Norman was most likely going to run for mayor. It also coincided with Roger Donoghue's birthday. Roger, a friend of ours, was an ex-boxer and a very good one, but quit fighting when he felt responsible for the death, in the ring, of his last opponent.

I was strangely irritated by the disparate vibes and the sense that the party was breaking apart like a string of spaced firecrackers. There were loud arguments, loud laughter, drunken shouts. There were so many young people I didn't know, all making their own party. The literary elite present, I was sure, felt threatened by the amorphous shape of the possibilities.

I left before Norman took his penknife to Adele, but the following night Norman and I drove around the west side of Manhattan. We were both silent. He finally parked a couple of blocks from his apartment. He calmly asked if I would go up to his place and get an open letter he had written to Fidel Castro. Christ, I thought, he stabbed his wife the night before and what was the uppermost in his mind? Getting that letter published.

It did not surprise me. The foundation of Norman's being is the sum of his writing, and that letter to Castro was a building block in that foundation.

Castro was in the news about the time of the party, and Norman wanted to get his thoughts known. I struck a deal with him: I would get his letter and he would hand me his penknife. The reason was simple: Norman wasn't clear on what to do. Should he turn himself in to the police, hide out for a while, leave the country? The alternatives to staying in New York to face the music, I knew, were going nowhere. So I convinced him it was a lousy idea to be caught with the weapon, no matter how small.

Norman did not want to risk running into the police at his apartment. He wasn't ready for that. The events of the previous night crashed down on me. I quickly found the letter and hurried out.

Norman reluctantly gave me his three-inch penknife, convinced he should not be caught with it. Convinced? But not for long— before he dropped me off, he wanted it back. I returned the knife to him, not willing to get into an argument.

The open letter to Fidel Castro was finally published months later, after the Bay of Pigs.

Years later, Norman remarked that he admired my courage the night I retrieved his letter. If I had encountered the police they very well could have charged me with harboring a suspect or aiding and abetting. But I never thought about that and if I had, I might have refused to jeopardize myself. Courage, I believe, is being aware of the danger and confronting it.

Norman did confront it. He didn't run for cover. After he left me that night, he went to the hospital to see Adele. He visited her the second night and that's when the police picked him up and took him to the precinct. It was then decided to transfer him to Bellevue Hospital for psychiatric evaluation. To New Yorkers, Bellevue was the nuthouse, a scary place to avoid when out walking. As befit its function, it was an ugly, forbidding building.

I have to admit, I dreaded the thought of going into Bellevue to visit Norman, but visit him I did. It was no ordinary sit-down visit. I stood facing a metal door with a foot-square grille. Norman appeared on the other side of the grille and we talked quietly for a few minutes. He was deeply concerned that the doctors would subject him to the frightful electric shock treatment and asked me to do whatever I could to prevent it.

I said, sure Norm, sure, but I hadn't a clue how to go about it. I left in a dismal mood. (He was later released without being subjected to the treatment.)

The New York tabloids were wild in their coverage. They all had banner headlines and photos. When Adele refused to press charges, Norman was put on probation and the reportage faded away.

Adele recovered and the marriage was over.

1961 Hollywood

Acting with Elvis Presley in G.I. Blues.

I n Hollywood the king is the actor who delivers the goods: big box office. Elvis the Pelvis was the number one delivery boy.

Before Elvis was born, Clark Gable was the king and what a difference twenty years makes. Gable in the 1930s was the man: Tall 'n' handsome, virile, romantic, and tough. In the 1950s, along came Elvis, a nice-looking country boy, pleasant, ready to please, and a new kind of singer. But he was authentic. The kids swooned, as they had done for Sinatra before him.

Hal Wallis, my former boss, signed him to a film deal. And the kids flocked to the movie houses. Long live the King!

Wallis brought me back to Hollywood as an actor in 1961. The blacklist was either over or Wallis, who had always disliked it, just went ahead and hired me.

The movie was G.I. *Blues*, with Elvis Presley. I was back in uniform, playing one of Presley's buddies. It was Elvis's first film after serving in the army in Germany, and he was in great physical shape, having studied karate seriously while in Germany.

He was proud of his karate skills, like breaking boards with his bare hands. Impressive. But his next demonstrations was even more impressive. When he was told that I had played the champ in a fight film, he approached me and faced me. "Try and punch me—go on, try—in the face."

"Forget it, Elvis," I said, "Hal Wallis would take a contract out on me if I damaged you."

Elvis smiled and insisted: "Go on, boy, try and hit me." I had no choice; he was the star of the movie. I swung at him, not hard, but it didn't matter; I didn't even graze him. I tried a couple of times and each time he slipped the punch. He reacted that quickly. That boy had many talents.

I asked him how he learned to move the way he did when he sang. "When I was a little kid I had a bunch of little black friends. I used to attend their church and I just did what they did when we sang psalms—moved to the rhythm. We didn't think there was somethin' wrong doin' it."

Being polite to everyone came naturally to Elvis. If a woman visited the set, he'd hurry to get her a chair. He wasn't showing off. He did it effortlessly, with instinctive good manners. I asked him where he learned his good manners and he said, his mama. Ever since he could remember she had taught him to always be polite. He was the genuine article.

We got to talking about karate. He had taken it up to defend himself. When he went on tour, before being in the army, there were often times he'd be confronted by some young nut, after the concert, who claimed his girl had dumped him because she was in love with Elvis.

However, in spite of his ability at karate, he had gathered several of his Southern buddies to travel with him. They became his entourage. But he said he was still being attacked despite their presence. His boys were always on the set with him. They were shy and rarely mixed with any of the cast. They sat around together and softly chatted between takes.

It's a mystery to me how, in later years and still young, Elvis changed so quickly. He was so proud of his physical fitness, of his talent. What happened? Was it his manager, the colonel? Was it drugs to escape the weight of his fame? I don't know, but from my experience of working with him, he was a fundamentally decent man.

1961 Brooklyn—Paris

Once again I was working on a Lumet film, adapted from Arthur Miller's play, *View From the Bridge*. Three of the leads were European actors and only one of them, Jean Sorel, spoke English well. He was French as was Raymond Pellegrin, who spoke little English. Raf Valone, Italian, had pitifully little grasp of English. He was the main problem, as he was playing the part with the most dialogue. Raymond showed some talent with languages (he also spoke Italian), but Raf had a tin ear. However, he, like Magnani, was strong-willed and determined to succeed. A couple of hours before appearing on the set, he would walk in Central Park every morning with a small tape recorder pressed against his ear, listening to the dialogue that I had recorded for him.

Besides being the dialogue coach, I also acted in the film, playing a waterfront hood. The film was being shot in English and French. It was produced by a French film company.

Working with so many foreign actors, I became aware of how difficult it was to act in a language that is not your mother tongue. I spoke French fairly well, was comfortable with the language in social conversation, but when I had to act in French, I found it an obstacle; I suddenly realized that my concentration was on the words, not on the action in the scene, thus interfering with the business of acting.

When we finished shooting in the old Brooklyn Navy Yard, we went to Paris to film the interiors. (I remained in Europe, for the most part in Italy, for thirty-five years.)

1961 Paris

The Longest Day *with a host of stars headed by John Wayne and Robert Ryan, produced by Darryl F. Zanuck.*

*T*he *Longest Day*—the longest job. Sidney Lumet's *View From the Bridge*, brought me to Paris to finish the film. Joan, my future wife, came along, eager to discover Paris. I had some cash in hand and when shooting was over on *View*, we stayed on, unwilling to leave Paris.

I ran into Gerd Oswald, a film director I knew from my Hollywood days. He was going to be the American director of Darryl Zanuck's ambitious project about Normandy landings on D-Day, June 6, 1944, and the bloody battle that followed. The German part of the film was going to be directed by Bernhard Wicki, the English by Ken Annakin. It was a difficult project considering the logistics: the large crews, thousands of extras, dozens of actors, tons of military equipment, and the complex planning of the landings.

Gerd got me hired as the dialogue director. It was great luck. I wanted above all to find something to keep me in Paris, and this job was going to last months.

My luck continued as we looked for an apartment. "Moustache" was a local character, well-known by American friends of mine who lived in Paris. He had a thick, drooping moustache, was a drummer, and later ran a restaurant for Sidney Chaplin. He had a large, two-bedroom apartment on the Left Bank and needed money. He was delighted to rent it to me and get a couple of months in advance while he crashed at a friend's place.

My first assignment on the film was to travel to several German cities and coach the German actors before the filming started. A few knew English fairly well, some not at all. The actor playing General von Runstedt had long speeches but spoke no English, and he was elderly, making him the most difficult actor I had to coach. I knew some German because it was close to Yiddish, so we could just barely communicate.

I left him a tape of his dialogue that I had recorded, as I did with the other actors. I would record the dialogue slowly, word by word, so it was absolutely clear, then record the phrases, still slowly, allowing space for the actor to repeat it, and finally I recorded the dialogue at its natural rhythm. It worked well enough for them to memorize the lines if I couldn't be there to work with the actors myself.

When we shot the scenes with von Runstedt, he came prepared, knowing all his speeches in English. The Germans were good that way. But he wasn't told what I had suggested to Zanuck earlier, that the Germans ought to speak in German and have subtitles in English. I offered the thought that the German language had more threat than English. Also the scenes had greater reality. Zanuck agreed.

When General von Runstedt was told, shortly before doing his scene, that he would be doing it in German, not English, he had a mild heart attack, fell into a chair, and almost passed out. All that laborious work, studying his words in English phonetically. Now he had to cancel it out of his brain and memorize his dialogue in German; at his age he was simply overwhelmed.

I also had to coach two famous French actresses—Arletty and Madeleine Renaud—who had cameo roles in the film. I went to Arletty's apartment first. She was a major star in the 30s and was quite a beauty in her best years. She was still strikingly attractive in 1961. She greeted my arrival wearing a dressing gown, exposing her famous legs when she crossed them after we sat down to work.

Arletty, during the Nazi occupation, had taken German army officers as lovers. It's not clear to me if she profited materially or if she followed her desire, or need, to lure men into her web of intrigue. In any case, after the war she suffered the anger and hatred of the Parisians. She had guts, she didn't apologize, and didn't bend when faced by the storm of fury.

When Arletty was asked to play a small part in *The Longest Day*, she was informed that Madeleine Renaud, also a well-known French actress about the same age as Arletty, had agreed to participate in the film. Before beginning the session with me, Arletty asked if Madame Renaud had a larger role than she. I told her both roles were cameos with about the same screen time. Gallic facial expressions in some ways rival the Italian art of communicating without the spoken word and Arletty's silent reaction was as clear as a shaft of sunlight. *Do you take me for a fool?*

Later that day I worked with Madame Renaud and she asked the exact same question about the size of Arletty's role. I was struck by the rivalry between those two aging stars, still envious of each other over a bit part.

Zanuck, no longer head of Twentieth Century Fox, wanted John Wayne for two weeks, no matter what the cost. He knew that his name would add to the financial success of the film, which in turn would hand the leadership of Fox Studios back to Zanuck. But the Hollywood guilds were, at that time, bitterly complaining about the runaway production—the shift of production to foreign locations, depriving American crews and actors of work. But the cost of shooting in Europe was much less than shooting in Hollywood.

Duke Wayne decided to stand with the guilds and refused to come to Europe to work, even for Darryl Zanuck.

John Shepridge, a Hungarian aide to Zanuck (and called Goulash by all), was assigned the task of collaring Wayne, using any wile, including money. But Zanuck wanted to be kept in the dark, no matter what arrangement Goulash made with Wayne's agent. In effect, Zanuck was ready to pay any amount for Wayne's name on the marquee.

Wayne's agent asked for twenty-five grand a day, a huge sum in 1961. Goulash did as he was told and agreed to the deal and Wayne, despite his principled stand, was in the movie.

Gerd Oswald was fired by Zanuck after the first few days of filming. Zanuck decided to direct the American sequences himself. I think it was his first shot at directing. In the late twenties he worked for Warner Brothers; in 1933 he cofounded Twentieth Century Fox, was the head of production, then became the president of the company.

To direct very complicated battle scenes, he had his right-hand man, Elmo Williams, an expert editor, help plan the camera angles. But Zanuck had one important deficiency: He didn't know what to say to the actors. He called a "rehearsal" in his office—the one and only time.

The scene he wanted to rehearse was between John Wayne and Robert Ryan. He read the complete scene flatly, quickly, hissing slightly through the gap in his front teeth, leaving the sense of the scene a mystery. "Mickey," he said, "take the Duke and Bob out and rehearse them."

Man, oh man, what an assignment. Was he kidding? I don't think so. He just felt inadequate and handed me the problem. Once outside Zanuck's office, the three of us went our separate ways, with never a mention of the word rehearse.

I hustled over to the cozy studio café for a glass of red. France is the only country I have worked in which the call for the day starts at noon when shooting at the studio. It's civilized; in other countries the actors, director, and crew, generally called at daybreak, are grouchy, half asleep, and slow to get up to speed. The French day goes from noon to seven with no lunch break. Everyone comes to the set rested, relaxed, and in a good mood, and the studio café is always open for a quick bite.

Wayne and I became fairly good friends. It was odd, given his Neanderthal politics. He was a big, amiable guy who enjoyed man talk. But I'm a political junkie and can't keep my big mouth shut when I hear thoughtless, indefensible crap, like the blacklist was a good thing and it kept the Commies out of the business. Wayne didn't say that exactly, but there was a lot of political rote that is frustrating when trying to breathe some logic into a conversation. But Wayne never showed any disrespect or anger when listening to me.

One of the reasons he befriended me was that he found out I was a chess player. It helped pass the time waiting between setups. I wasn't very good, but I was better than Wayne, which ain't saying much. After we had had a particularly disconcerting argument, I concentrated on beating him on the chessboard. I won five games in a row. Then he got mad, almost mad enough to stomp me.

Bob Ryan was a man to be respected. He was an impressive actor, always believable, always a powerful screen presence, and had been an intercollegiate heavyweight boxing champ. Wayne must have known that. Ryan told me that when he was in Mexico on a film with the Duke, they got into a hot political argument, until finally Bob invited the Duke outside. Now, Wayne was famous for his supposed bar fights, but that day his fame was tarnished; he turned his back on the invite and ordered another drink.

He and Ryan hadn't spoken to each other until years later when they met again on the set of *The Longest Day*.

Before coming to Paris for the filming, Bob read the John Birch Society manifesto on the radio without adding any comment; he let the manifesto speak for itself. The John Birch Society was politically far right and, to many, racist. Bob was warned by the Society not to read the manifesto on the radio. The threat was clear, but didn't stop him.

While in Paris, Bob's wife called, panic in her voice. Someone identifying himself as a John Bircher had phoned to warn her that their house was going to be set on fire.

At the studio, the word spread quickly. The Duke hustled over to where Bob and I were talking. After many years, Wayne finally broke the silence between them. "Bob, it can't be the John Birch boys. They're really good fellas. I know some of them. They would never harm your family."

"I'm glad you told me that, Duke. Excuse me, I have to make a call." Bob phoned a private security agency in L.A. to protect his home and family. He wanted to leave the film for home immediately, but was assured by the security people that his home would be protected around the clock until he returned. His house wasn't torched, but it gave him pause to think.

A few days before Wayne and Ryan finished their filming, Zanuck gave a large dinner party for the company. Wayne called and asked if he could come with me to the party.

That was how he put it. I understood it was his way of repairing our short-lived friendship. I said, "Sure, come along." Did I mind coming to his hotel? We could use his car and chauffeur.

At the party, we sat at the same table. After dinner I wandered around to chat with some of the guests. I then joined Ryan at the bar. He was drinking Coca-Cola. He told me he was on the wagon (he was a pretty good boozer in his day), but I noticed a slight wink to the bartender as he ordered another Coke. Rum and Coke? Yessiree. Wayne appeared and sat next to Bob. The two of them began a friendly conversation, so I split.

I was ready to leave. The Duke and Bob were nowhere to be seen. That was Saturday night. Monday morning, at work, I heard that Bob and Duke had disappeared. Zanuck figured they were on a weekend bender and didn't seem too concerned. "Boys will be boys," he said.

The next day they both reported for work, a little worse for the booze. They made no excuses and no one commented. But the Duke and Bob were once again friends.

Robert Mitchum was also in the huge cast. He was unique. "Never apologize, never explain," he often said, and lived by it. On screen, one felt a threat the moment he appeared. Although he was laid-back and often seemed sleepy, there was a sense that danger lurked behind those half-closed eyes.

We talked about his short stay in a Los Angeles jail, years earlier, when he was busted for smoking pot. He enjoyed the stay, laughed at the scandal and never told the authorities he would quit pot. As we sat in his dressing room talking about pot, he told me he never bought the weed. Someone always offered him a stash.

A knock on the door and a young Arab, who was on the crew, came in and offered Bob a small pack of hash. He didn't want any money; it was a gift. Mitchum looked at me and smiled. It did occur to me that he might have staged the little scene for my benefit; the timing was too good to be true.

While driving to dinner on the Left Bank with Mitch one night after a few drinks, we stopped at a red light. A seedy-looking drunk stood on the corner waving at us. In a sudden rage, Mitch started out of the car and yelled, "I'll kill the bastard!" I grabbed his arm and told the driver to get going. The light had just turned green or Mitch would have jumped out of the car and, no doubt, done damage.

After dinner, Mitch disappeared. The following day, a gleeful light in his eyes, he told us he had picked up a bag lady, brought her back to his hotel (the Raphael; exclusive, elegant) and took her up to his room. She was encrusted with dirt. He ran her a bath, had to peel the stockings off her legs, undressed her, dumped her into the tub and scrubbed her clean. Oh yes, she had no front teeth.

In the morning, on the way to the studio, the manager of the hotel had a civilized word with Mitch; the hotel would appreciate it if Monsieur Mitchum would not invite madame to his suite again. Mitch agreed and the manager bowed in gratitude. Fact or fiction? Only Robert Mitchum, the enigma, knows.

The next time I saw Mitch was in Madrid, in 1972. He was checking into my hotel. He seemed pleased to see a friendly face. I invited him to share a bottle of Jack Daniels I had bought from an American air force pilot stationed in Spain. On the way to the elevator, we passed a large public room off the lobby. Mitch stopped to look in. The place was full of well-dressed bridge players engaged in a tournament. Mitch shouted, "All right, you greaseballs, everyone out." I pulled him away and quickly led him to the elevator.

While drinking my booze, Mitch, a good storyteller, told me why he happened to be in Madrid. He had been working on a movie in North Africa, directed by Otto Preminger, an American citizen who held onto his German accent and shaved his head, no doubt thinking it added to his authority. And he was hard-driving. I never worked for him or met the man, but his reputation was known in the industry.

The morning before Mitch came to Spain, he got up late for work. He was taking his time having breakfast in the tent provided for the crew when an angry Preminger strode in and bawled out Mitchum for being late and having a leisurely breakfast. Mitch told him to shove his film and took the first plane out. It brought him to Madrid. When I asked if he feared being sued, he grinned and said, "Not a chance." He'd claim Preminger insulted him in front of the crew, making his stay there absurd. He was not sued and another actor replaced him.

Elmo Williams had been given an Oscar for editing *High Noon*. He was an excellent editor, but a strange man. When *The Longest Day* company moved to Normandy for exteriors, Joan, my future wife, was with me. Naturally, we lived in the same hotel room. Elmo let me know, through a second source, that he disapproved of our living together unwed. He said his wife and children were living in the same hotel and it was not a good example for the little ones.

A puritan yet. I shrugged it off. It was a joke. The crew and cast kidded me and had some dandy names for Elmo.

Most of the cast stayed in the same hotel when we shot in Normandy. The English contingent was great fun. They assembled in the warm, inviting hotel pub every evening after work. They were loud, deafening, in fact. In order to be heard, everyone had to shout, which kicked the decibel count off the chart. But the atmosphere, although boisterous, was not threatening.

After work one evening, Peter Lawford and I entered the bar. We spotted his wife, Pat Kennedy, sitting with a colonel who was the British army advisor on the film. The colonel had organized his own battalion of Scottish farmers into a fighting force that landed on

D-Day. The adventure made him famous. However, soon after landing, he took a bullet in the buttock and hid out in a barn until rescued. Peter Lawford played him in the film.

Mrs. Lawford and the colonel had taken a tour of the battlefield earlier in the day. The colonel showed Pat the barn where he took refuge after being wounded. To Peter, their tête-a-tête at the end of the bar seemed suspect; what happened in that bar? Peter turned to me and said, "The party's over . . ."

The colonel was very British and very handsome. His thick gray hair, well-tanned, sharply chiseled features, and tall slim frame would turn any husband or lover a shade of green. Peter never told me if he had found straw clinging to Pat's skirt.

Zanuck had great faith in Elmo Williams. He trusted him as an editor and advisor. Elmo, on or off the set, barely acknowledged my presence. When I was asked play the small part of a downed American aviator being hidden from the Germans by a French family, I put a bandage over one eye as a disguise because my actor's ego resented playing a small part. Elmo, looking to stick it to me, neglected to add me to the cast credits, or credit me as a dialogue director. Now I regret not getting the credit. It's a film I'm pleased to have been a part of.

"We wuz robbed"—literally. The cast and production people were staying in a hotel in Cean, Normandy, while shooting the battle scenes. Every room was burglarized, including mine, but I only lost some toilet articles. Others lost jewelry, money, hairpins, and books. George Segal's wife had a watch stolen, given to her by her grandmother.

Nothing much was done about it until a box of expensive Cuban cigars and a few hundred dollars were taken from Zanuck's room. Then the shit hit the fan. It wasn't the money, it was the box of cigars. Those Cuban cigars set a serious search in motion to nab the culprit. Mr. Zanuck went into action. After all, he chomped and smoked seven to eleven of them a day.

Zanuck insisted the police be brought in to uncover the thief. The only detective with the town's police was called in to take charge. He declared he'd round up the usual local suspects. Zanuck was steamed. He was convinced it was an inside job and ordered the detective to start with the employees of the hotel.

He and an assistant began the interrogations. One of the first was a bellhop, a kid about seventeen. He nervously lit a cigarette with an expensive-looking lighter. The sharp-eyed detective plucked it out of the kid's hand and tried to read the inscription on it, but it was in English, so he handed it to his assistant. She read it aloud. "Stolen from Paul Anka." She translated it into French.

The detective gleefully shouted. "We got our man!"

Indeed they had. Paul Anka was in the film and was delighted to recover his lighter. The bellhop confessed all. He was living with a woman in her thirties, looking for a ticket to Paris for herself and the kid to maker their fortune. But they needed money. She coached the kid how to be a successful thief. He probably wouldn't have been caught if Zanuck hadn't been stung by the loss of his cigars. All the loot, including the cigars, was found in the woman's one-room apartment.

The hotel manager and city authorities wanted to prosecute the kid, but Zanuck saved his ass. He told the police neither he nor anyone else would press charges. If they jailed the kid he was sure to learn how to be a proper thief. Zanuck understood that a horny kid would do anything to keep from losing a steady lay.

The bellhop was let go with a warning, as was his lady love. George Segal and his wife had returned to the States prior to the discovery of Anka's lighter. Before he left I told him I'd send him his wife's watch if it ever turned up. Mrs. Segal was delighted to receive her treasured watch.

Since the editing of the film kept up with the daily shooting, when the principal photography was completed so was a rough cut. Zanuck invited the production people to attend a showing. That meant no music, no special effects, no fine-tuning the sound or final editing.

After the showing, Zanuck, seated in the front row, turned to face us and asked what young actor in the film would most likely reach stardom. There were about twenty-five actors with small roles. Some names were mentioned. I named George Segal, then unknown. He was a friend, but he was good even in a small part. Zanuck's choice was no surprise: Richard Beymer. Richard was a Fox actor who had the lead in *Five Finger Exercise*, a Fox film. Is he remembered? How about George Segal?

A couple of weeks before the filming was completed, I was at my favorite watering hole, the bar at Hotel George V, having a dry martini. I would drop in from time to time, sit at the bar, and get my fix.

A hand clapped me on the shoulder. I turned around to see the unforgettable face of Carl Foreman. "I been looking all over for you. I'm going to direct my first film from a screenplay I wrote, *The Victor's*, and I need your help."

I should have said, "Flattery will get you nowhere," but the ole' ego got a hard-on at hearing I was needed by Carl Foreman. Carl was considered a top screenwriter in Hollywood. He had written the screenplay for *High Noon*, which opened many doors for him after the film came out in 1952.

But he got smacked right in the gut by the blacklist. He was proud of his reputation and hated to see it evaporate, not due to failure on his part, but by an amorphous, hidden power.

Gary Cooper, star of *High Noon*, respected Foreman's talent. Although his politics were to the right of Carl's, he suggested they form a company to produce several films to be written by Carl. Carl was elated. But the film moguls checked their secret blacklist and were quick to react: Cooper got calls from every studio head, "advising" him to drop his compact with Foreman. There would be difficulty in getting financing for any project connected to Carl Foreman.

Cooper met with Carl and told him about the problems they'd have to overcome, but said, "I want to fight them. Let's go ahead, we'll work it out." But Carl convinced Cooper it would be hopeless and they reluctantly dropped their plans.

Foreman was effectively removed from the blacklist by a smart labor lawyer, Sidney Cohn. Sidney was married to Robbie Garfield, John Garfield's widow. Robbie was intelligent and never feared to speak her mind. I was in New York in 1962 after *The Victors* was completed and asked her if she knew how her husband, Sidney, had cleared Carl of the blacklist. He lips were sealed, she said, and could not divulge what happened when Sidney and Carl met with the House Un-American Activities Committee.

Carl was cleared before he wrote the very successful, *Guns of Navarone*, in 1960, hence the greenlight by Columbia Pictures for *The Victors* in 1961.

Back at the George V, I told Foreman I was working on *The Longest Day*, but would be free in a couple of weeks. Carl asked if I would see if Zanuck would release me immediately. I declined, but Carl didn't seem to get it.

"What if Carl Foreman called Zanuck and asked him to release you?" It takes a Mae West or Greta Garbo to speak in the third person, and Carl Foreman was neither.

"I'd rather you wouldn't, Carl. I been on the job since the beginning and I want to finish it," I said, trying to convince him.

My words were in vain. Persistence, for Carl, was the name of the game. The following day, Zanuck had me in his office. "Got a call from Carl Foreman, wants you with him on his picture, asked me to release you, wanna go?" Zanuck asked.

"I would like to remain until *The Longest Day* completes its schedule, Mr. Zanuck."

"Glad to hear it," Zanuck replied.

Carl started *The Victors* three months later.

It came down to Paris or Joan. Joan won out. It was painful to leave the City of Light, but I had no choice. Joanne was having a difficult time. When she did fashion photography, she would be paid, finally, with a check that was *barre*, meaning it could only be cashed by the payee if the payee has a bank account. By French law, only a citizen or a permanent resident could have a bank account. So, the payee was stuck with a useless piece of paper. Catch-22.

I had to make the rounds with her to get cash for her work. She had a difficult time with the Parisians. They made foreigners feel unwanted, invaders of their beautiful city. The French models also gave her a hard time. In New York I saw how the American models showed concern and aided the foreign models, including the French. No reciprocity when in Paris.

The proverbial straw did it one afternoon. I went with Joan to shop for shoes. The saleslady had a pinched, unsmiling face, a bad sign. Joan indicated the shoes she wanted. She tried them on and said they were too tight. The saleslady glared, her voice tight, and said, "It's not the shoes, Madame, it's your feet."

Tears quickly followed by a direct order: We leave France immediately. Three days later my Renault, packed to capacity, was headed south. We were going to Italy.

1962 Rome

An expatriate, I live in Rome for thirty-five years.

A nd so I became an expatriate for three and a half
decades living and working in Rome, but also filming
throughout Europe and many parts of the world. And I
never looked back, never gave the blacklist a second thought.
Rome was my home and America was a place to visit—to para-
phrase Gertrude Stein.

And I had a life the blacklisters didn't intend for me. I fucked 'em
royally. I was king of the hill. In Rome it was *la dolce vita*—the sweet
life. (Not Fellini's fanciful *Dolce Vita*, but the literal sweet life.)

For the first two years Joan and I lived on the Piazza Farnese next
to the French Embassy, partially designed by Michelangelo. (Competition was stiff in the sixteenth century and Michelangelo had the
clout to get the original architect bounced when the huge building
was almost completed. Michelangelo redesigned the top floor
façade.)

It was a fine old area; we were next to Piazza del Fiore where the
daily open market sold all kinds of vegetables, fruits, meat, fresh fish,
and flowers. Miraculously, by early afternoon each day, the large
Piazza was empty of stalls and pushcarts and the ground was swept
clean and washed.

Then Joan got pregnant (we tried hard enough) and we needed a bigger place. Lady Luck winked at us and we found our home on Via Gregoriana in 1964.

Saying I was in love with my Rome apartment sounds like a punch line, but there it is. I had love for that apartment, if love can mean waking up in the morning and reveling in the space and beauty of the place. And is the yearning to return after being away love? It sure is.

Via Gregoriana is a narrow one-block street that begins to the right of the top of the Spanish Steps and slopes down to the end, about three football fields away. It's a beautiful street, lined with elegant, Roman-pink buildings. I lived in number twenty, next to a large, walled villa where, it is said, Henry James wrote a part of *Daisy Miller* in 1878.

Via Gregoriana 20 is a square, three-story building a couple of centuries old. It still belongs to a family called Dante Alighieri de Serego, descendants of the Dante. In my living room hung three large, magnificent paintings, framed in centuries-old, gold-leafed molded frames, of Dante's eighteenth-century descendants. Count Alighieri, the owner of my apartment, lived in Dante's original castle in Perugia, north of Rome.

The apartment had two floors, a garden, and a terrace over the garden. The ceilings were high and the floors were all tiled in polished terracotta. The kitchen was huge, with a fluted ceiling and French doors leading to the garden.

My two daughters were born while living there—one in 1964, the other in 1965—and were brought up in Rome until their midteens. They are now grown adults and still have fond memories of Rome. And so do I.

Roman restaurants spoiled me. Waiters are courteous, patient, and proud of their métier. And why not? It pays well and they enjoy serving consistently savory meals.

There were good reasons to eat out in Rome—it was cheaper than eating in, all things considered, but the conviviality was the key reason. Dining out with friends lasted until closing time or later. We were rarely asked to leave, though at times a waiter would hover nearby with a slightly pained look.

For thirty-five years, my Roman adventure was a time of much film work, optimism, and a secret delight in living in a city of beauty.

1962 Italy—London

The Victors *with George Hamilton and Eli Wallach.*
Directed by Carl Foreman.

Carl Foreman had planned on starting his film, *The Victors*, several months before I actually got the call that filming was to begin in ten days in Salerno (about one hundred and sixty miles south of Rome), then on to London. There was one hitch: Columbia Pictures had reduced his budget. He was forced to cut back. Either I take a salary cut, along with others in the company, or I agree to work only the first six weeks of shooting on my contracted salary.

It pissed me off. Carl originally said he needed my help since it was his first directorial job. The studio bosses put the squeeze on him and he crumbled.

I wanted to quit, but I had a problem; I had refused to work in Rome due to a conflict in dates with *The Victors*. If I didn't work on *The Victors*, it would raise questions within the small Roman film community; why wasn't I working on Foreman's film? It was simply bad news. The other factor was Joan. She liked the idea of going to London after the Salerno shoot. Her wish, at the time, was my command. So I accepted full salary for six weeks.

Off to Salerno I went. *The Victors* was about G.I.s in World War II. The cast included George Peppard, George Hamilton, Eli Wallach, and Jeanne Moreau. Aside from being the dialogue director, I was cast as a G.I.

One funny incident in Salerno is worth describing. We were shooting an intricate action scene. An infantry patrol, including the leading actors, was in a firefight with the Germans. During the scene, they found themselves crawling over a small bridge under fire. Vince Edwards, part of the patrol, suddenly jumped up and shouted, "Hold everything! Get a doctor! Goddamnit!" For a long moment, everything did stop. Then the assistant director sprinted to Vince. I walked over and saw that he had scraped his hand. It was bleeding and he had turned pale. "I need a tetanus shot right away," Vince wailed. Carl was seething and muttering curses. Vince, a big, husky young man, at the loss of a few drops of blood turned out to be a crybaby.

A local doctor appeared, carrying an old-fashioned doctor's black bag. He cleaned the scrape and was about to give Vince a tetanus shot. Vince rebelled. He slammed his helmet down and insulted the whole Italian medical system for still being in the Middle Ages for not using disposable needles. The Italian doctor didn't have disposable needles. But the Navy did. He suggested they take Vince to the U.S. Naval Base in Naples, about forty miles away.

So shooting stopped while Vince was driven to Naples, suspending the rest of the day's work. It was a time to stay clear of Carl Foreman.

George Hamilton is a superb comedian. I knew that in 1962. It took the film industry a long time to discover his comic talent. He's a likeable, even-tempered guy. He takes great care of himself. He is always tanned. And he knows the right things to wear, classy yet casual-looking. He arrived to begin *The Victors* bringing his weights and personal barber.

Every major city in Europe that I know has its own character. London has it in spades. It would take a troglodyte to dislike London. The cities in Europe grow outwards from ancient centers, with each century showing its ring of style as part of that growth.

Being in London to work on *The Victors* was like a welcome gift. Joan and I took an apartment in the White House, a homey, rambling hotel, anticipating a pleasant stay.

But the first day on the set was about to be my last.

Vince Edwards and a beautiful young Italian actress had a delicate scene of discovering each other. It was going nowhere; it was flat and didn't ignite. I was standing in back of Foreman. He had told me before we started the film to tell him any ideas I might have before he printed the take, not afterward. Out of frustration with how the scene played, he turned to me and asked if I had any thought on how to get the scene off its ass. Boy, did I put my foot in it.

"Carl, there's too much dialogue, these actors can't handle it. The scene is long. Cut some of it or it won't work," I quietly suggested.

But Carl had written the dialogue! "Fuck you!" he shouted, enraged.

Dead silence on the set. All eyes on Carl and me. I closed my script and left the sound stage.

That afternoon, I told Joan I had quit. "You quit?" she asked coolly. "We just got here."

I described what had happened and told her to say I was out if the phone rang. It rang. It was Eva, Carl's personal secretary and aide. Joan told her I wasn't in and repeated that the next three times she called. Then Eva said the magic words, "Carl will kill me if I don't speak to Mickey."

I got on the phone. "Carl wants to invite you to a dinner he's giving tonight for the stars of the film. Please come."

"Not a chance," I replied.

"Please, do it for me. You know Carl, he'll have my head if you don't come."

I pleased both Joan and Eva by going to the dinner. The guests were grouped at the bar. Carl was at the near end, so I drifted to the far end. I arrived late. Before I could order a drink, we were informed that our table was ready. Everyone slowly left, except Carl and me.

I started to join the others, but Carl stopped me. "You disappeared this morning. What happened?"

"'Fuck you'? I quit. You obviously don't respect me and I don't respect you, so it's mutual."

"I only say fuck you to my friends. I say fuck you to Sidney Cohen all the time and he's a close friend. I apologize if I offended you. Come back to work, I need you." I didn't say anything. I shrugged ambiguously. He took my arm and started to lead me to the dinner table. "Let's join the party. I hope you're all right about coming to work tomorrow. I am sorry about this morning."

Getting an apology from Carl Foreman was a small victory, but still a victory. I showed up on the set the next day.

Eli Wallach and his wife, Anne Jackson, were old friends of mine from the early Actors Studio days. Both are talented Broadway actors. It was fun having Eli on the film; he's a good companion, easy to talk to and be with.

On location, one day, Eli had a representative from his agency join him for lunch. Lunch break, while away from the studio, is a casual, although a somewhat rushed meal. Eli, his guest, several others, and myself sat at the same table. As we began lunch, the assistant director came to our table and leaned down to whisper to Eli. He was flushed, uncomfortable, embarrassed. "Eli, Carl asked me to tell you we are not allowed to have guests for lunch. I'm sorry. I hate to be the messenger on this one." Eli was confused for a moment, then angrily got up and left, followed by the young lady represenative.

It was absolute bullshit. Everyone in the crew and cast on all the films I worked on have brought guests to lunch at one time or another. And this particular lunch was as cheap as the production could make it, mostly thin white bread sandwiches.

I went out and found Eli sitting against a tree, growling and muttering to himself. I didn't say anything. I sat, joining him in missing lunch.

Communication between Eli and Carl became chilly at best. I got to know Carl pretty well, and to this day I can't understand why he was so stupid as to needlessly get on the wrong side of one of his leading actors. It was something an experienced director would never dream of doing.

It was the only film Carl directed.

1962 Rome

Gore Vidal's party. Greeting Rome.
John Huston makes his move.

In the winter of 1962, Gore Vidal rented an apartment on Via Giulia in Rome. He gathered a group of friends and acquaintances to celebrate his arrival in the Eternal City. John Huston was one of the notable guests.

Joan and I, earlier in the year, had settled into a small penthouse apartment on Piazza Farnese. At Gore's party, Joan's classy appearance stopped the music for a moment. She wore her runway disdainful look, as she usually did when among strangers. As a kid in Brooklyn, she was called a "spick" and never forgot the shame, the guilt, and a lingering hurt.

She was left alone when I headed for the bar. As I returned with our drinks I heard John Huston say to her, "Well now, whom do you belong to?"

"She belongs to me, John," I said.

"Well, how would you like a cigar," he asked, quick as a tomcat on the prowl.

"Sure," I answered, too damn pleased because I was a smoker who valued a good cigar and I knew Huston would have only the best. And he did. He withdrew a long cigar from an inner pocket, put his drink on the table, balanced the cigar across the rim of the glass, lit a match, warmed the cigar with its flame, then grandly handed it to me. Ever the artiste.

Later that evening, primed by a few ounces of booze, I sauntered up to the fellow who was John Huston's casting agent. We had met earlier and his surly puss put a chip on my shoulder.

"You here to help cast John's film?" I tried not to sound too aggressive, but I didn't succeed.

"Yeah," he replied, close to a snarl.

"I got to know a lot of casting agents and most know fuck-all about acting," I said, meaning to incite him.

"So what? To me actors are just hunks of meat."

I threw a punch. He lunged at me. We wrestled for a few seconds and were pulled apart.

Gore was pleased, saying the scuffle made the party. And all I wanted to do was bust the asshole in the chops.

That year began a long residence in Rome and later in Ravello for Gore and Howard Austin, his companion. Gore and I had known each other, though not well, since 1959. In Rome, however, we saw each other fairly often. When the occasion arose, he would suggest me for movie work, and he was always generous with his dinner and party invitations, which were spirited and amusing. Gore was never a slouch at entertaining his guests with his sharp humor. He could vocally imitate anyone. President Franklin Delano Roosevelt was his favorite, and he was as pleased as his audience to hear himself repeat, "The only thing we have to fear is fear itself."

As far as I could see, he had one deep friendship—Howard. No matter how often we saw each other and had conversations, Gore and I were what I would characterize as local friends.

I had worked with Elio Petri, an intelligent, first-rate Italian film director. Gore also admired his work and I suggested that Gore write a screenplay for Elio with me trying to produce it. He did have a terrific idea for a movie and in due time wrote it and handed it to me, saying, "It won't be easy, but go ahead." Now, that's class. A screenplay by Vidal, directed by Elio Petri, a name actor or two and the film is a go.

Gore was incredibly prescient. The script was about an attempted assassination of Pope John Paul. He wrote the screenplay during 1976 and the Pope was wounded in 1981. The timing would have been perfect with the film coming out shortly before the shot that was heard around the world.

But events can turn even a diamond into a zircon. Elio got hit with a heart attack and left the earthly scene. It was a blow, but elements did seem eventually to brighten only to slowly dim and sputter. I did get financing from a young Swiss gentleman. Jim Coburn and Lauren Bacall were supposed to play the leads, but the project was doomed. It is too depressing to go into why it never got off the ground. Gore thought the Swiss spent a lot of money on the project for one reason only—tax evasion. We'll never know.

1963 Rome

Bette Davis in Rome to make The Empty Canvas.

Bette Davis came to Rome to be in *The Empty Canvas*, a film adapted from a book by Alberto Moravia, *La Noia*, (ennui, boredom). I met her the first time in her suite at the Grand Hotel. I was with the director of the film, Damiano Damiani, a talented, no-nonsense director. He spoke little English and I was with him to interpret.

"Are you a communist?" Her tone was her signature, clipped and clear.

Damiani responded calmly, slowly, "Madam, all intelligent people are of the left." Italy had a strong Communist Party, averaging a third or better of the nation's vote in all elections since the end of World War II, so her question didn't surprise him or me. She smiled and let it pass.

I was the dialogue director (the film was being shot in English) and mainly worked with the other lead actors, Horst Buchholtz and Catherine Spaak. Of course, I was also at Damiano's elbow interpreting when Davis was working.

Early on, we were rehearsing a long dialogue scene with Bette and Catherine. I know when an actor goes up (forgetting dialogue) and Ms. Davis went up. It's not unusual while rehearsing. I waited, giving Bette time to recall the line. Finally, I threw her the cue. She turned to me, glared for a long beat, then let me have the full Bette Davis delivery, sharp and loud, "How dare you cue me? I always know my lines and don't you forget that!"

I banged my script shut and walked off the set. I wasn't angry; I was amused and did a bit of showboating. For the next two days I ignored her. The third morning she approached me and said, "Don't you say good morning, Mickey?"

"Sure Bette, good morning."

She smiled and said, "That's fine, now let's get to work." Well, she was friendly and always available for the rest of the film.

She showed an interest in my career. She knew I would have liked to direct and I agreed with her. She was planning on doing a TV series when she returned to the States and if the deal worked out, she said she would certainly give me a shot. Her tone had changed, her voice was soft as she suggested we would do some fine work together.

Bette heard that I had worked with Anna Magnani and asked me about her. She thought Anna was a marvelous actress. Could she meet with her? I asked Anna if she'd like to invite Bette for a drink or a meal. "Of course, I like that actress."

The three of us gathered at Anna's friendly Rome apartment in a huge palazzo. The two ladies were modestly dressed, Anna in black, Bette in gray. They were cordial but cool at first. Leading players in movies are usually cautious and diffident when meeting. They rarely have close friends who are fellow stars. But the vibes were good between Anna and Bette.

They soon warmed to each other. I translated:

BETTE

Anna, you are the greatest actress.

ANNA

No, Bette, you are the greatest.

BETTE

Anna, do not contradict me, you are the greatest.

ANNA

I do not contradict you, I say you are the greatest.

BETTE

All right, I say we are both great.

Anna laughs her deep-throated, vibrant laugh.

BETTE

You know, we must make a film together.

ANNA

Yes, we must. There are only two like us.

BETTE

Before time interferes.

It's a rare event when two actresses of such fame and talent freely and feelingly enjoy each other. When the evening was over, they embraced warmly and I drove Bette back to her hotel.

Anna asked me to come up with an idea for a movie she and Bette could do together. After being with the two ladies at their one and only meeting, I realized that they didn't need newly created characters. Nothing would be more interesting than playing themselves.

I wrote a short treatment: Anna and Bette are making a movie (within a movie), embodying the proposition that has in real life happened with actresses in the past: They both fall in love with the young director, and conflict ensues. Surprise—Anna hated the thought of playing herself, and so was cool to that idea.

Ella Fitzgerald was in Rome to perform for one day. I asked Anna if she would like to attend the concert and she readily agreed. After the performance, Anna said, "Let's go backstage to see the great Ella Fitzgerald."

Seeing them together, I knew I was right about Anna playing herself. Ella knew who Magnani was, and responded to her with honest respect. "Ella Fitzgerald knows Anna Magnani for a great woman and actress and she is pleased to see her," Ella said.

"And Anna Magnani says she is happy to be in the presence of Signora Fitzgerald and tell her how much she loved her performance." They spoke to each other in the third person! And it sounded perfectly natural.

1963 Paris—Venice—Belgrade

Marco Polo *in Yugoslavia with Orson Welles and Anthony Quinn.*

*A*nd *God Created Women,* the French film announced. But who created Raoul Levy, the wily French producer of the film? With an apology to God, Bridget Bardot, the woman in the film, through the mysterious ways of natural forces, created Raoul Levy.

Raoul Levy was as quick and sharp as a whiplash and should have become a rich, famous film producer. But Raoul, it turned out, had a built-in grenade on the verge of being detonated to self-destruct.

He had a deep memory bank. He knew the details of every film being produced in France. When I first arrived in Paris on Sidney Lumet's film, *View From the Bridge,* I met Raoul. And when I went to work on *The Longest Day,* he kept in touch. Not because I was so scintillating, but because I might fit into a future plan.

A year later he contacted me. He was about to start a film about Marco Polo and needed me as the dialogue director. Alain Delon, the French movie star, had agreed to play Marco Polo.

My wife, Joan, was with me. We started shooting in Venice and Alain Delon, thinking himself God's gift to women, made his move. But Joan was, at that time, pregnant and delighted to be my wife. And what Alain could not understand is that, as Joan was a one-man woman, he never had a chance.

After the second week, the production shut down. Raoul's financial dealings were serpentine at best, but in this film they were hidden in a subterranean maze. He had tried the Italian sleight of hand: Complete at least one week's shooting while trying to convince the banks to invest in an ongoing production. Bills and salaries go unpaid. Promise the crew and cast the money is on its way, that a second week's production will bring the financing. When the second week's shooting passed and still no cash was seen, Raoul attempted to cajole a third week. But the French aren't easily fooled. They had learned the Italian lesson and decided to accept the loss and decamp.

Back to Paris we went. About ten days went by and I got a call from Raoul to come to his office. I was surprised that he still had an office. He said he was putting the film together again with Yugoslavian financing and wanted me to go to Belgrade with him and a new French director, Denys de la Patelliere. (Yugoslav financing? Now there's an oxymoron!) So, off we went to Belgrade on a prepaid flight with a Yugoslav airline.

We met with the government men who ran their nascent cinema industry. Raoul introduced me as a writer and expert acting coach, telling them the movie would be made in English, as they had requested. Raoul's best argument was what the Yugoslavs wanted to hear: Their small investment would bring an avalanche of dollars to cover the total production cost and enough profit to raise the standard of living for all Yugoslavs.

After a dramatic pause, Raoul pointed at Denys and said, "This man, this fine director, will bring that avalanche of dollars to your country. He has brilliant ideas about how to turn the screenplay into an Academy Award winner that will guarantee commercial success. Denys, tell them, tell them in your inimitable way what you have in mind."

This came as a frightening surprise to Denys, a pleasant, workmanlike director. Raoul, of course, hadn't done Denys the courtesy of telling him he was going to be called on to save the project. Denys hadn't even read the script. I swear, the shape of the man's eyes changed two times, wondering how the hell he was going to handle this assignment. First his eyes became as round as large marbles, then they became slits as his brain went into overdrive. He began, slowly at first, then faster and finally in rapid-fire French. As the interpreter fell far behind, the Yugoslavs, confused, looked from Denys, to Raoul, to the interpreter, to me. He was talking "creative rubbish" but fast enough to confuse the gentlemen at the table.

Denys finally concluded, flushed but happy with himself. Raoul wound up the matter. "My friends, can you believe what this good man did? He has laid the blueprint for a great motion picture. Now that is cinema! Monsieur de La Patelliere is a genius. I have always been a great admirer of his!"

He applauded Denys, joined by the three Yugoslavs. Even I applauded. The bullshit in that room was knee deep, and no one seemed to smell it.

Raoul told the Yugoslavs he had important actors for the filming of *Marco Polo*, including Orson Welles, Anthony Quinn, and Omar Sharif. Horst Buchholtz, a young German actor with some name recognition in Europe, would be Marco Polo. He did not have the allure or magnetism of Alain Delon, but he came a hell of a lot cheaper. In order to get Tony Quinn, Raoul had to accept Tony's demands. Tony is one actor who knows when he has a producer by the short curlies. He demanded and got his own man to write his scenes, an extra expense hard to cover, and he demanded a substantial amount of his payment up front.

European producers were hardy souls, always on the prowl, ready to romance, con, beg, lie, or do whatever it took to get a movie rolling. They were the unsung heroes of post-war European cinema.

Raoul was a remarkable salesman. He had charm, spoke virtually every European language, was quick to grasp the situation and turn it to his benefit, and was shrewd and intelligent. I admired his skill in Belgrade in bringing *Marco Polo* back to life. The Yugos never had a chance. Financing was difficult to get. There were producers I knew who started films on promises and no money, hoping and praying that they could convince someone, anyone, to come up with the cash.

A month later, we were to start shooting in Belgrade (the Venice sequence was cut out of the script to save money). The day I arrived at the hotel was November 23, 1963. The desk clerk couldn't wait to tell me the rotten news: "Your president was shot in Dallas." I didn't believe him and called the American Embassy. The dreaded truth hit hard and I had a sense of deep foreboding. That day was the birth of doom for our country.

Working on *Marco Polo* was just another job until Orson Welles arrived for a week's work. He had a short but concentrated part. He was a presence. Impressive. A big man, well over six feet, and weighty in body and mind. Years earlier, when Orson was in his twenties and trim, he was considered one of the best-looking men on anyone's ten best list.

He brought several makeup boxes with him. In one of the compartments there were countless noses made of undertaker's wax, of all shapes and characteristics. I later learned that he wasn't too fond of his small nose and enlarged it whenever he worked as an actor. To wit; *Touch of Evil,* one of his best films, he created a nose that immediately signaled, upon meeting Sheriff Welles, that he was scary and up to no good.

That nose. It was a beaut. If one can say a nose has a built-in sneer, that nose had it and only Orson could have sculpted it. I saw a sketchbook of his with designs for costumes for a Shakespeare play. They not only were accurate to the period, but were rendered by an artist.

Orson and I had never met before this film and I had no intention of imposing myself on him, so we had no conversation for the first couple of days. On the third day, after the director shouted, "Cut! Print!" Orson didn't seem pleased with the last take.

He caught my eye and beckoned me to him. "You have something to tell me? " he asked.

I stared at him for a moment, wondering if I should tell the great man what I thought. Finally, I spoke. "Your first take was the one. You lost energy and concentration in the last one."

His voice boomed. "I want another take, don't print that!"

"But Orson, it was very good," Denys sang out in a high-pitched French accent.

"Let's have another take, shall we?" Orson's tone allowed for no further discussion.

He got his take and gave me a slight nod. Later that day he approached me and said, "You're worth your weight in gold. I'd like to have you with me on my next film." I was taken by surprise and didn't know what the hell to say, so I smiled. I did what I learned to do when I started in the world of show biz: in one ear, out of the other, to coin a cliché.

A friend of mine, Noel Howard, was hired as a second unit director. He was half French, half American, a talented painter. He and I hung out with Orson after the day's work. We felt honored to spend time with him. But I couldn't keep up with them, since I had to be on the set early. I'd leave at about two in the morning and try to get Noel to split too, since he had to get up even earlier than me to travel to a location out of Belgrade. He had one reply, "Leave the company of Orson Welles? You must be crazy." He lived to drink and had a deep capacity, as did Orson. But I didn't.

Orson enjoyed Raoul's stories and the way he operated. During the war, Raoul told us, he was a tailgunner in a B-17 Flying Fortress. What saved him from serious injury or the final wound was the way he used to pad the B-17's tail with a mattress. He was a skinny kid and was able to slip into the narrow space. True or not, Raoul spun that story for every humorous nuance.

Omar Sharif was a hot actor at the time. Raoul wanted him in the film, even in a cameo part. But when Omar read his scene, he told Raoul to forget it. It stunk. So Raoul turned to me. He wasn't about to hire a writer, even a cheap one. He asked me to rewrite the scene, in which an Arab sheik tried to convince another Arab sheik to join him in battle. I wrote a speech I knew Omar couldn't resist. I dreamed up the corniest images I could think of: "You, oh great sheik, have the grandeur of an eagle gliding along the horizon, the swiftness of a leopard, hungry for a gazelle, the wisdom of an owl."

Omar bought it, thinking it would be amusing. He speaks perfect English, so he must have known how corny it was, but I supposed he liked its flair.

He later came through for me when I was refused a visa to enter Egypt, where we had two weeks of filming *Marco Polo*. Omar, before leaving for Cairo, said to me: "You get on the plane without a visa. I assure you, you will have no problem." I'm not a great fan of flying and told him I didn't want to fly to Cairo and be turned back to Belgrade just for the fun of it. He replied, "I am the king of Egypt, I can do anything I want!"

He was right. Two men in dark suits came aboard when we landed, and politely invited me to disembark. Nasser was then president, a tough anti-Israel Arab and somehow a Jew slipped into Cairo. However, I learned that a movie producer, even Raoul Levy, a Jew, could go anywhere, including a country at war with Israel.

I was in Cairo. I had worked in many European countries, lived in London, Paris, Rome, Madrid, and worked on a movie in Thailand for a couple of months, but Cairo had a smell, a nerve, an aura. I knew about the extraordinary history of the country and I marveled at the exquisite artistry of ancient Egyptian artifacts exhibited in the Cairo Museum of Antiquity.

We were put up at the Mena House Hotel, at the foot of the Pyramid of Cheops. It first opened for guests in 1869. The rooms were large and airy, the corridors were wide, and the wood floors squeaked. It put modern hotels to shame. Winston Churchill was an expert on cigars, brandy, and, what is little known, hotels. When in Cairo, Churchill's choice was the Mena House.

There was a sizeable terrace in front of the hotel where people gathered for Turkish coffee, aperitifs, or just to gossip. After the day's shooting, I would sit there for half an hour, sipping the sweet, thick coffee and staring at the pyramid or people watching.

I was aware of a man in a dark suit, white shirt, and tie sitting at the nearby table. I had seen him on previous evenings, alone, watching me. I was sure he was one of the men who had met me when I arrived at the Cairo airport. One evening I went to his table and asked, "Are you following me?"

"Yes," he answered, and invited me to join him.

He was polite and never lost his small smile as he explained that he worked for the government and was assigned to report on my activities. He hoped I understood he was merely doing his job. For the remainder of my stay, his smiling presence was always nearby.

Raoul Levy knew "Le Tout Paris," the highest social strata of Paris. Rubirosa, one of his socialite friends, visited with his lady, a former model. He was a well-known playboy who had married the woman reputed to be the richest woman in the world—Doris Duke (tobacco money). Although he was a sometimes diplomat from the Dominican Republic, his claim to fame was the magnitude of his schlong and his ability to put it in play.

We were shooting in a wide, deep sand pit. Rubi, as his friends called him, was standing on the edge of the pit with his lady friend, about eight feet above us. The local crew slowly stopped work to stare up at them. I glanced at the lady and forsooth, it was a vision: The lady's white, skintight pants sculpted the contours of her erogenous zones to exciting perfection. It was uplifting, to say the least.

Some years later they were both killed in an automobile accident in the Bois de Boulogne in Paris. Rubi was driving and evidently plowed into a tree in the early morning hours after a night out on the town.

Marco Polo didn't fare well. It disappeared. The script and its execution were indifferent. It had attractive locations, lovely costumes, Orson Welles, and Anthony Quinn, yet it had very little to intrigue the audience.

Omar Sharif and I became fairly good friends, and later worked on a movie, *The Appointment*, in 1968, in Rome. It costarred Anouk Aimee and was directed by Sidney Lumet. That one died too. I don't believe it ever had a general release. Omar went to Cannes during the Film Festival when the producers exhibited the film in the cinema out of competition. He showed poor judgment by attending the showing. The film was booed. When the lights came up the audience, seeing Omar, whistled to show their displeasure.

Omar and I would play gin rummy while waiting for the next set-up. He's a superb bridge player, loves to gamble, and thinks he plays a great game of gin. I can't tell, I'm a lousy gin player. While playing with Omar, I had a run of spectacular luck that I hated to see wasted on gin rummy. We played for small stakes and I won about a dozen games in a row. Omar's pride as a card-player took a nosedive. He became grumpy and even a bit nasty. He wouldn't pay up. As I recall he only owed me about twenty-five bucks. He was a generous man and the only thought I had was that by not shelling out, he could cancel the stupid loss from his mental file. When I told him I would tell everyone that he refused to pay up, he tried to make me promise I wouldn't stoop so low. Boy, did I stoop so low.

Once, when Omar and I were having a drink in my apartment in Rome, the thought hit me that Omar was right for an actor's dream part: Che Guevara. I told him that Franceso Rosi, a well-known, serious movie director and a man I had worked with, was planning a film about Che Guevara to be shot in Cuba, I thought Omar ought to meet Rosi, who lived across the street from me. I called Rosi and he invited us to come right up.

Omar was full of surprises; he showed little enthusiasm. He reluctantly followed me to Rosi's apartment. They talked for a while and Rosi agreed that Omar was indeed right for the part. Back at my place, Omar confessed to me that he would never play Che because he didn't believe in his revolutionary zeal and simply didn't like the man.

Now get this: 1969, I was working on *Justine* at Twentieth Century Fox Studios in Hollywood. On my first day, I entered the studio commissary for lunch. Who do I see sitting alone? Omar Sharif. He greeted me warmly and invited me to join him. I asked what he was working on and he said (guess what), "I'm playing Che Guevara."

After a mildly surprised moment (he was wearing a military uniform) I said, "You told me you'd never play Che. You disliked him, how come?"

He didn't answer immediately. He looked puzzled. I felt he had forgotten the meeting with Rosi. Finally, he said, "Oh, but this is Twentieth Century Fox, not a left-wing Italian director shooting in Cuba. I never would have worked in America again. With Fox, I'm safe."

1964 Rome—Spain

In Spain with Orson Welles on Chimes at Midnight.
Jeanne Moreau, John Gielgud.

Get your ass out of bed, run out and get the *Daily American*," a friend shouted into the phone. The *Daily American* was the local Rome newspaper in English. Orson Welles had called the paper from Madrid and given them a short interview, including a request for Mickey Knox to call Welles.

So I called the master. He greeted me warmly in that incredible voice and said he was pleased that I was still reading English newspapers. He told me he wanted me on his next film project in Madrid. I was to start immediately if I was free. Man, that was the frustrating part of film work. You can go for months sitting on your ass, then you get two terrific offers at the same time. I told Orson I had already agreed to work on a film for Charley Feldman. Orson asked if I could get out of it and I told him I'd see and let him know.

A few weeks earlier I had indeed agreed to work on a film called, *What's New Pussycat*, produced by Charles Feldman, a smart, likeable former agent. If one remembers the film, it was loaded with gorgeous women and it also was to be Woody Allen's first film as an actor. He came to Rome and we walked around the heart of the city, talking acting. He was timid and listened closely. I liked him immediately.

Feldman had changed plans. Instead of shooting the film in Rome it was to be Paris. I love Paris enduringly, however—Orson Welles or Paris? No contest.

I met Charley Feldman in Hollywood a couple of times when I made all those films the first five years I was there. He was then an agent and I found that agents, producers, and directors knew me just as they got to know all the new working actors. They wanted to know what fresh face might move ahead of the crowd.

I told Feldman about the Welles offer. He was understanding, as I knew he would be. He said he didn't want to lose me. The film needed an experienced dialogue director, given all the different nationalities in the movie, but the chance of working with Orson was not one to be missed. I thanked him, went home, called Orson, and told him I was free.

Orson had a deal with the Spanish producers to make two films: *Treasure Island* and *Chimes At Midnight*. The latter was to be a movie about Prince Hal, Falstaff, and their friends, taken from Shakespeare's *Henry IV*, part I and II.

The Spanish producers, not having much faith in the commercial possibilities of that one, insisted Welles make *Treasure Island*, to cover their investment. The clincher? Welles agreed to film the pirate picture *first* with himself as Long John Silver. In Spain, Orson was more than just another celebrity; he was a world-famous icon who chose to live and work in their country. He was also a serious bullfight aficionado. But they knew his reputation: There were films he had started but never completed, the most noted being, *Don Quixote*, after having shot eighty percent of the movie.

It wasn't because of a lack of money. Darryl Zannuck told me he had offered Orson all the financing he needed, if only he would complete the film. Orson refused. I once asked him why he didn't want to complete it and he said writers sometimes don't finish a book when it's not working out, and he felt he had the same right.

So, Orson agreed to film *Treasure Island* first. He was going to use most of the same cast of English actors for the two films to save money.

My first assignment was in Rome. I was to immediately start looking for a boy who could play Jim Hawkins, the lead in *Treasure Island*.

There are a number of English and American private schools in Rome, attended mostly by the children of diplomats, businessmen, and foreigners. I visited all of them and interviewed hundreds of boys. I took photos of the kids who might be right and sent them to Orson with my comments.

A week after starting to film *Treasure Island*, Orson suspended filming, claiming that the pirate galleon needed a lot more work before he could film it. To save time, he'd start *Chimes* while work was being done on the galleon, then return in a couple of weeks to complete *Treasure*. He never did.

I was hired to work on *Chimes at Midnight*, as his personal assistant and to cast and coach the Spanish actors. (By contract, Orson had to use a certain number of local actors.) I was summoned to Madrid. Valentina, my daughter, was four months old at the time and I wasn't about to leave her or my wife in Rome. Orson had the production rent an apartment for me in a residence hotel. It worked out fine. The place attracted mostly Americans, and Joan soon had a gaggle of girlfriends.

The first morning I started work, I fucked up. It cost me. Orson was a tough taskmaster. One misstep and the respect barometer dropped a degree. Orson wanted me at his house at ten. I was twenty minutes late. In that commanding voice of his, directed right at my eyes, Orson let me know he was pissed off. I had no excuse and said it wouldn't happen again. He assured me of that. He had been Mr. Nice Guy in Belgrade when he told me I was worth my weight in gold, and then again on the phone when he wanted me with him in Madrid, but at that moment I felt I was worth my weight in tin.

Among the Spanish actors, Fernando Rey was the most accomplished and talented. His English was excellent. He had made several films for Luis Buñel, Spain's most famous and talented director. During the Spanish Civil War, Ray was a loyalist opposed to

Generalissimo Franco, the leader of the Fascist side, and so was on Franco's shit list. Ray was barred from working in Spain or leaving the country. But Orson, so admired and loved by the Spanish people, that only he could dictate to the dictator. "Either Fernando Rey acts in my film or I make it in France," he said. Franco got the message. Rey was in.

One of the minor parts I cast was a walleyed actor named Israel. I told Orson about him and showed him a photo. Orson agreed he was a good type. I hired him, but the production refused to sign him. It didn't take long to figure that one out. He was Jewish; they had no other reason not to hire him.

I met with Orson and told him the production didn't want Israel. "What!" he bellowed. He got the production manager on the phone and read him the riot act. Israel was in the movie.

Orson could always command a first-rate cast and this was no exception. He had the best English Shakespearean actors, including John Gielgud. He also got Jeanne Moreau. Although her English was good, she did have an accent. But Orson liked the lady, so she was in the movie. I had worked with her on *The Victors*. She was one of those women who is hard to define. In my short time with her, I found her to be seductive, singularly beautiful, and effortlessly alluring: a mythic temptress.

At lunch one day, I asked Orson if he had read *Henderson the Rain King*, by Saul Bellow. He hadn't, and I suggested he read it. He was the perfect choice for the part of Henderson. A couple of weeks later, he found the book and read it. He was impressed, and thought *Henderson* could make an interesting film; the part appealed to him. He seriously thought of trying to get the project going, but nothing ever came of it. But he did admire the book.

I must have worked with a hundred directors during my career in the theater and movies over a stretch of more than sixty years. One man stands out: Orson Welles. No one was more inventive, more creative, or paid more attention to the smallest details.

On the day the filming of *Chimes at Midnight* was to start, Orson called it off. He was concerned with the "patina" of the main set's interior of the inn, where Falstaff, Prince Hal, and their chums drank, argued, and proclaimed. It had to be properly aged, not have the look of a movie set (which it was.)

A crew of workers labored for a weekend and aged every inch of the inn until it had the look that Orson wanted. Unlike most construction of movie sets, that inn was constructed of real wood, beams and all.

Orson designed the costumes, armor, and weapons, all true to the period, months before the filming started. His sketches were beautifully executed and if signed could have hung in the Prado.

Fearful of showing my ignorance, before leaving Rome, I researched the period of *Chimes*. I studied the royal lineage of the times. After all, a little knowledge could make me seem knowledgable. But Orson didn't give a damn what I knew about the Plantagenets or Henry Bolingbroke, so I kept my big mouth shut. A good lesson, not to appear knowledgeable unless you got the goods.

We went to the Basque country for location, where we were snowed in for a few days. Orson, the French director of photography, his camera operator, and I, sat down one evening for serious drinking. Orson ordered a bottle of tequila. He filled the shot glasses and down the hatch. I wanted to sip but Orson wouldn't hear of it. Well, the bottle went fast, and so did the second one. I couldn't keep up with Orson. I downed one shot glass to his three. But I couldn't avoid getting drunk and fading away.

Orson and Toshiro Mifune, the wonderful Japanese actor who was Kurasawa's favorite, were the only men I worked with who could kill a bottle of brandy before lunch and show no signs of slurred speech, stumbling, no incoherence, no problem working.

Orson loved to eat and was discerning about the food he ate. He said the best cuisine was Basque. Long before the French discovered food, the Basque people were cooking the finest meals in that part of the world. I was told about a good, small restaurant in a village not far from Pomplona, where we were staying. That's the way it looked on the map, take the short way over the mountain and there it was. I told Orson about it and he immediately ordered two cars and drivers. Since we still couldn't shoot because of the weather, we started out at noon to have lunch. Orson was in the lead car with the director of photography and I was in the second car with the camera operator. Orson disliked crowded traveling.

The day was overcast and cold. I was looking forward to lunch at the best little inn in Spain. We drove up a narrow mountain road that was a continuous series of curves. At one point, we had to slow to a crawl due to a truck ahead of us. Soon it was one o'clock. Finally, the truck had space to pull alongside the road and allow us to pass.

But we kept driving up the mountain. I checked the map and realized we should have taken what appeared to be the much longer route, a national highway that circumvented the mountain. But the village looked so much closer going over the mountain. So much for my ability to read maps.

About one-thirty, Orson's car horn began blaring, echoing across the mountain. His car stopped, the front door opened, and this enormous leg slowly came out, followed by Orson's torso, and he was mad. He shouted at me. "Where the fuck are we going?"

I answered quickly but stupidly. "To lunch." Orson just glared, and glared, and glared, then slowly eased back into the car and started off.

I had made a mistake, but Orson's anger was overblown. Beware, a large man suffering hunger pangs can give you serious indigestion.

Two o'clock and we finally reached the village. Not a sign of man or beast on the one street. We drove slowly, looking for the restaurant. We didn't find it. I felt sick; I lost my hunger. Where the fuck was the restaurant? I kept asking myself. This was the right village. There was a welcome sign when we approached it. But within moments the village was behind us.

Man, was I in trouble. Where food was concerned, Orson had no humor. (I found out a week later, when I returned to the village with a couple of crew members, why we didn't see the restaurant. It looked like all the other houses in the village. It had a sign, but the sign was on top of the roof, not visible if one was in a car. I cursed that sign and whoever painted it and the person who planted it on top of the roof. The pity is, the meal at that little restaurant was indeed memorable.)

Orson's car sped down the mountain road and we followed. We reached the main highway, where we pulled into a gas station. Orson asked the gas jockey where six hungry men could dine. That was all he could think about, that goddamn lunch.

We were directed to a nearby parador (one of a string of government-run inns across Spain that are generally clean, stylish, and provide acceptable food and at the best, excellent meals.)

We arrived at the parador after three, and were told the dining room was closed. However, on seeing Orson, the manager bowed and said he would summon the chef and open the dining room for us.

We trooped into the empty dining room and were seated at a large round table. We were a glum group, except for Orson; he was grim. I felt sure it was my last meal on the film. I had just never learned to keep my mouth shut. Why? Because I was born and raised in Brooklyn where all my friends and neighbors were Jews and everyone loved to talk—talk back, talk to each other, talk to ourselves, talk together, talk at the dinner table, talk in the classroom. I never got over the habit and it rarely failed to get me into trouble. I feared that after a potluck meal and a joyless ride back, Orson would fire me.

Wrong. The meal was not just a meal; it was a feat. Only the presence of Orson Welles, beloved by all Spaniards, could have inspired the chef to create such a magnificent spread.

Out came huge platters (there were six of us, including the two drivers). Dozens of lush oysters, clams, mussels, strange, delicious seafood I'd never seen before, shrimp, lobsters, all exquisite and fresh. Then came a huge cold roast beef, a couple of roast hams, French fries, potato salad, cole slaw, heaps of fresh vegetables, and finally, several desserts: crème caramel, a large pan of flaming goodies, nuts and fruit, sherbet and ice cream.

One of the perks of being world-famous in a country you love is you get treated like a king. Of course Orson was not just ordinary world-famous, he was, in size, intellect, talent, and magnetism, head and shoulders over anyone else. I hazard a guess that only Picasso would have been greeted in like manner upon returning to Spain.

Orson dived right in; his appetite seemed endless. Under his cape he had a lot of space to fill. He ordered brandy after the meal and I knew things were right with my world when Orson, one of the great storytellers, spun a few tales and had us laughing and applauding. He had eaten well and had an audience; he was happy.

The chef and a couple of his helpers came out to meet Orson. He praised the chef as only he could, making allusions to the seven wonders of the world and other superb achievements. The chef beamed, bowed in respect, clasped Orson's hand in his two hands, and thanked him.

I slipped away to pay the bill, hoping I'd have enough money on me. The two French cameramen soon followed and insisted on chipping in. I was surprised at how small the bill was.

Orson never mentioned the incident, but I'm convinced it became a part of his bag of stories.

When the main photography was completed, the actors returned home. Only Orson, playing Falstaff, was left with the camera crew and me. Although Orson made up including his mortician's wax, bulbous nose, and put his costume on when he was on the call sheet for the day's shooting, he would stage the scene so that he could be filmed at a later date and still seem to be present in the scene with the other actors. He had me keep notes on each scene, noting his exact position as Falstaff so at a later date he could fit into the scene, already filmed with the other actors.

As an actor, I was surprised by his reluctance to perform. He really didn't enjoy acting. He avoided it until he had no choice if he wanted to complete the filming.

The last two weeks were as grim and difficult for me as they were for Orson. He was in a constant state of anxiety and discomfort and had lost his sense of fun. I had to cue him by reading the off-camera lines. It wasn't easy. I had no experience or training in

Shakespeare. I knew my readings annoyed him, as did my Brooklyn-tinged New York accent, but I wasn't about to put on a phony English accent.

Finally, it was all over. Orson was to shut himself into the editing room to put it all together. He had shot the film knowing what the finished movie would look like. He didn't cover the scenes with too many angles, thus saving the producers a lot of pesos in raw stock.

Orson did send me a note of gratitude for my participation in the making of the film. I expect he did the same for the other crew members, something that's rarely done by most directors or producers.

I saw him twice before he died. He had taken over as the host of a TV talk show while the regular host, David Frost, was on vacation. He chose Norman Mailer to be his first guest. After the program was over, I greeted Orson. He seemed genuinely pleased to see me and embraced me warmly, pulling me to his enormous chest.

The last time I had a chance to see him was in Hollywood. I had heard that he took lunch every day at an "in" restaurant at that time, Ma Maison. I was with a friend and we sat on the terrace so I could spot Orson when he arrived.

He soon came down the path to the main entrance with an old friend of his, a man I had known in Italy, Sandro Tucci, a Sicilian prince. I was shocked; Orson seemed wrapped in melancholy. He had lost that special look of his: subtle defiance, audacious spirit.

I delayed, to my deep regret, not jumping up and greeting him right then. But he seemed too remote. After a meal, I thought, his mood would be friendlier. But it was not to be. He must have slipped out the back way after having a very quick lunch.

The experience of working with Orson has left its impression on me, never to fade from my memory. I had often played the silent game of "what if"—what if he had gone into politics? I've rarely seen anyone in politics with Orson's resources—his power to convince, to attract, the power of his intellect, and the force of his personality. The man could have been president.

Orson Welles died in 1985. He was seventy years old.

1965 St. Paul de Vence, France
La Colombe d'Or.

I n 1964 Joan gave birth to a sweet, alert girl, named Valentina after the first woman rocketed into space. She delighted us with her happiness at being alive, and we decided to try our luck a second time. So, the following year, Joan had a round, smooth belly once again (Melissa, a lovely girl, was born September 23rd, 1965).

An idea was born in my head that a pregnant woman would be more apt than not, to send good vibes to the fetus in her womb if she were to visit a peaceful place of beauty. La Colombe d'Or in St. Paul de Vence, an inn in the South of France about half an hour drive into the hills behind Nice. I had been there in the past, and its rare charm and beauty never failed to be enchanting.

St. Paul de Vence is an ancient, changeless village at the top of a hill that overlooks a painter's vision of a dream countryside—deep green vegetation, absorbing the hot undulating rays of the sun. The shaded patches of grass invite a picnic with a nude woman for a summer afternoon of intense but lingering lovemaking.

The village dates back to the glory days of Rome, with its stone houses overhanging narrow stone streets. A short walk outside the village is the renowned La Colombe d'Or. The inn is classic Cote d'Azur architecture, the hospitality is warm, and, needless to say, the food is excellent.

La Colombe d'Or—The Golden Dove—is aptly named. As the sun begins to set, a flock of pure white doves appear, literally out of the blue. They circle the inn, then, as they glide down to skim the valley below, the sun transforms their plumage into shining gold, hence, La Colombe d'Or. No one seems to know why, but the doves arrive every day at the same time to catch the setting sun's rays.

The outdoor tables of the inn are on the saddle of the hill overlooking the valleys on either side of the hill. Indoors, hang painting by Impressionist painters. The painters were lured to the top of the hill for a couple of good reasons: Even without a sou to their names, they were welcomed with open arms by the innkeeper. From the inn's vantage point, the view provided the kind of light worshipped by the Impressionists. Unable to pay for room and board, an artist would leave a painting or two to settle the bill.

Joan explored the wonder of the old town. She bought a lovely birdcage, enameled in white and decorated in Picasso pastels. She had that cage until the day she died more than thirty years later. It never imprisoned a bird.

Sidney Buchman, the executive producer of *Saturday's Hero*, and I had become friends during the shooting of the film, and lady chance pulled a pleasant surprise. There was Sydney and his wife sitting at an outdoor table of the inn about to have lunch. We embraced and he invited us to join them.

He asked about my activities and was pleased that I was working regularly and facing life with a few bucks in my jeans. "If only I had a cushion of about twenty-five grand, man, I'd then feel pretty secure," I lamented. (Not a bad bankroll in 1965.)

Sidney quickly answered, "If I were down to twenty-five thousand dollars I'd have a heart attack!" He laughed, but then he meant it.

1965/90 Rome

An American Mafioso exiled to Italy.

J erry Chiericchio was a Mafioso with one of the New York Mafia families. He had violated a serious Mafia code (he never told me the details) and was marked as a dead man by a rival family. He was told by his capo that a deal had been made: If Jerry left the country for good, he wouldn't be hit. But if he ever showed his face anywhere in the States, it would be good-bye Charley.

Shortly after World War II ended, Jerry came to Rome. He opened a small joint on the Via Veneto that served the best steaks in the city. Food was scarce those days, but leave it to Jerry.

He romanced the army chefs on American military bases in Italy, offering them cash if they would supply him with prime beef. What the hell, the war was over, time to make some extra moolah. And Jerry had a thriving little steak joint.

Jerry moved up in the world. He opened the Luau, off the Veneto. It had a pleasant bar and a spacious dining area. Jerry, always friendly, told me if I ever needed any help, no mater what the reason, to let him know. You wanna break a guy's leg, fifteen hundred bucks, put a guy in the hospital, three thousand, put him under, ten grand. Sonofabitch, he already had his own gang. He was so open and friendly I never thought of him as being all that tough. I was mistaken.

While having a drink with Jerry in his bar, I saw how brutally tough he could be. Three young Embassy marines were at the bar making threatening sounds. The drinks were watered and they weren't going to pay. The bartender turned to Jerry. Jerry told the Marines the drinks were not watered, but he'd buy them a round anyway.

"Fuck you," one of them snarled.

Jerry advised them to get the hell out of his joint. "Make us," the jerk replied, and threw a punch. Jerry hit the Marine so hard he broke the front door. He then took on the other two Marines. I watched in awe as he beat both of them to the punch and they quickly split. Jerry was then about sixty.

He had a running gin game after closing time. And he was good. He made a bundle every week, and the suckers kept coming back.

One night, he sat at a table in quiet conversation with about eight kids, still in their teens or a bit older. When he came over to join me, I asked who they were. "My boys," he said. "They deliver stolen cars to me and I export them. They pay good money in North Africa for the fancy ones."

About a year later, my beautiful fire-engine red Super Mini Cooper I had bought in England was stolen. When my rage subsided, I remembered Jerry. My fucking luck. Jerry was away in Switzerland for about a month. Good-bye to recovering my red Mini.

He finally returned and I complained bitterly, "Where were you when I needed you?"

"What happened, Mick, you got trouble?" he asked.

"They stole my car. I could strangle those bastards."

"Aw, come on, Mick, they gotta make a livin' too."

I stared at him in disbelief.

He had a pained look on his face. He said mournfully, "I could have gotten the car back for you if I was in town, you know that." The pity of it is, I'm sure he would have done just that.

After forty years in Italy, Jerry was a free man. By chance he and I were on the same plane to New York. He didn't have to look over his shoulder any longer, he said, he was allowed to go home. He asked if

I wanted a ride to the city when we landed. A limo would be at his disposal.

Waiting for our luggage, his name crackled out on the loud speakers. He was wanted on the phone. I went to the phone with him. He listened, said, "Yeah," and hung up. He apologized for not being able to take me to Manhattan. "I gotta catch a plane right away to New Orleans; I got a meet with the boys."

Jerry Chiericchio was back in the family business.

1965 Around Europe

Grand Prix. *Shooting Formula One races round Europe, directed by John Frankenheimer. James Garner, Eva Marie Saint, Yves Montand, Toshiro Mifune.*

A race car movie? Should be fun. An old friend, Richard Sylbert, a respected, sought-after production designer in Hollywood, was in Rome and got in touch with me. He wanted to know if I was free to be the dialogue director on *Grand Prix*, a film about Formula One. I was free. He introduced me to the director John Frankenheimer; we talked for a few minutes and I was hired.

The cast included James Garner, Yves Montand, and Eva Marie Saint. An Italian, Antonio Sabato, was cast, as was Françoise Hardy, a young, popular French singer. Neither knew much English and had to be coached. Yves Montand also needed serious coaching.

Then Frankenheimer dropped a depth bomb: Toshiro Mifune, who was the great Akira Kurosawa's favorite actor, had been added to the cast. He knew not one word of English. I groaned. Mifune had long speeches; he alone would be a full-time job.

After working with him for a couple of weeks, I was complaining to his interpreter, a young American of Japanese descent, who replied, "Don't feel bad, his Japanese is pretty awful, too." Swell!

We followed the Formula One season, shooting the races in Italy, France, Belgium, Germany, and England. What I remember most is the excitement in the pit—the shouts of encouragement from the crew, the smell of fuel, the roar of powerful racing cars as they sped around the track.

Mifune and I started work about six-thirty every morning. I had other actors to work with during the day and I wanted to give as much time as possible to Mifune, hence the early start. When I got to his room, he'd have ordered a bottle of brandy, a dandy way to start the morning. A couple of hours later, more than half the bottle would be gone, but I never saw him drunk. His eyes were always focused, his walk steady, and as far as I could tell he didn't slur his words.

He played a wealthy Japanese industrialist who had organized and financed a Formula One team. He had the screen presence to convey a tough industrialist, but could he convince the audience he really knew English or was he parroting it?

Before we started filming, I spoke to Frankenheimer about simplifying Mifune's dialogue. His speeches were long and written in perfect English. Frankenheimer looked at me with a bully's eye and barked: "You do your job, I'll do mine," and strode away.

Mifune had a line in one of his speeches: "We all know the sound of two hands clapping but what is the sound of one hand clapping? Get the problem?"

The day came for the "clapping" scene. The ambiance was a Japanese rock garden. Mifune wore a traditional robe. I took a walk. A couple of minutes later, Frankenheimer's voice rang out loud and clear: "MICKEY . . . MICKEY!"

I slowly walked back to the set as John's voice continued to boom my name. He ran toward me, flapping his arms wildly, "Crapping? Crapping, Mickey? What the hell is that?"

"You want clapping?"

"You're fucking A—I want clapping!"

I took Mifune aside and whispered *clapping,* emphasizing the "L." His eyes lit up. He nodded and tried to pronounce the word, but the L was a serious obstacle. He worked at it several times until I thought he just might work it out.

John called action. When Mifune got to the nonsensical line, he visibly placed his tongue against the back of his upper teeth, but the tip of his tongue curled backward and seemed to get stuck there. In an effort to get the "L" out, his mouth and face contorted into a picture of desperation until he finally snapped out: "Clapping." He then broke into a wide, happy grin that he vigorously displayed to his right and left.

John: "MICKEY?"

"You want crapping or"—I imitated Mifune's contortions—"clapping? You take your pick."

John, for once, could not speak. Frustration nearly choked him. Mifune finally got a fairly decent take, ending his and John's agony.

The production gave a dinner in a large, French country restaurant for cast and crew. The wine and food were plentiful and good. Crew and cast members stood to speak, make fun of each other, tell obscene jokes. There was much laughter and banter.

I, of course, sat with Mifune. He didn't understand the words being spoken but he understood the laughter and the jolly mood. He turned to me, a question in his eyes. I shrugged. He nodded slightly, stood up, walked to the space for dancing in the middle of the room, clapped his hands to get everyone's attention, and bowed deeply.

He then sprung into a samurai fighting stance, grunted a hoarse battle cry, whirled to his left, to his right, leaped ahead, and spun around, slashing the air with an imaginary sword, battling imaginary opponents.

It was a graceful, fierce dance accompanied by fiery-sounding Japanese. No one in the place moved. All were transfixed. The performance must have lasted a full minute. Finally Mifune bowed, ending his contribution to the evening. He got a standing ovation. It was the highlight of my time on the film.

Yves Montand was a much easier actor to coach; he did speak some English. We became companions, dining together, gossiping about the alliances in the film.

Yves spoke rapidly in French and in the little English he knew, which made him difficult to understand. Once I got him to slow down by concentrating on listening to what the other actors were saying in the scene, he did well.

He had made a film with Marilyn Monroe and he told me he had had a serious affair with her. She would show up at his hotel room wrapped in an ample mink coat. Once inside, the mink coat would fall to the floor and there she would stand in all her nude glory. Yves had thought about leaving his wife, Simone Signoret, the talented French actress. "How can I leave a woman like Simone?" he asked, rhetorically.

What could I say? I didn't even know Signoret, but I did mumble, you can't leave her. We did meet several times after we completed the film; she was intelligent, witty, attractive, and treasured her hidden bottle of booze. He didn't leave her; she died some years later, leaving him.

Yves was addicted to cards: gin rummy and poker. He lost his salary on the Monroe film to 20th Century Fox gin sharks. In Paris he was a welcome member of a high-stakes poker game, more often loser than winner.

Actors have a lot of free time between setups or when they're not in the scene being filmed. On our set, Yves organized a modest-stake gin game with James Garner, Garner's stand-in, me, and the production doctor.

The doc was a friend who lived in Rome. He had been a Mafia doctor in Brooklyn. He broke some Mafia rule and found himself on the hit list. The capo of his family worked it out with the capo of the other family; if the doc disappeared, left the country, and never showed himself again he wouldn't be hit. (Like his buddy, Jerry Chiericchio.)

So he came to Rome. When we met, he had such a pronounced Brooklyn accent I didn't believe he was a legitimate doctor, but he was, and a good one, too. He opened a medical office, played a lot of gin, and never had to look over his shoulder.

But Doc was a skilled card shark and in due time he and Yves were playing for high stakes, head to head. Before long, Doc owned a handful of markers that amounted to about ten grand.

Yves was in a controlled, maddened state. He sensed that Doc was cheating, but didn't know how, so he kept playing. Then he figured it out. He brought me into the showdown as his interpreter to make sure Doc got the picture.

Finally Yves noticed the subtle spots on the backs of the cards. Even though a new deck was opened for every gin session, Doc, being an expert, applied the spots without anyone seeing him do it.

The last game was set up. Yves said nothing until the game was over. He picked up the deck, spread the card face down and pointed to the spots. "You have been cheating, Doc. Look at this spot, and this one. You knew every card I held." He must have practiced that line because there was no need for me to translate.

Doc was a card shark, but he had class. "You found me out, Yves. How about I do this?" and he tore up the markers. Yves was speechless, obviating any translation. He shook hands with Doc and that was the end of it.

Jim Garner was generally genial, unassuming, and a special kind of actor who, no matter what the role, always appeared at ease, believable. That takes talent, and Garner is abundantly graced in that department.

Yves and I remained friends long after the film was completed. Toshiro returned to Japan knowing one word of English—"good-bye." He sent me elegant cards every New Year.

By the time the filming was ended, John Frankenheimer and I were not great friends. A good director, he worked hard and was in no mood to make friends, but he, at times, showed his bully side; not pretty. But the film was successful.

I was in Paris working on a film for Sidney Pollack about ten years after *Grand Prix* when I got a phone call from John. I didn't recognize his voice, which annoyed him. "Who is it? Jesus, Mickey, it's John."

"John who?" I meant it.

"John who? Frankenheimer, for Chrissakes," he said angrily, clearing that up.

He quickly changed his tune; now he was friendly. "I got a problem. I'm here dubbing with Marte Keller; she was in my last film. You worked with her, so you know the problem. Can you give me an hour or so in the dubbing room with her?"

I liked Marte and agreed to help out. John was pleasant and appreciated my effort.

The next time I saw John was in Rome more than a dozen years later. He called and we went through the same routine: John who? He was staying in a hotel around the corner from where I lived. He asked if I could join him, as he wanted to talk to me.

He was going to film *Across the River and Into the Trees*, adapted from the Hemingway book. He introduced me to Gene Hackman, who was to play the main character. John wanted me as dialogue director. But there was a conflict of dates; I had an Italian movie lined up during the same time he planned on shooting his film.

"Get out of it, I need you, this is a go." A "go" usually means the film is financed and thus will be made.

Hackman joined in.

"John told me about you. I believe we could use you on this one. It should be an interesting job."

"But John, I agreed to work on another film," I repeated. And John repeated: "Get out of it, it's a go." So the next day I found someone to replace me in the Italian film, called John and told him I was clear to do his movie. "Okay, I'll get in touch with you soon."

"Soon" was many years ago. He still hasn't called me. His film was not a go, it was a go fuck yourself.

1967 Rome

The Tenth Victim, with Marcello Mastroianni.

T he Italian icon: Marcello Mastroianni! We had met several times socially before I worked with him in *The Tenth Victim*, a futuristic film about a national game of killing that assigned victims for prizes. It was directed by Elio Petri, who was highly respected in the industry. I acted in it, playing a TV producer-director. Not a bad part. I also coached the other actors, including Ursula Andress.

Marcello was a handsome charmer, accessible, modest, and a hell of an actor. Italians adored him, proud of his international fame, proud of his good looks, his talent, and most of all, proud of his reputation as a gracious cocksman.

After the release of *La Dolce Vita*, American film moguls beckoned. I had lunch with Darryl Zanuck in Rome. He asked if I knew Mastroianni. I told him I did. "Tell him I'll pay him a million dollars if he'll act in a film for me, but he has to learn English."

"That's not too good at present," I reluctantly told him. (A million bucks was a large payday then.)

When I met with Marcello, I told him of Zanuck's offer. "In Italy I am a big fish, in America I will be a little fish, you understand?" I thought he was probably right, but I suggested there was the possibility he might become a big fish in the American pond.

He made one of those expressive Italian gestures, meaning: it's doubtful, and anyway, who cares? He then asked, "Here I have Fellini, who will I have in America?" Good question. I couldn't and didn't answer.

When we started filming *The Tenth Victim*, Marcello asked me to give him a short English lesson every morning. I agreed. I imagined he wanted to test the water. The first morning we worked, he quit after ten minutes; "I'm tired, tomorrow, yes?" So I said yes. That was the first and last formal English lesson Marcello endured. He did tell me that he was just too lazy to continue to "break my brain butchering the beautiful English language."

However, he wanted to say something in English in the film, so we worked on a short phrase in which he was selling a product on television. We worked on it every day for a week. The time came and he seemed nervous; he was. This is what he said on camera: "Da de da do deedle deedle do . . . " and continued for a few more seconds. I asked him what the hell happened and he said, "I forgot the English, but what I said is easy to dub."

After filming was completed, all films in Italy were dubbed into Italian, then if required for exportation, dubbed into English. (I was a charter member of A.R.A., the American dubbers cooperative.) All the dialogue was dubbed (revoiced) by an expert group of Italian dubbers and not necessarily by the actor appearing on the screen. Marcello always dubbed himself in Italian, but not in English. In Marcello's case, it didn't matter what he said when filming as long as he got the right length so it would synchronize with the proper dialogue to be dubbed.

He was one of those rare actors who was admired and genuinely liked by women and men. Especially women. He was admittedly lazy, so women usually made the first moves. He had a serious affair with Catherine Deneuve and they had a daughter together. He always said he would never divorce his wife and I don't think he ever did. I believe that Deneuve wanted more than just an affair. When that didn't happen, they finally broke it off.

I also worked with Ursula on her English dialogue. I had met her for the first time years earlier. When I was under contract at Paramount Studios, there was a group of young actors called The Golden Circle. A laughable name for mostly inexperienced actors. Ursula was part of the group and did qualify as golden; she was gorgeous with her long golden hair.

I was asked, as an actor who had been on the stage, to speak to the Circle about acting. I did, and couldn't take my eyes off Ursula. After the session I invited her for coffee. "Oh, I'm with Marlon Brando. He's my boyfriend." I bowed to Marlon and retreated.

I went to her Rome apartment one day to work with her. The maid said she was sunning on the roof. Boy, was she sunning. Totally nude. When she saw me she nonchalantly stood up and slowly put a robe on. She had a perfect body. And she knew it. I figured that's why she languidly covered herself, giving me enough time to appreciate her magnificence.

It was inevitable; Ursula and Marcello quickly became lovers. However, Jean-Paul Belmondo—a major French movie star—was Ursula's beau at the time. But we were in Rome and he was in Paris. A bird like Ursula cannot be left out of the coop too long. Belmondo must have known of Marcello's irresistible charm. Or perhaps Ursula, while on the phone with Belmondo, playfully described Marcello as sweet and sexy? Belmondo cannonballed to the airport. As told to me by Ursula, I reconstruct the scene after Belmondo's arrival: Ursula pretended to be surprised when he showed up. He sniffed around the apartment and picked up a large man's umbrella. He judged its weight and said, "This belongs to Marcello, n'est-ce pas?"

"Oh," she answered, "he visits now and then."

"He visits your bed?" he asked innocently.

"Sometimes when I'm in bed he sits next to me and we talk."

Belmondo responded with juicy Parisian slang as he lifted her up and carried her to bed, pretending to be angry. However, as has been noted, the French are rarely indignant over a sexual detour.

1967 Rome

Robert Katz writes a grim story of Nazi horror in his book,
Death in Rome. *Pope Pius XII's niece takes Katz to court.*

One day, somewhere during 1967, I met Bob Katz. My doorbell rang and I buzzed the front door open. A stranger stood in the doorway, about fifty feet down the corridor. "Mickey Knox?"

"Yeah, what can I do for you?"

"I'm looking for Pete Hamill, I was told I might find him here."

"He ain't in Rome any longer," I said, "but come on in and have a drink."

He said okay and slowly walked the length of the corridor and cautiously entered my apartment. I handed him a scotch on the rocks, the first of thousands of drinks we would have together through the years. He and his wife, Beverly, have been close friends of mine since that day.

Bob is an historian, novelist, investigative author, and screenwriter. He and Beverly come from Brooklyn, my teenage playground. But Bob is a cool character, unlike the raucous Brooklyn kids I knew. In conversations he tends to listen, then when he hears an outrageous assumption or statement, he loses his cool and loudly objects to the bullshit.

Beverly is a classic *balabusta*, a talented housewife who keeps a clean, efficient home and is a great cook. She has opinions, judgments and ideas, none of them kept secret, which makes her good, lively company. I should have been as lucky as Bob to have had a wife who is as loyal and protective as she is.

In 1970 they had the foresight and smarts to buy a three hundred-year-old farmhouse in Tuscany for a song, now worth the whole opera. They produced olive oil in an area deemed to be the best quality oil anywhere and their grapes produce good earthly table wine. On summer evenings, Beverly creates wonderful-tasting meals over an outdoor wood-burning grill. And her olive oil-coated pasta begins a meal only found chez Katz.

Through the years, they have worked to make it a most *gemutlich* home and a joy to the friends who are lucky to be invited to their "Paradise Found."

I love that place almost as much as I loved my Roman apartment. The stone farmhouse sits high on a hill above the village, with a spectacular view of the green fields that stretch way to the distant range of mountains.

At times I would drive the two hours from Rome just to stand on a rise near the house to feel the giddy thrill of watching a slowly moving sunset as the gold changed to glowing orange and the mountains assumed pastel shades.

Bob and I would witness the sunset, a scotch on the rocks in our hands, neither of us speaking. Beverly would pause in her dinner preparations to join us and say something like, "Not bad, huh?"

Among the historical books Bob wrote, there are two about the Nazi occupation of Rome during World War II. One titled *Black Sabbath*, relates the events of the roundup of Jews by the Nazis, the other, *Death in Rome*, describes the resulting horror of what became known as the "Via Rasella attack."

On the 23rd of March, 1944, at 3:45 in the afternoon, a bomb exploded as a column of 156 Nazi SS troops marched along Via Rasella in Rome. Thirty-two of them were killed outright.

A cell of sixteen partisan fighters, members of the Italian Resistance fighting the Nazi occupation of Rome, planned and carried out the attack. They were, in the main, university students, and included a professor, a couple of workers, and a few young women. They were all Communists, as were most of the partisans fighting the Germans in Italy.

The reaction was swift: Hitler ordered that ten men be taken and executed for each German soldier killed unless the partisans who planted the bomb turned themselves in to the German high command within twenty-four hours. The partisan fighters rejected Hitler's order, declaring that they were at war with the German army of occupation and decried the execution of noncombatants. Furthermore, they claimed the Germans would execute the hostages in any case.

Men were rounded up at random, among them teachers, workers, Italian army officers, students and a priest. When the 33rd SS soldier died, they rounded up ten more victims, all Jews. Out of rage, five others were also picked up.

The following day they were taken to the Fosse Ardeatine, a series of catacombs, sacred to Christians, on the outskirts of Rome. In all, 335 men were to be executed inside the galleries.

Lt. Colonel Kappler was in charge of the executions. He and several of his fellow officers quickly planned the operation: Sixty-seven SS troops were used to stand behind the victims as they were brought to the caves in groups of five and made to kneel, facing the wall. They were then each shot at very close range in the back of the head.

The execution of 335 men, including 75 Jews, began at 3:30 in the afternoon of March 24, 1944 and continued into the night until all 355 men were had a hole blasted through their heads. A 9mm German army pistol was the operational weapon.

All entrances to the catacombs were blown up and blocked. But daylight was destined to illuminate those dark caves of death.

American troops liberated Rome June 4, 1944. A few days later a commission of Italian and American officials was given the task of opening the caves and exhuming the bodies for identification.

A somber monument was constructed above the catacombs. 335

coffins, each containing a victim, lies on a marble platform about three feet above the ground. The coffins all display the name, age, and photo of the victim. High above them, a roof shelters the coffins, although all sides of the monument are open to the day and night.

Robert Katz's book *Death in Rome* was published in the States in January 1967. The Vatican claimed Pope Pius XII was unaware of Hitler's orders. Bob, not having documentary proof at the time he wrote the book, could not and did not clearly state that the Pope knew about Hitler's orders but did nothing to prevent the executions.

That was important because Pius XII had considerable clout with the German high command and thus an urgent message to Berlin opposing the executions would have had real weight. The Pope had always been a Germanophile, having spent years studying in Germany. Although he might have disapproved of Hitler, he believed that Hitler's armed forces were a powerful bulwark against despised communism and the godless Soviet Union.

Carlo Ponti, the Italian film producer, bought the film rights to *Death in Rome* and Bob wrote the screenplay. The film starred Marcello Mastroianni and Richard Burton. It set in motion years of litigation.

The film was called *Massacre in Rome* and was released in 1973. It didn't take long for Countess Elena Pacelli, the niece of Pope Pius XII, to file charges against Carlo Ponti, director George Cosmatos, and Robert Katz for defaming the memory of the Pope.

Ponti, the old fox, smelled trouble and split for France where he became a citizen and out of reach of the Italian judicial system. Cosmatos turned tail and ran, leaving Bob to face the music.

The first trial began in 1974. Although the Vatican did not officially bring charges against Bob, they clearly backed Countess Elena Pacelli. I don't know much about judicial matters, but I remember telling Bob the sun would shine in hell the day he could prevail against the Vatican.

The countess lost the first trial, won the appeal, then after a mistrial, won the next two appeals.

The trials lasted ten years. However, in 1980 the Vatican released a huge volume of past official documents. Bob thought he had found the smoking gun—a memo from the Pope's personal secretary alerting the Pope to the following day's executions. Like every document in Italy, it was stamped with the date and time. It was delivered to the Pope on the eve of the executions.

The Pope had known about the reprisal, but made no attempt to forestall it. The judge was blind to the smoking gun and ruled against Bob.

Thirty-six *carabiniere* (national police) escorted Bob to the court for sentencing after he lost his last appeal. He was given a suspended fourteen-month sentence plus court costs, a bit more than pocket change.

But the last note was yet to be heard: in 1984 Bob had one more appeal—the Italian Supreme Court. The judges, wearing their fairness robes and after seeing all the testimony, vacated the previous decision and dismissed the case.

Bob became a celebrity among Rome's intellectuals and the sympathetic political community. An American who took on the royalty of the Roman Catholic Church, including the Pope? What chutzpah!

1967 Monte Carlo

I act with Vittorio De Sica in The Biggest Bundle of them All.

Monte Carlo, here I come! Wait a minute—I had one small problem—I was working on *The Tenth Victim* in Rome. However, the Monte Carlo film, *The Biggest Bundle of Them All* was one job I did not want to miss; one long scene playing opposite the fabulous, charismatic actor-director Vittorio De Sica. The role they wanted me for was that of a discharged G.I. living in Italy, selling used World War II tanks.

In the film, De Sica was part of a gang that was planning to rob a train. But they needed a tank to stop the train and De Sica was given the task of finding one. Also in the film were Edward G. Robinson, Robert Wagner, and Raquel Welch.

I cornered Elio Petri, the director of *The Tenth Victim*, and prevailed upon him to let me go for one day to act in a scene with De Sica. It didn't present a problem. DeSica was a legend in Italy and Elio was happy to give me the day off.

In the thirties, De Sica, a tall, handsome man, was one of the leading actors in Italy, playing both romantic and comedic leads. When he turned to directing, he made a number of the most memorable films after the war. In the late forties and early fifties, he made such classics as *The Bicycle Thief; Miracle in Milan,* and *Umberto D,* thus creating, with Roberto Rossellini, The Italian School of Neo-Realism.

De Sica was an inveterate gambler and his preferred casino was in Monte Carlo. In those days, when Europeans needed a passport to cross borders, De Sica, when hiring a driver, had only one question, "Do you have a valid passport?"

But he was a lousy gambler. He constantly lost and was always in need of money. In his later years, he would take any acting job and usually it was for a day. They would film him for ten, twelve hours, because they had to get all his scenes in the can without running into a second day. De Sica would not leave his dressing room in the morning until he was handed his daily fee—ten million lire (about fifteen thousand dollars at the time.) In the main these were small budget comic films, then the rage in Italy.

The director of *Biggest Bundle* was Ken Annakin, who had directed the British effort in *The Longest Day*. The English actors referred to him as "Panickin' Annikan." Ken did have a panicky streak. However, in my scene with De Sica he was a cool cat. How anyone could direct De Sica, even forgetting the fact that Ken didn't know De Sica's language, was a mystery to me.

The scene in the film: I am perched on top of a battered tank, wearing G.I. fatigues, smoking a cigar, and trying to clean the dirt off the tank. An elegantly dressed Italian approaches and asks if the tank is for sale. My eyes light up—a sucker. After a bit of conversation, I tell him the price (let's say a million lire). In a familiar Italian gesture; his hands come together in prayer and he beseeches God to help him obtain the tank because he's almost broke. Tears appear in his, oh so sad, eyes, his voice gets weepy as he tells me his young soldier son was killed in battle and his town wants a monument to commemorate a hero's final sacrifice for his country.

I'm impressed and cut the price in half. But still no sale. "My God, for my son I would pay a fortune, but I do not have fortune, I have much, much less than a fortune. Just think what it would mean to my dear, dead son to know that he is being honored by the people in his hometown with this glorious American tank, proudly displayed in the village square."

He is now weeping a rivulet of tears, and I too am beginning to tear. "How much can you pay for the tank?"

"I have the pitiful sum of ten thousand lire ($15) . . . please, for my dead brave son?"

Now I'm weeping rivulets and I say, "Sold."

De Sica miraculously stops weeping and laughs joyously. Then he asks, "Does the cannon shoot?"

I say, "Sure it does." But it puzzles me and I ask him why does he want a tank that can shoot when it will be planted in the village square as a memorial to his son?

"Oh," he says, "for the children. When they play on the tank, they will mock it if the cannon cannot shoot."

"Oh, okay, it shoots," I tell him.

So he gets his tank, I get the measly ten thousand lire and I am happy to have contributed to a father's fond memory of his brave son.

De Sica is an historical figure in the evolution of cinema. As a film director, he defined the postwar period in Italy with sensitivity and artistry.

1967 New York

On stage with Mailer's play, The Deer Park. *The making of two improvised films:* Wild Ninety *and* Beyond the Law.

T he *Deer Park* was going to come alive on a New York stage. Norman Mailer adapted the play from his novel of the same name. He called it, "an existential play. It is a surrealistic comedy about the nature of tragedy. It is a play about sex and love." Late in 1966 he got in touch with me in Rome to ask if I would come to New York to begin rehearsals of the play for an off-Broadway production.

The year before it had been a project at the Actors Studio and I had played Marion Faye, a pimp. I was now to play Carlyle Munshin. I quote a description of Munshin from the published play: "A producer 40 to 45. Has a broad heartiness. His voice is an appurtenance; it booms, it bleats, it whines, it shouts, it attacks, it groans, it runs away, and all the while he is hiding behind it shrewdly estimating his next move."

When it was a project at the Studio, Anne Bancroft had been in it, as was Patrick O'Neil, but he didn't last long. It must have been humiliating to be removed from a Studio project.

It was disappointing that Anne wasn't going to be in the off-Broadway production due to prior commitments. Yes, she was a fine actress, but she was also a woman who had humor, intelligence, and unadorned appeal. But I was delighted to find that Rosemary Tory, who played the part, was close to being a look-a-like for Anne Bancroft and proved to be excellent in the play.

Rip Torn played Marion Faye, and an old friend from my Hollywood days, Hugh Marlowe, played Charles Eitel, the doomed movie director. He was good, but not ideal casting. (John Huston would have been my choice.) Hugh and Rosemary fell in love on and off stage. After the play closed, they got married.

I wasn't about to leave Joan, Valentina and Melissa, my two daughters, for what probably would be several months. I had to get a place big enough for all of us, including our Italian nanny. Although Norman offered me the maximum he could pay, I couldn't afford an apartment in a hotel. But I lucked out. Ben Gazzara, a Studio friend, had a large, marvelous apartment on Riverside Drive. I finally contacted him in Hollywood and he immediately came through. His apartment was free for several months. All I had to do was pay his rent (an unbelievable four hundred a month, rent-controlled).

A young director, Leo Garen, was chosen to direct the play. Norman was present at most rehearsals, sitting in back of the theater, fidgeting but rarely interfering with the director. Sure, he had private conversations with Leo, but I knew from experience how a writer suffers watching all the repetitions during rehearsals, at times boring, at times achingly off-key.

We opened to a full house, including critics, in February 1967 at the Theatre de Lys. One of my scenes was an actor's dream. It ended with a blackout and got a hand every night, thanks mainly to the writing.

I stand accused of being immodest; The following is a quote from *The New Yorker's* Edith Butler's review of the play:

"The second-funniest character is a youngish producer, a self-bemused man and a gamy nonstop talker, tenderly nurturing his own clichés, who is very well played by Mickey Knox. His fast synopsis of the script, immediately followed by pragmatic suggestions for emendations, is something I shall not soon forget."

Will Lee, a good actor, played Herman Teppis, the head of the film studio (could have been L.B. Mayer, former boss of MGM). I was his son-in-law in the play and I had a scene with him in which he read me the riot act for being untrustworthy, a schemer, etc. I quote one of his lines: "You think a man can break the laws of society?" he was seated at his desk and I was standing facing him. This is what I heard as he forgot the last word: "You think a man can break the laws of BONG?"

Bong? He was so good an actor that he kept the action going and didn't lose his concentration, so the audience didn't get it, didn't react. But I did. I couldn't stop laughing. Off stage I saw Marsha Mason waiting to make an entrance, laughing so hard she had to cover her mouth. When Lee got to that line every night, he purposely hesitated before saying "society," knowing I was going to break up. I loved him dearly but, oh, what a sly fink.

During the run of *The Deer Park* Norman and some of us in the cast would meet after the show in a bar to cool down, drink and poke fun at each other. No intellectual colloquies there. The core of the after-theater group was Norman, me, and Buzz Farber, a good friend of ours who had a small part in the play. Some of us were displeased with the bar we regularly went to. It had that half-attempt at being ritzy: red silk walks and soft plastic chairs to match. I went looking for a friendlier, unpretentious place. I found it.

It was a bar/restaurant in the Village, Casey's. The name was Irish, but it sounded like the name of the rich Chinese who owned the place. He must have been told that an Irish name would bring in the drinkers, but a Chinese name would keep them away. The first night I wandered into Casey's, it was late and there were few customers, but there was something that quickly attracted me; the warmth of good wood. The bar itself was possibly mahogany. The stools had some art in their design and three round, heavy oak tables in the bar area were solid marvels. I looked into the small dining room past the bar. There were no diners, but the place had a good smell to it.

I sat at the bar drinking. The other drinkers drifted away, leaving only the bartender and me. He locked the entrance door. He had been drinking too and we got into some argument. It's ridiculous, but when one drinks enough, the dumbest, most inconsequential argument takes on a grand reason to defend your end of it.

Mike, the bartender, was suddenly red-faced and angry. He

snarled, "Don't fuck with me, buddy boy." I was in no condition to get into a fistfight with a tough-looking bartender. But I knew there was not going to be a fight when he added, " You know what karate is? Huh? I'm a fucking black belt. I break bricks bare-handed."

I had studied karate briefly and I knew a few things: no karate expert threatens, or brags, or declared he can break bricks. I tapped one of the oak tables and said, "Okay, buddy boy, let's see you break this with your hand." I was relieved he was drunk enough to try it.

His hand curved in the karate knife-position. He whacked the table hard. He went pale with pain; the table didn't tremble. I encouraged him: "Go ahead, give it another shot, you can do it."

He tried again. His arm went limp and he smiled weakly. I barely heard him say, as he breathed the words, "The drinks are on me."

It was late and I was lucky to find a cab. The next day I went back to Casey's before the play to check the food. The bartender was happy to see me: "Some night, huh pal?" He then introduced me to the man who owned the joint. He was about thirty, and had two front teeth missing. His long, coal-black hair was sleek and he was friendly. He sat with me while I ate and explained that the restaurant was just a hobby. He wasn't in it to make money, it was fun and he met interesting people. Casey had inherited a fortune from his father's tungsten mines in China and South America so the investment in the restaurant was like amusement money for him.

He had hired a well-paid French chef and he spared no expense to make the restaurant top-grade. We began to meet there almost every night after the play. At times, Casey picked up the tab or lowered the prices for us, making it indeed, an agreeable gathering place. Norman was the only one not pleased with Casey's. I never knew why.

Word spread among show-biz folk. Recognizable faces became regulars. However, they also attracted the suits. After a couple of drinks, noting the fun we were having, they would pull up a chair and uninvited, join our table. That put a damper on the good mood.

Casey's became a huge success, crowded nightly with tourists and young Wall Street operators looking for any kind of action. Casey was bewildered. It was his first business venture, undertaken out of boredom and loneliness. The place lost its intimacy and its fun. And Casey lost interest.

Some of the regulars from Elaine's famous bar and restaurant joined us at Casey's. They introduced Casey to Elaine's. Soured by his success, he spent most nights there. He was even permitted to play poker with the poker crowd at Elaine's. Being rich, Casey could afford the constant losses he suffered. He was playing with sharks, but he was happy to be one of the players. When he sold Casey's, he moved to the Hamptons to keep up with his favorite crowd.

Out of those nights, after the play, came our first movie, *Wild Ninety*. Norman suggested to Buzz and me that since we were so brilliantly witty during our nightly razzle-dazzle repartée, we should make a movie. He conceived of the premise: Three hoods go to the mattresses (hood-talk for hiding out). That was it, leaving the field of action wide open for us to improvise, be funny, wild, crazy, or inventive. Buzz got a well-known underground filmmaker, D. A. Pennebaker, to shoot the movie. A small loft was found and we were off to the mattresses.

In 1967, I had been working in films for twenty years, but this was a novel experience. After acting in a play that was almost three hours long, off we'd go to our loft to improvise for a roving cameraman until dawn. It was fun. The result was patchy but remarkable, given no script. Norman fired the scenes, giving them heat.

The dialogue was tough and loaded with obscenities. We also had friends join us who contributed to the action. Jose Torres, a former world boxing champ, brought a growling German shepherd. Norman bent down and matched it growl for growl and bark for bark. He was nose to nose with the dog and I was concerned for a moment that one of the noses was going to be shorter.

Buzz, the amateur, slept through a good part of the shooting, leaving the stage to Norman and me. Hard to believe, but he didn't understand that not being in front of the camera means you ain't in the movie. When we saw the finished film the first time, Buzz was mad as a bee. "Why did you guys let me sleep? Why didn't you wake me?"

He quickly learned. Our second film, *Beyond the Law*, was more ambitious. We were now detectives. Norman was Irish, laying on the brogue and squinting fiercely. Now Buzz had his big nose so close to the camera that at times it blocked out other actors.

I quietly encouraged him to take a nap. "Are you kidding?" he answered.

"Well, take your face out of the camera, ferchrissakes," I said.

"I ain't napping on this one," he replied haughtily.

We had a large cast, all improvising. George Plimpton played the mayor (Central Casting couldn't have done better.) On a visit to the film's police precinct he behaved as if everything was just fine, while all around him there were junkies, whores, small time hoods, everyone shouting and cursing and fighting. Plimpton was a smiling, cool mayor through it all.

But Lt. Mailer had the Irish glint in his eye and he wasn't smiling. This time he was nominal director and his sense of drama never deserted him. For a nonactor, he was a formidable presence.

In this scene he cornered Buzz in the bathroom, stared at him hard and snarled: "You been toolin' me wife." His eyes flashed danger and Buzz, I do believe, was scared. "You been toolin' me wife!" he repeated.

Buzz, pressed against the wall, threw his hands up, protesting his innocence. "I don't know what you're talking about, Lieutenant, you know I wouldn't do anything like that." Man, it broke me up and I had to walk away.

The third movie, *Maidstone*, I wasn't in. I was back in Rome with my wife and kids. Norm shot it in color on Long Island on a friend's estate. It was wild. In one scene, Rip Torn hit Norman on the head with a hammer, they wrestled and Norman bit Rip on the ear.

Like the other films, there were lapses, some nonsense, and some improvised very good moments. Where there's Norman there's sure to be sparks, at times flames, at times laughter.

1968 New York—Rome—Spain

Sergio Leone creates the spaghetti western. The Making of Once Upon a Time in the West, *with Henry Fonda, Charles Bronson, Jason Robards and Claudia Cardinale.*

I got know Sergio Leone, who practically invented the spaghetti western, when he asked me to go to New York and dub his film, *The Good the Bad and the Ugly*, into English.

The Good the Bad . . . was a difficult and tiring film to dub; difficult because it was long and was shot with very little soundtrack, and United Artists had made it clear that nothing less than one hundred percent synchronization of the words and lips of the actors would be acceptable; tiring because it took me six weeks, sitting over a hot Movieola to accomplish the writing of the dialogue and synchronize it. I'm not a genius at dubbing, but I proved that with perseverance it can be done. The film came out in the States and not one review mentioned the fact that it had been dubbed.

The following year, Leone took me to New York to help cast one of the leads in *Once Upon a Time in the West*, the film Leone was scheduled to start next. The actor he wanted more than anyone was Charles Bronson, but there was a question of availability so Leone wanted a backup actor.

Sue Mengers started with the William Morris Agency as an office worker and was soon promoted to agent status. I had met her through a mutual friend and called her when I arrived in New York. I described exactly what Leone wanted, using Charley Bronson as an example, and we made an appointment for the following day to meet with Leone.

She arrived with an envelope of photos which she spread out on a table—all Anthony Perkins. Leone gave me a Mafia look, questioning my judgment. I stared at Sue blankly as she rattled on about Perkins's fabulous talent and how perfect he was for the part. Leone, who didn't understand a word of English, turned and went into the bedroom without saying a word.

"Sue, are you out of your mind? I said tough, muscular, a man to reckon with, a powerful individual you wouldn't challenge. Is that Tony Perkins? I worked with him, a lovely guy and a good actor, but not a Charley Bronson. Now, go back to your office and come up with someone who would fit the bill, okay?"

"Got it," she said and we made an appointment for the next day.

Anticipate me reader and you'd be right. Sue came into the hotel suite smiling and said, "I gave it a lot of thought and I'm convinced he is your man," and, yes, once again she spread out half a dozen photos of Tony Perkins.

I was speechless, but Leone wasn't. In Italian he said, "She has a great ass, but get rid of her," and once again he left the room.

I had plenty to explain to Leone to avoid looking like a dolt. He admired Sue's ass (he was an admitted ass-lover)and the vision of it helped him dismiss Sue's youthful enthusiasm as part of the business.

Like almost everyone who works in show biz, Sue was fiercely ambitious and within a few years became one of Hollywood's power brokers. But the girl was intelligent and after years of deal-making, she accumulated enough wealth to retire at a relatively young age.

Leone was not the sort of man to panic, no matter what the situation, but he was concerned enough when he was informed by Henry Fonda's agent that after reading the script of *Once Upon a Time in the West*, Fonda found the dialogue so bad that he would not act in the film unless it was rewritten to his satisfaction.

Italian screenplays are in two parts to allow the cinemas to have an intermission in which to sell popcorn, ice cream, and cold drinks by vendors walking up and down the aisles. Leone had me rewrite the dialogue of the first part in order to send it off to Fonda as quickly as possible. Casting was suspended until I finished. I worked twenty-four hours straight though and a couple days later Fonda informed Leone that he was pleased with the rewritten dialogue and would be happy to do the film.

Henry Fonda was the actor Leone had always longed to have in one of his films. Why? Well, John Ford, the director Leone most admired, had used Fonda in several of his westerns. Fonda's starring in a Leone western was sure to add to Leone's status in Hollywood. Also, Leone shrewdly cast Fonda as the bad guy and Charles Bronson (who eventually signed on) as the hero.

Though Fonda showed interest in working with Leone, he almost got away because of a badly translated screenplay. In all the years I adapted Italian scripts into English, it never failed to amaze me why a producer would jeopardize his project by hiring an inadequate translator in order to save a few bucks.

During the shooting of *Once Upon a Time in the West*, Fonda told me that Leone wanted him for his first western, *A Fistful of Dollars*, but Fonda's agent thought, "An Italian Western? Are they nuts?" and dumped the script into the wastebasket without telling Fonda about the offer. (Fonda told me he would have jumped at it.) The agent couldn't be faulted. There had been no Italian westerns before Leone, and he was loath to bother Fonda with such nonsense.

Finally, the cast fell into place. Fonda, Bronson, Jason Robards, and Claudia Cardinale. Not bad for any film.

I must have worked with at least seventy-five directors and Sergio Leone was among the most inventive. He was attentive to detail in everything related to what appeared on-screen. It was amusing and fascinating watching him select the actors' costumes. Hank Fonda, for example, tried on over twenty hats until he and Leone were satisfied they had chosen the right one. Leone was among the first to feature long dusters in westerns. He had a pile of books of photographs of the American West that he used for research, and they included photos of ranch hands wearing dusters.

Sergio told me he lost five years of his life on every film. Watching him work, I believed it. He never wanted to quit and would shoot until the production manager told him we had to wrap it, the crew and cast were worn out. Some days we worked sixteen hours and more, but Sergio would insist we had worked only eight hours.

He never printed a take until it was exactly what he wanted. He had the entire film in his head before we started shooting. It was the first film I worked on where the music was composed and recorded before the filming had commenced.

And Ennio Morricone was the perfect composer for Leone. His strange, seductive, original film music set the tone for the audience and seemed to foretell the coming action. Many times, Leone would play the theme music for a scene during rehearsals and it effectively helped the actors in creating the proper mood.

One of the reasons the actors were excited about working with Leone was that he filmed them in very tight close-ups to emphasize their eyes. A good actor can convey whatever emotion or thought is required in the scene through his eyes.

But Leone was in essence a cold man. He didn't appear to warm to anyone. When he worked, he was consumed only by the needs of the filming. Oddly, in between films, he would constantly have large numbers of people at his home, but he never cozied up to any of them. He didn't like people but seemed to need their presence; it's no fun being alone if you're famous.

We started shooting in Rome and a problem surfaced that disturbed me, but there was little I could do to resolve it without jeopardizing my position in the Italian film industry. I had coached Anna Magnani in *Rose Tattoo* when she didn't know any English and in spite of that, won the Academy Award as best actress. I also coached her for the film she did with Marlon Brando, *The Fugitive Kind*. We worked well together, but she called me after I had started the Leone film; she was about to begin a film in Rome with Anthony Quinn and wanted me as her coach. I told her the timing was lousy. I had started a film and it would be difficult getting out of it, but I would ask Leone to release me.

I knew it was a bad way to start a film; if he let me go, the word would spread that I was a quitter, and Rome is a small town. It would destroy my reputation of trust that I had in the industry. Also, just asking him put my loyalty in question. I was fucked no matter what the outcome. Leone turned me down flat with one word—no.

Magnani's producer, Stanley Kramer, a man I had known in my Hollywood days, met with me and said Anna was insistent. She wanted me on her film. He offered to pay me anything within reason if I'd leave Leone and join them. I told Kramer I could have done that before the Leone film had started, but in any case Leone had rejected my request to leave his film.

Then Magnani asked would I mind if she personally spoke to Leone. I said give it a try. But she failed, too. Leone told her he needed me and that was the end of it.

One day, Sergio asked me to join him for lunch at the commissary at Cine Città, the Rome studio we were shooting in at the time. He had an appointment with an American movie producer who had come to Rome to convince Sergio to direct two films based on books by Dashiell Hammett. Sergio was the key element in getting the project off the ground. Once he signed on, the financing was guaranteed. I was asked to lunch to interpret for Sergio.

We got to the studio commissary a bit early. Sergio couldn't remember the producer's name—English to him was Chinese and who could remember a Chinese name? I was startled to see Harold Hecht, Burt Lancaster's ex-business partner, approaching our table. He had aged badly; he was stooped and looked decrepit. "Vengeance is a dish best eaten cold," a Mafia chieftain once remarked. I had waited a long time for that lunch.

I had refused to speak to Hecht after his appearance as a witness during the House Un-American Activities hearing twenty years earlier. He was the friendliest songbird; he sang and sang, naming friends as Reds from his WPA days in the thirties to his recent friends in Hollywood. He then got on his knees and kissed those fathead interrogators' asses.

He finished his testimony by pleading with the committee to call him back for any help he could render them in the future. No doubt he would have cleaned their toilets if asked.

Harold had cashed in on his friendship with Burt. He made big bucks, but as wealth usually does, it bred fear. Gone were first principles and the main necessity in life was to protect the estate.

Burt stuck by him. I didn't understand why. Harold was, to put it mildly, a fink. Burt in his politics was liberal. When Dukakis ran for president, he was accused by his Republican opponent of being a "card-carrying ACLU member." Burt got on the radio and said, "I am a card-carrying member of the ACLU and proud of it."

Of course, Burt and Harold had close business ties; they had formed an independent movie company together. Still, Burt could have booted him or could have cut their social connection, but he didn't.

At the lunch in Rome, Harold could not hide his dismay and pained surprise at seeing me. He tried to smile, but only succeeded in disfiguring his mouth.

I didn't greet him. A slight nod of recognition was sufficient to shake his faltering confidence. He was disconcerted by my presence as he weakly laid out his case: if Sergio agreed to collaborate in writing the scripts and directing the two films, he could name his price.

After Harold left, Sergio asked, "You know him, what do you think?"

I knew if I waited long enough it would be done, and I did it. "He's a crook." Sergio nodded and added fuck him in Italian.

About a week later, I got a call from an agent I knew in New York. He had a message for me from Harold Hecht: Harold felt I hadn't been very helpful during our meeting with Leone, but he would give me an envelope containing twenty grand if Leone would agree to commit himself to direct the two films.

"Who me, not helpful? How could Harold think that? I'd love to make twenty grand, but Sergio makes up his own mind," I responded to the agent. Harold never produced another film, that I know of.

We went to Spain for the tough location shooting on *Once Upon a Time*. I prefer working in a studio under controlled conditions. Two events stand out while in Spain: a suicide and the news of the assassination of Bobby Kennedy in Los Angeles.

The film had a large crew and our base was in Guadix, a small, hot, dusty village that had minimal accommodations. Most of us were staying in a three-story building that passed as an "accommodation." We had returned from a location shoot, some distance from the village, and I happened to glance out the window to see what looked like a body shooting by—it *was* a body, and it belonged to an actor who appeared only in the opening sequence of the movie.

He was still wearing his western costume and Leone, upon hearing of the suicide, told the production manager, "get the man's costume before they take him away." The actor hadn't completed his role and they needed someone to fill in, but that would be no problem if they had the dead man's costume. Anyone about the same height and shape would do.

Actually, the man was not quite dead, but Leone didn't ask if he was still alive. He was only concerned for the next day's shooting. What finally killed the actor was the ride in a production car over a bumpy road to the distant hospital. He should never have been moved. A broken rib pierced his lung during the drive. We later learned that the actor was a drug addict and couldn't get a fix in Guadix. Desperate, he went up to the roof and took a dive.

On June 4, 1968, we were in Almeria, a town on the southeast coast of Spain. It was a favorite location for many Italian and American westerns. The hotels were first rate and the surrounding country was similar to the American West. Film companies poured enough money into Almeria's economy to make it a prosperous town.

When the news of the Bobby Kennedy assassination hit, we were filming some distance from the town. Fonda, Robards, and Cardinale were working that day. When the messenger insisted the dreadful news was true, Fonda, angry, shouted: "That's it, I'm moving out of America. It's too much. John Kennedy, Martin Luther King, now Bobby Kennedy. What's happened to our country?"

Jason Robards openly wept. Jason was the most prominent interpreter of Eugene O'Neill's plays. From the moment he appeared onstage, he seemed without great effort to capture the audience's attention. Jason wasn't at all "actorish." He was always in the skin of the character and totally believable.

And in his drinking days, he was a hell of a drinking companion, never mean or combative, always in good humor, ready to sing his favorite: "Casey at the Bat." We had many fine, relaxed evenings while lifting a couple of cool drinks.

Charley Bronson was a phenomenon; he became a movie star in his middle years after playing a series of featured parts for a couple of decades. After *Once Upon a Time*, Charley's position as a major screen player was solidified.

A reticent actor? Yes, sir, the one and only Henry Fonda. And the complete professional, always prepared, never late and at all times giving a hundred percent of his talent. He was obviously deeply moved by the Kennedy assassination, as his rare show of emotion proved. Unlike my life outside of work, I had learned to be discreet on a movie set. I try not to gossip (not easy) and to not impose myself on the actors. Generally, actors are friendly and seek out someone to hang with, (certainly on long location work).

Fonda wore the mantle of stardom with ease, but without waving it in your face. After a couple of weeks of filming, Fonda opened up a bit and talked about his children, about his wife Shirley who was with him in Spain, and even about politics. He didn't exactly approve of Jane's trip to Hanoi during the Vietnam War, but he sure admired her courage.

I had seen Utah's Monument Valley in most of John Ford's westerns but I was now going to see it in the flesh, so to speak, because finally, Leone was going to film in Ford's favorite terrain. It seemed all of Leone's shots included that one looming formation, so placed that it can be seen from miles around: a huge sandstone square on top of a high mound of red earth. There were more interesting formations in bizarre shapes, but they didn't take up as much space or could be seen from all camera angles.

Leone hated to fly, but he had little choice if he wanted to keep to any kind of shooting schedule. On the flight there his heart must have lost a couple beats that it never recovered when he suffered a fright he never forgot. his plane had to make an unscheduled stop in Chicago, because there were serious problems with one of the motors, and Leone could see flares of fire shooting out of it.

The plane landed all right, but Leone wasn't about to transfer to another plane for the remainder of the trip. He was with one of his production assistants, who tried to calm Leone and get him on the replacement plane, but it was useless. Leone told him to hire a car. They were going to drive all the way to Monument Valley. That malfunctioning motor was a sign—don't fly. It didn't matter that the drive from Chicago to Monument Valley was about fifteen hundred miles.

They drove straight through, stopping only to gas up. Leone feared flying, but I can testify that he was in more danger of cashing in his chips behind the wheel of a car than flying with one motor out. I drove with him for the first couple of days on the way to our location in the Valley from our motel and it was scary. He pushed the car to the limit, at times exceeding a hundred miles an hour, not to be done in a lightweight Chevy. Okay, the roads were straight and there was hardly any traffic, but the car wandered from side to side.

After the first day, I told Leone I'd give him one more day but if he went over eighty again, that was it. The second day he relentlessly kept his foot on the floorboard, grimly gripping the shimmying steering wheel as if to prevent it from flying through the windshield. The goddamn car started to shudder and I was sure it was going to fall apart. You can place a bet that I never got into a car with Leone at the wheel again.

We all stayed at a motel run by Indians on the Navajo Reservation in Monument Valley. It was the only game in town, and the only place to eat after a day's work. We sat at a large table that accommodated all in the cast and crew. The waitresses were young Indian girls and their service was fast and friendly. I noticed that Leone was the only one at the table who didn't leave a tip.

Anyone who visited Italy would know that the tip—at least eighteen percent—is, in most restaurants, included in the bill. I explained to Leone that it is hardly ever the practice in the States and that the Indians working in the restaurant lived on tips. He said the tip was included and showed me the state sales tax on his bill. He smirked and never did leave a tip.

The last day we were there everyone left a generous tip for the Indian girls except Leone. Like a fool, I stood up and blasted him in front of everyone for being the cheapest man in the universe. He didn't say a word, but he gave me a look of future payback. It eventually cost me.

Like many Italians who are schooled in the writings of Machiavelli, he concealed his anger and was friendly enough after the film was completed. He still needed me. But he was going to pick his moment.

He took me to New York to meet with Bludhorn, the head of Paramount Pictures at the time, and the company that financed the film. The execs at Paramount wanted to see a rough cut of *Once Upon a Time in the West*, even though it was only dubbed into Italian at that point. Since none of them understood Italian, I was asked to interpret the dialogue as it was being screened in the Paramount projection room.

I was faced with simultaneous translation, a tough job only undertaken by the trained and gifted few; way beyond my ability. But I didn't know that until the film started to unreel. I was always a couple of speeches behind or simply missed some of them.

The result was confusion and annoyed sounds made by the studio executives: "What the hell . . . what'd he say?" "Oh shit, I missed that." "What?" I couldn't answer any of that. I was *farblunget* (for the

Gentiles—lost). I must have sweated out five pounds. The film was three hours long in that version. Finally the torture was over and one of the execs said, "Tough assignment, old boy." (An exec's way of saying, "You fucked up, *schmuck.*")

I was worn out and the day wasn't over yet; I could have used a boiler maker to put some fuel in the engine. After the showing, Leone and I went up to Bludhorn's office. I was there to interpret for them. Bludhorn thought the film was a masterpiece, but too long. Leone defended the length of the movie, explaining that he had tried cutting it, but found the story was too tightly woven to remove any scene or sequence. (After the film was released, I was on the Via Veneto in Rome with Leone. A friend of his stopped to chat with Leone and told him the film was fine, but too long. Leone turned to me and said, "Tell him how I begged Bludhorn to cut the film, but he refused, said the film was great as is, isn't that so?" I didn't answer, taking it as a rhetorical question, and Leone went right on as if I had agreed with him.)

Paramount had bought the film rights to the book *The Godfather,* and Bludhorn asked Leone to supervise the screenplay and direct the movie for a million bucks, enough money in 1968 to buy a small island. Leone turned the offer down, saying the book was old-fashioned. He hadn't read the book but relied on his brother-in-law, no literary maven. Bludhorn pressed Leone, but Leone was the Rock of Gibraltar—nothing doing.

Once out of the office I told Leone I had read the book and thought it was the perfect blueprint for a film, that it was not at all old-fashioned, but a hell of a fascinating book about the Mafia.

My take was that Leone had earned the respect of the Hollywood captains and didn't want to jeopardize his reputation with the possibility of making a bomb. It was not only difficult to make, but Leone knew little English and the film would have to be made in English, in direct sound, something he had never attempted.

But when *The Godfather* became such a blockbuster, Leone decided to show Hollywood that he too could make a gangster film that would rival *Godfather*, to be called *Once Upon a Time in America*. I, of course, was on his shit list, so I had no part in that project. Except for his first choice of screenwriter—Norman Mailer. Leone had asked me what American screenwriter would be the right man for the job and I said "If you want the best writer in America, try Norman Mailer." He knew about Mailer and they worked out a deal.

Before starting *Once Upon a Time in America*, Leone got a rare meeting with the real but elusive head of the Mafia in the States— Jimmy Blue Eyes. Jimmy Blue Eyes avoided all publicity and was unknown to the public; as they say in professional circles, he kept a low profile.

How Leone got the meeting with Jimmy is unclear. In speaking about the meeting, Leone inferred that he had arranged it with a lawyer who handled Mafia legal affairs, but I had the sense that this wasn't the whole story.

Leone sat across from Jimmy at a back room table of an Italian restaurant in Brooklyn (where else?) Leone told him that he was going to make a film about gangsters in the twenties. Jimmy listened, his eyes staring down on the table, never looking at Leone. When Leone finished, Jimmy spoke in little above a whisper: "You no makea dat movie."

Leone quickly got the message and added, "My movie is about Jewish gangsters in the twenties."

Jimmy Blue Eyes slowly lifted his eyes to Leone and replied, "Dat movie you make." (Jimmy Blue Eyes had very dark brown eyes.)

Leone played by his own rules and they were usually unprincipled, at times cruel. Leone's favorite actor to work with was Eli Wallach. He loved him, as much as he could love anyone, because of his performance in *The Good the Bad and the Ugly*, a performance that helped make the film such a huge success.

When Leone planned on producing, but not directing, a western called, *Duck You, Sucker* he made a verbal agreement with Eli's agent to star Eli in the film. But United Artists, the company that was to distribute the film, had a previous picture deal with Rod Steiger and they wanted to exercise it by having Steiger play Eli's part. After all, Leone did have a verbal agreement with Eli and in Hollywood that's as good as a written contract. Steiger played the role. So much for Leone's loyalty and gratitude for Eli's performance as the *Ugly*.

Sergio waited over a year to stick it to me (he would have made a tough, feared godfather.) and like a Mafioso, he never forgot what I said to him in front of the cast and crew for being so fucking cheap.

I got to know Alberto Sordi, one of Italy's most famous actor-comedians. I had adapted a script from Italian into English for a film he was in. In all comedy scripts it was always a problem adapting Italian humor into something equivalent in English; it took patience and imagination.

Alberto Sordi asked me if I'd be interested in collaborating on a screenplay with him and I said, of course I would. But Sordi was a constant visitor to Leone's Sunday gatherings. There's little doubt that Sordi spoke to Leone about using me and Leone, finally tasting revenge for my insulting attack on his moronic stinginess, signaled thumbs down.

Leone planned on making one last major film, an enormous project to be filmed in Russia, based on the book *Stalingrad*, about the battle for that city during the invasion of Russia by the German army during World War II.

The last time I saw Leone was at the movie studio, Cinecittà, in Rome. He was always overweight, so I was surprised to see he had shed a lot of fat and had lost his heavy belly. I figured his doctor had found that Leone had high blood pressure or a heart problem and warned him to drop forty pounds or he'd croak before the next full moon.

My last words to him were: "Sergio, where's the other half of you? (he laughed) But this doesn't make you just half a shit . . . (he didn't react) but I have said and will continue to say that you're a hell of a good movie director."

Sergio worked on the script and preparations for filming the Russian film for a couple of years before he died in bed, apparently of a heart attack. The year was 1981. He was sixty years old.

1968 Tunisia—Hollywood

Anouk Aimee's magic moment. Meeting Albert Finney in St. Paul de Vence. Justine *intervenes.*

L awrence Durrell was a writer I admired. He had written a trilogy set in modern Egypt. *Justine*, one third of the trilogy, was going to be made as a film by 20th Century Fox Studios.

When a film is adapted from a book, the actors often are not cast to represent the characters in the book; the box office draw counts. However, the casting of the characters in *Justine* was faithful to those in Durrell's book. The main actors were Anouk Aimee, Dirk Bogard, and Michael York. Joseph Strick was engaged to direct the film. Strick came from a wealthy family (Strick trucks) and had probably financed *Ulysses*, an indie film he directed.

Richard Zanuck, the head of Fox at the time, had a special place in his heart for Anouk; he thought about making her a major star. Anouk had requested me as her coach. Zanuck must have told the production manager to give her anything her sweet heart desired and she desired, for her personal use, a hairdresser and makeup artist, both Italian. I had worked with Anouk before and her English was excellent, but there were also several French actors who needed serious coaching, including Phillip Noiret, a marvelous French actor (*Cinema Pardiso, Il Postino*). He had one of the principal parts but knew little English. So my plate was full.

The location was Tunisia. I always anticipated with a measure of excitement, going to any country I hadn't been to. And rarely was I disappointed.

Soon after arriving in Tunis, I met with Strick. It surprised me to learn that he had his yacht transported from the States by ship to Tunis. Directing a film is all consuming—long hours, not only concentrating on what's in front of the camera, but also dealing with the inevitable problems behind the camera. Did Strick plan on midnight yachting?

I soon found that in spite of his lack of experience, the man was arrogant rather than humble. Eavesdrop on our first conversation: "There are three great directors making films today: Bergman, Fellini, and Strick." He's joking, I thought, but the guy meant it. "And that's the truth," he added.

Anouk insisted I stay at her hotel in Carthage, some distance from Tunis. The other actors stayed in a first-class hotel that included bungalows on the beach.

One evening I was invited, along with the English crowd, for drinks and dinner in Dirk Bogard's bungalow. The newlywed Mrs. Ken Tynan, an attractive young woman with a fetching smile, was the guest of honor. She had come from London to write a piece about *Justine* for an English publication.

The "show biz-English" are fun to be with. They like to drink, gossip, laugh and duel jocularly. Mrs. Ken Tynan was the center of the evening, telling us about her new husband. She was amusing describing their honeymoon and provoked a lot of laughs, that no one found awkward or embarrassing. I didn't know Ken Tynan well, but I didn't think he deserved to be the caricature of the evening. In England and America he was a respected and feared theater critic, theatrical producer (*Oh Calcutta*) and author.

We started shooting and things quickly went wrong. Strick was abrasive and curt with the crew for no apparent reason. He was not only unprofessional, he was insensitive. You don't antagonize the crew gratuitously. They fucked him royally. Every other take, the film would run backward in the gut of the camera, creating a "salad"—useless as food or film. An electrician can be a magician when necessary.

A couple of weeks into the shoot and I got a call from Howard Koch Jr., the producer of *On a Clear Day You Can See Forever*, soon to begin filming with Yves Montand and Barbra Streisand. Yves had asked Koch to hire me as his coach on *On a Clear Day . . .* However, there was that ubiquitous fly in the ointment—the film's schedule would overlap with *Justine*. I was pretty agile, but not enough to work two films at the same time.

Koch, a note of anxiety in his voice, told me Yves insisted that he find me. He found me and offered to double my salary if I could get out of *Justine*. Since I'd have more fun working with Montand, doubling my salary made the offer doubly attractive. But too many years had gone by being a professional and I just couldn't violate my personal code and break loose. Koch called me two more times, but as painful as it was, I turned him down.

Anouk was of the feline family. She loved cats more than people. At dinner she would order two filet mignons, half of one for her, one and a half for the cats that gathered from near and far for their evening meal. We sat at a garden table next to the wire fence so she could surreptitiously sneak them strips of filet. Our waiter would watch from a short distance with sad eyes. Telling her it was a poor country and few could afford any kind of steak fell on dead ears. "Doesn't that embarrass you?" I asked.

"Oh no, I love cats and they must eat."

Before starting the movie, Anouk had met Albert Finney at La Colombe d'Or in the South of France. And love's magic wand touched them both, or so she told me. I didn't know Finney then, but I did know that he was, like Brando, a superb, one of a kind actor.

Love has many demands and Anouk was not shy in calling on me to compose her thoughts in English so she could cable Finney, which she did every day. There I was writing love notes to Albert Finney for Anouk. Little did I know the consequences.

Before the company left for Hollywood to continue the shoot, Richard Zanuck returned to the studio after attending the Olympics in Mexico City. He hadn't seen any of the rushes until then. He saw them and fired Joseph Strick. Zanuck replaced him with George Cukor, famous for his success in directing Oscar-winning actresses.

Off to Hollywood we went. But Anouk was missing. I was grilled by the production people, knowing I would be the one who knew where she was. They were right, but I wouldn't betray her. (She was with Finney on the Isle of Corfu in Greece.)

Right off the starting line, Cukor looked on me as a traitor. His only words to me were, "Where the hell is that woman?" When I denied knowing, he angrily turned away and never spoke to me again.

Anouk finally showed up, a week late. Boy did she pay. Cukor made her life miserable, and daily had her in tears.

But Anouk was tough. She shook off Cukor's ire like rain off a cat's fur. She was consumed by her crush on Finney, thus Cukor was only a mild irritation. Her refuge was the phone in her dressing room and hotel suite. Free time on the set would send her racing to her dressing room to dial Finney in London. "Say hello for me," I once said.

Finney, reaching for a life line, asked to speak with me. "Please tell Anouk I'm working. I just can't spend hours on the phone. I would think kindly of you if you could help me on this."

But I knew it was useless. Her phone bills at the studio and hotel were astronomical.

I saw Yves Montand several times. He was doing the movie with Barbra Streisand at the nearby Paramount Studios and was still unhappy with me for not leaving *Justine*.

He did invite me to a roof garden party. An orchestra played romantic music. It was a clear, moonlit night and I was introduced to Marilyn Monroe by Yves, her ex-lover. I invited her to dance. Then I knew it was true: she wore no underwear. She had on a sheer evening dress, my hand cautiously slid down her lower back; only skin was under the gown. The dance was over, she graciously said thank you and went back to her table. Now, I have worked with and gotten to know international movie legends, and for the most part it was hello and good-bye and onto the next film. But one short dance and Monroe left an ache somewhere inside me.

Justine did not make a big splash at the box office. The directing credit went to Cukor. Joseph Strick, as far as I know, was not heard from again, blowing his chance to join Fellini and Bergman in the film directors' hall of fame.

Anouk, soon after *Justine*, married Finney. She told me she would quit work and dedicate herself to her husband, home, and her many cats. I wished her well. But nothing is as constant as change.

A year or so later she and Finney were in Rome, staying at a hotel around the corner from my apartment. We had lunch and he told me he was planning on doing *Hamlet* and *Tamburlaine* for the Royal Shakespeare Company. *Tamburlaine*, the Christopher Marlowe play, is about five hours long and rarely performed. It treats a heroic theme of a Mongol conqueror in the fourteenth century.

"Come to London," Finney said, "and I'll invite you to see the plays." I had always admired his talent as an actor, but his personal warmth, his humor, and his openness revealed an unusual *mensch*.

I was, at that point, a wounded mensch. The story is too long and still too painful to recount. The hard facts are that I was away on movie locations for weeks on end, giving an Italian "friend" the time to worm his way into the heart of my wife. On June 15, 1969, she took our two small girls and moved out of via Gregoriana to via Cassia, on the outskirts of Rome. Eventually, divorce number three.

I got to London with my then live-in woman companion. First we saw *Tamburlaine*; Finney was majestic. I had seen him do *Luther* on the stage before I knew him so I knew of his range and power as an actor.

Wandering around London, I ran into an actor I had worked with. He suggested I might like to house-sit his mews home for a few days while he was away. Yeah, man, are you kidding? No, old, boy, I am definitely not kidding, he said.

London never failed me. To put it simply, I felt good being there.

For aesthetic reasons, I suppose, cities split by rivers are appealing and offer walks and perspectives.

After Finney's brilliant performance as Hamlet, we went backstage to see him. He asked us to have a drink with him. I told him I had to move that night and he suggested he drive me. We went to where we were staying, loaded our bags into his mini station wagon, and drove to the mews address.

We were lugging the bags up a narrow stairway of the mews house, when Finney stopped midway and said, "I can't believe it, I just finished four hours of Hamlet and here I am being Mickey Knox's baggage boy."

"I told you I'd take a taxi, but you insisted."

He laughed and said, "Right you are m'boy, I did do that."

Although Anouk was, at one time, wildly in love with Finney, the heat of her love cooled and the marriage fell apart. She went back to Paris with her cats and back to work. I saw her in Paris and she raved about her new love, an assistant director on a film she was doing. He was, she proudly announced, fifteen years younger than she.

Finney always spoke of her kindly and with affection after the breakup.

Every film I've worked on has had its surprises, but *Justine* is a contender for the championship. A producer hates surprises—they're usually expensive, but for the salaried hands it's at least amusing, and at best hilarious. Surprises make for a lively day on the set. And on *Justine*, the drama and fun were not in the script. But the book is great.

1969–70 Klosters, Switzerland

Irwin Shaw lives the good life in Europe.

I rwin Shaw wrote, *The Young Lions*, a World War II novel, one of three war novels that were published in the first years after the conflict. Like *The Naked and the Dead*, by Norman Mailer, it was, "don't see the movie, read the book." Only James Jones' novel, *From Here to Eternity* was made into a movie that was compelling and successful, yet also a powerful and moving first book.

Irwin and I had met in London sometime in 1943 during the war. I was a private, he was a warrant officer, but we hit it off quickly. He was a fine drinking companion and being with him, you were treated to wit and intelligence.

After the war, he lived in France and during the years I lived in Italy, we wrote to each other occasionally or met up in Paris or Rome. He told me, as did others, how beautiful Klosters, in Switzerland, was. Klosters was "discovered" by Anatole Litvak, a well-known film director. He and his group—Shaw, Peter Viertel and Debora Kerr, among others—had bought homes in the village and were there mostly during the skiing season.

I was tempted to join all those fun lovers, but never made it until my brother Carl, having dug himself in a business hole, came to stay with me in Rome to heal his wounded pride.

He was rightly depressed and miserable. I couldn't cheer him up with booze—he didn't drink—so I suggested we spend the new year, 1969-70, in Klosters. He was more than willing. We decided to drive up the Italian boot to Switzerland in my fire-engine red Super Mini Minor.

The trip was mostly silent as Carl was deep in thought and suffered a fast-developing flu. He didn't feel too well when we checked into a charming small hotel. I called Irwin Shaw that evening and he asked me to lunch the following day.

Lunch was not a barrel of laughs. Irwin was shacking up with his girlfriend—a German yet. His wife, Marion, a splendid woman, was in the process of divorcing him and Irwin complained bitterly that she wanted the whole kit and caboodle: the cash, bank accounts, the property, leaving Irwin, for all practical purposes, broke.

Irwin was a "shtaker"—strong as an ox, physically and mentally. And he surprised me—tears popped up! Man, he was hurting. All I could give him was sympathy.

Peter Viertel, author of the excellent *White Hunter, Black Heart*, about film director John Huston, had planned a New Year's Eve party at the Village's best-known hotel, the Chesa Grischuna. Carl was in bed with a full-blown flu, so he missed the fun.

There were probably fifty or so guests in the large lounge, taken over for the party. Irwin and I spent much of the time at the bar. It wasn't a rowdy affair; on the contrary, it was subdued and ended about two in the morning.

Peter Viertel's mother, Salka Viertel, was well-known in Europe and Los Angeles. She was an author and an articulate intellectual. As a close friend and confidante of Garbo, she was involved in writing her films.

About twenty years earlier, I had gone with Mailer to Salka's salon for an evening. Now, at the New Year's party in Klosters, Peter introduced me to his elderly mother. She said, "Oh, I remember you, Norman Mailer brought you to my home in Los Angeles." She obviously remembered me because I came with Norman, but I was impressed by her memory.

The party broke up and we went to reclaim our coats hung on a rack in a nearby hall. Irwin couldn't find his newly bought sheepskin jacket, and it angered him. Ever ready to help out, I said, loud enough for all to hear, "Hey Irwin, Marion came and took it away with her." It got a laugh from everyone but Irwin. The next day, he revealed sheepishly that he had left it at home.

Irwin had the "good life." He lived in Europe during the best years—soon after World War II ended (I should know, I was there). For the most part, he preferred living in Paris; the French respect writers. The dollar was king and with the buck, everything was a bargain. Irwin worked in the morning, then tennis, then lunch with friends, after, a "matinee" or a snooze. The evening began with drinks, followed by a good meal with excellent wine.

Irwin gave "the good life" a true meaning.

He died in 1984. He was 71.

1970 Rome

Poet Norman Rosten writes an ode to Rome.

Norman Rosten, poet, novelist, and playwright, was born and raised in Brooklyn and we hit it off right away. He wrote a novel, *Under the Boardwalk*, about Coney Island, my birthplace. He was sensitive to his fellow man, always in a gentle mood, but however, he tended to gush with optimism.

He came to visit and stay with me in Rome several times, and delighted in his love for the city. He slept under a large French window facing my garden, shaded by several trees. He would lie in bed in the morning and stare up at the sunlight peeping through the leaves and branches, enjoying the intricate play of light.

Rosten and I would walk for several hours a day through narrow cobblestone streets and piazzas, large and small. He never lost his enthusiasm or his sense of awe for the city.

We often walked down the Spanish Steps, just up the street from me. He enjoyed watching the Italian sharks insouciantly hustling the girls and the travelers taking the sun, snoozing, or quietly strumming guitars. He later wrote this poem about Rome, his friend, and the Piazza di Spagna.

Norman Rosten died a few years before writing of these memoirs and I still miss his "happy to be alive" face.

Rome: First View
by Norman Rosten

(for Mickey Knox)

They tell me the swallows of Rome
Move from point to point
Across the city in search of food.
I'm like those swallows,
My heart pulsing in all directions,
Hungry for color, the water of fountains,
Kisses if possible - the works.
Because it seems if any town
Can kill the clock and cure the shakes,
This must be the place.

My horny friend Mickey
Slides in and out of the past,
A joyful juggler, guides a red chariot
Down streets of the inferno,
His exhaust setting the trees on fire.
Following his example
I track a girl in a dark piazza
But she goes up in smoke
Just as I close in.
Mickey says it's to be expected,
Snatch is the most perishable commodity
Here as elsewhere. Keep trying.

Could it be that half of the town
Is looking for the other half?
In the Piazza di Spagna
Tigers stalk and lounge upon the balustrades.
It's a forest of possibilities.

Two are eating a third in the bushes,
A fourth is bargaining for a necklace,
A dozen cling like bees to the marble,
Fifty more are skipping the steps
In a wild Jargon.
Keats at his window,
1821, dying, shouts, "Get those damned tourists
out of here!"

To which Mickey would say,
"Keats needed a change of scene
But this wasn't right for his English blood.
Come on, let's join the night
And catch some live birds for dinner."
(To Mickey—Aventi! Norman—July 15, 1970)

1971 Budapest—Rome

Filming Bluebeard *with Richard Burton. Elizabeth Taylor accompanies her husband. Joan splits—I meet Iris.*

In order to bring in hard currency, the countries behind the Iron Curtain offered advantages film companies couldn't resist. Movie crews there worked for less than western European crews. Location sites, costumes, transportation, hotel accommodations, catering services, were all much cheaper than their Western counterparts and added up to real savings for below the line expenditure. In a movie budget, actors, writers, the director, and other related costs are above the line. Production costs are below the line. The main advantage of shooting in an eastern bloc country was that they picked up most of the local charges for either a percentage of the profits of the film or an outright payment, becoming coproductions and bringing in much needed foreign hard currency. It all made for a happy and profitable experience for everyone.

In the case of *Bluebeard*, a rich man who killed his wives, a French company made a favorable deal with Hungary to shoot the film in Budapest. Richard Burton was to be Bluebeard, and if his name wasn't enough to bring in the moviegoers, a bevy of young beauties chosen from around Europe were also in the cast.

A French friend connected with the production called me in Rome to ask if I'd like to be the dialogue director. I was free and Budapest was a new location for me, so I accepted the offer. I didn't regret it. It was fun and interesting; the girls were beautiful, the Hungarians affable. The food was lousy.

Like most capitals in the eastern bloc, Budapest has its charm. The Danube flows between Buda on the west bank and Pest on the east. Pest is the older part of the city and that's where much of its beauty can be seen. Most of us were put up in a newly built high rise hotel, the Intercontinental, on the West Bank, but our evenings were spent dining across the Danube in Pest.

The restaurants had old world charm and low-key cheerful service. The national dish, goulash, was okay if it suited your taste, which it better had because that was it. The other dishes were inedible, unless you like desserts.

The eastern bloc authorities had their sex police. Surprising how puritanical those governments were. I took a local girl who worked on the film up the hotel elevator on the way to my room. As we entered the room, the phone rang. It was the hotel security ordering me to send the girl down to the lobby immediately. I told her to stay; she had nothing to fear. She looked at me as though I were crazy and rushed out. How the hell did they know which room we went to? No one was in the corridor and there was no one operating the elevator.

But sex police can be dumb. They neglected to block the most obvious point of entry, the rooftop nightclub. I quickly figured that one out. Take a girl to the club, have a drink, then toddle down to the room via the stairway.

Elizabeth Taylor was named the Phantom of the Corridor. She was visiting her husband, Richard Burton. Many evenings she would go in search of Richard, who would often be in Natalie Delon's room. One night, Elizabeth knocked on Natalie's door. Natalie, having an instinct and wide experience in such matters, sensed it was Elizabeth and rushed Richard out onto the balcony, locking the French window.

Natalie was married to Alain Delon, the French movie star. She was witty, attractive, and bright. She did spend time with Richard while on the film. But was it more than just flirting? Who knows? She flatly said she was a great lay and by her tone and eyes, she left little room for doubt. But I don't believe Richard was looking to sat-isfy a sexual urge. He liked women and enjoyed talking to them. He also was drinking pretty good and battling with Elizabeth.

When I arrived in Budapest, I was told that Richard was on the wagon. Like many of his English mates, he was a social drinker. However, socializing started early in the day, and continued until the publican called, "Time, ladies and gents."

I was with him in his mobile home one morning, running a scene. He poured himself a screwdriver. Then a second. He offered me one, but I stupidly said it was too early in the morning for me—not meaning to reflect on his drinking. "This, m'boy, is merely grapefruit juice with a splash of vodka, a decent morning drink."

He was a subtle charmer, a man you had to like and want as a friend. He was tuned into literature and regretted he wasn't a born writer. We talked often about writing. It was indeed a pity he wasn't a writer, given his love of language. He was, after all, Welsh.

As a young actor on the London stage, he was thought of by most of his fellow actors as the future Hamlet, an honor not bestowed on many. But he deserted the stage for Hollywood and the silver screen. He had made a few films in England and a couple in Hollywood before making *The Robe,* one of the few movies I have ever walked out of halfway through the showing. It was boring and incoherent. But Richard was handsome and forceful, and his film career was on the road to movie stardom.

Natalie Delon was a little nuts. She dropped acid most every day. And she was funny. One night I was with her when she collected a pile of shoes left outside the hotel rooms to be shined. We went back to her room where she tossed them all out the window onto a jutting roof halfway to the street, laughing happily as each shoe sailed out.

One of the girls in the film had a cocktail party in her room. Due to a lack of chairs, many of us sat on the floor. I sat next to a pretty German actress. We chatted a couple of minutes and I took her hand. She not only allowed it but squeezed my hand in response. Oh boy, my lucky night.

Not to be. Natalie, my friend, pulled the chain: "I would not hold his hand, my dear, he has syphilis, you know," she lied, her face beatific. The speed at which the German girl whipped her hand out of mine caused a skin-burn. (No, I never had syphilis.)

A month later, the Burtons gave a New Year's Eve party at the classiest hotel in Rome, the Grand. Strangely, it was a subdued party. Quiet talk, champagne at midnight, embraces but no real gaiety. Except for Iris, my dearest girl at the time, who drank her fill and got very drunk. She was fun and jolly until the booze hit her and she rushed to the ladies' room. It took me about twenty minutes to realize that Iris hadn't returned. I went to the ladies' room and knocked on the door. No one answered. So I bravely went in. Iris was lying on the floor, out cold. I got her up, splashed cold water on her face until she revived.

When the party was over about an hour later, Iris, once again up to speed, pleaded with me to take her dancing. What a girl. I didn't take her dancing. I had other things in mind.

Iris filled a gap in my life at a crucial time. Joan had left me for a persistent Italian. I was alone and dazed. Lionel Stander, a good friend, knowing my woeful emotional life at the time, saved me further pain by calling one afternoon soon after Joan flew the coop and suggested I come see his new apartment—as it turned out, a ploy to get me there. Luckily, I had nothing better to do. He introduced me to Iris, who found him the apartment.

She was an American living in Rome, working as a real estate agent. At that time she was in her midthirties, pretty, with beautiful skin. She exuded warmth along with clouds of cigarette smoke. Being vulnerable, I was taken with her on first sight. And I liked her slightly pigeon-toed walk; it added to her natural sex attraction.

We became constant companions. I truly adored Iris; she was generally gay and convivial, hardly ever moody, always adventurous.

For several years, Iris was an important part of my life in Rome. But love is an obsession, and when the obsession is deeper in one lover than the other, the affair is headed for a reef, to flounder and break apart. As my love for Iris deepened, hers diminished, and she became cocky. I cut loose and stopped seeing or talking to her. A couple of years later, we became just friends.

After being on both sides of love's dignities and indignities, I found the obvious; that love can be an exhilarating trip, or it can turn wretched. What is not so obvious is that there are no free tickets.

Once again, I digress—to digress is not always a bad thing. If the forces of nature hadn't digressed, we still might be monkeys or, better yet, amoeba:

Lionel Stander was a remarkable man and a talented stand-out actor, he was the first one in Hollywood to be blacklisted for political reasons in the late 1930s, ten years earlier than the House Un-American Activities Committee began its Hollywood hearings.

He appeared before the Committee and was probably the only witness to overpower the Committee's attempt at intimidation. Using his heavy, buzz-saw voice, he accused the Committee of being un-American and proceeded to inform them of every amendment to the Constitution, several of which they were violating. They could not shut him up and finally dismissed him. On the stand, Lionel was a marvel; he had beat them at their own game.

Being smart, intelligent, and articulate, he survived beautifully. He became a stockbroker, accumulated some money, went to England, played a leading role in Roman Polanski's huge success *Cul-de-Sac* and then went to Rome to begin working on Italian films.

1970s Rome—New York

Norman Mailer vs. Gore Vidal. The clash of literary titans.

T he Hatfield-McCoy feud it wasn't—no one got shot dead, but the Mailer-Vidal feud, begun with Vidal's weapon, the printed word, lasted all of fourteen years.

During the many years I lived in Rome, I saw Gore Vidal from time to time. One afternoon he called. He wanted to show me an article he had written. When I got to his apartment, he handed me a scotch and a few typewritten pages.

I read it. "You're not going to publish this, are you?" I asked. He assured me he was indeed going to publish the article. It was titled, "The Three Ms: Miller, Mailer, Manson." Gore explained he was merely showing a progression. I honestly didn't know what that meant. I found it was sophistry at its best—clever and plausible, but finally misleading. (Gore would certainly reject that thought.) Every writer I have known is tough on the competition and Mailer was in the front line.

Gore's article was published in the *New York Review of Books* early in 1971.

The feud was exacerbated when Gore and Norman were invited to appear on a TV talk show, hosted by Dick Cavett, in November of 1971. Janet Flanner, a writer with *The New Yorker*, was also included.

Norman was seated in the dressing room being made up before the show. According to Norman, Gore entered, and what happened after that is unclear. But Norman did butt Gore on the forehead.

Gore, more often then not, is devastating on TV talk shows; he's sharp-tongued and more articulate than most talk-show showoffs. Norman can be formidable in the talk-show format; he's tough-minded, never relies on the cliché and is able to eloquently express complex ideas. My thought is that Norman, that night, using a lot of inner energy to control his anger, was not at his best.

Janet Flanner, a smart, quick-witted woman, hit Norman a couple of shots; when he's in an existential mood he can leave himself open to a fast jab. When he takes center stage and isn't completely focused, he can get hit.

The times I visited Gore in Ravelo, we'd drink into the early morning hours. Gore would be critical of Norman's actions and writing and I would try to counter. Howard Austen would cash in early, saying, "I heard it all before, over and over again. Goodnight," and head for his bedroom.

Norman called me in Rome in the early 70s, asking me to deliver an insulting message to Gore. I refused, telling him I wasn't a messenger boy. Two years went by before he spoke to me again. We finally agreed to meet in a New York restaurant. Buzz Farber and Rip Torn were witnesses to the reconciliation.

1971 Rome

Martin Balsom conquers Italy.

Now Martin Balsom fell in love with Italy . . .

It began with a call from the Italian director, Damiano Damiani. He asked if I knew Eli Wallach. Knew him? Will twenty years of friendship do? Damiano said, "Good, then you could be helpful. I have a screenplay I would like Signore Wallach to read, would you get the script to him? Time is important. Tell him it's for the part of the Police Commissioner. Okay?"

Eli had become an actor in great demand in Italy after Sergio Leone's film, *The Good the Bad and the Ugly,* in which Eli was beautiful in the part of the ugly. The picture was an international smash and Eli's salary ballooned.

Damiano got me the script, titled *Confessions of a Police Commissioner,* and I gave it to Eli. He was staying around the corner from my apartment, in the Hotel de la Ville. He read it, liked it, but Eli apparently had a play to do in the near future, so he turned Damiani's film down.

Damiano, an inherently angry man, added an octave to his voice as he scolded me when Eli passed. I asked him, "Why be angry with me? Call Eli and shout at him." Damiano said if he knew enough English he could have convinced Eli to do his film. And he probably would have.

And it was a hell of a good story. The part of the Police Chief of Palermo was a terrific part for an actor. It involved the Mafia, but in an intriguing, intricate way. Franco Nero, a well-known Italian actor, was to play the chief prosecutor.

Damiano was a superb director and was highly respected in the Italian cinema community. Given the excellent script, he just couldn't understand why Eli was not going to be in his film. He needed an American actor with a solid name to satisfy the investors. In order to comfort him, I put my head to the matter and came up with a brilliant idea—Ben Gazzara. Ben was not a kid anymore. In fact his hair was turning gray and his background was Sicilian. He had an excellent reputation as an actor and he was known internationally. Perfect!

Ben accepted the job. But he insisted the production hire his writer to work on his part. Reluctantly, the producers agreed, even though the budget was tight. I met Ben at his hotel the day he arrived in Rome. He was not in a merry mood.

His writer complained that he had been refused the right to change the structure of the script or even its title, that the structure was sacrosanct. He wanted the title to be one word: the name of Ben's character. That idea was shot down, so he quit.

Ben was angry. I told him the script was almost flawless and should not be tampered with. His writer was paid to work on the English dialogue—period.

Ben asked me what I thought the chances were of the film being sold in America. I didn't have the slightest idea and he said, "That's where fifty percent of my money would come from and if it isn't distributed in the States I'm doing the movie for peanuts. I'm going home."

"Ben," I said, now pissed off, "I suggested you for this movie. I live here and make a living here; I insist you go down to Palermo and tell your problems to Damiano. Then you can take a walk or stay and do the film."

"Is he tough?" Ben asked.

I made the mistake of telling him the truth: "He was the intercollegiate wrestling champ of Italy."

"Well, I don't care about that. I'm still going home," Ben said.

That was Saturday and Ben was expected in Palermo on Sunday. They had anticipated Ben's arrival by starting the shooting a couple of days earlier. I told Ben I wasn't leaving his room until he promised to fly to Palermo the next day. At three in the morning he promised. I left, feeling I had done my duty. But Ben flew back to New York several hours later.

The actor's agent in Rome representing Ben was Roger Beaumont, an ex-actor I helped convince become an agent. Representing Ben Gazzara for the Damiani film was Roger's first important negotiation and he was due to collect his first substantial fee. When he called me Sunday morning telling me that Ben had split for New York, he was in a panic. The producers had called him from Palermo asking when Ben was going to arrive. Roger mumbled something about Ben not feeling well, that he'd arrive the following day. But he was desperate; his first big deal and it had fallen apart in the worst possible way. His actor, after signing a contract, had walked. It was a hell of a way to start an agency. "What am I going to do?" Roger wailed.

I got a hundred watt flash: Martin Balsam. Marty was an old pal of mine and a very good actor.

Roger's first reaction made sense: "He's unknown in Italy, they want a name."

"For Chrissakes," I said, "he won the Academy Award for best supporting actor a few years ago, that ought to impress them." The producers (two young worriers) were going to be in serious trouble if they didn't find an actor immediately.

On Monday, the shit hit the fan; Damiano and the producers went ape. They couldn't afford to delay the shooting any longer and unless an acceptable actor suddenly appeared out of the blue, they'd be ruined.

But Roger had his ace—Martin Balsam. I had already called Marty in New York and, without seeing the script, he jumped at it. Roger calmly told the producers not to worry; he had the best actor for the part—Martin Balsam.

"Martin who?"

Roger, sure of himself, scolded the producer. "He won an Oscar, for God's sake. And you don't know him? For shame!"

"The Oscar? Oh. Can he come tomorrow?"

"He's on his way." Roger was now in control.

They accepted all of his terms. Before hanging up, the producer shouted, "Take his passport away as soon as he lands!"

But Marty had a problem—his wife. She had recently broken her leg ice-skating in Central Park. Marty had hired a full-time nurse, but she complained and demanded he turn down the job. Marty was not so easily moved by a wife with a broken leg. "You married an actor and you know that an actor goes where the work takes him. You're going to be well taken care of while I'm gone. Case closed." And Marty went to Palermo.

I was hired to write the English dialogue, interpret for Marty, and coach some of the actors.

The film was a smash hit in Italy but neglected by the small-time U.S. distributor. They had bought a film they simply didn't know how to handle and failed in their effort to get good screen time. So Ben Gazzara had a point.

The two young producers made a bundle. They produced a couple of more movies that went nowhere and quit before seeing the profits from their one success vanish.

Marty and Ben had the same business manager in New York. Their photos were hung on the wall and each time Marty visited his business manager, he bowed to Ben's photo and thanked him.

After the success of *Confessions of a Police Commissioner*, Marty became well-known in Italy and subsequently made about twenty-five Italian films. He was recognized wherever he went, usually greeted by strangers calling out. "Ciao, *Commissario!*"

Whenever Marty got bored in the States, he'd fly to Rome and stay in his favorite hotel for a month or two. His last stay in Rome was in 1996, where he was found dead in his apartment one morning.

My old friend Marty was a constant companion when in Rome. I can still imagine hearing his hearty laugh and his wry wit. Ciao, Commissioner!

1972 Rome—Spain

My Italian adventure producing a spaghetti western.

I fell for the Italian dream—to become a movie producer. As Mel Brooks might say, put your hand on a rock and shout, I am a movie producer! I had the connections, all I needed was the story.

For several years, spaghetti westerns were being made by the dozens, raking in money from all over Europe. I found a paperback western and contacted an active film producer I knew who made a fortune with westerns, all comic. He was unknown outside the industry; his name never appeared in the credits. For fiscal reasons it was a good ploy. And so, a fictitious name for my future partner—Luigi. He didn't read the paperback (it was in English), but he agreed to make the movie with me. He would need an American name actor and that actor was Eli Wallach, who was in great demand in Italy. Luigi knew Eli was an old friend of mine and so more prone to be in a movie I produced.

I called on a lawyer I knew who specialized in movie contracts to deal with Luigi for me. Luigi agreed to give me an executive producer credit, ten percent of the profits, and a small fee for following the film as the line producer.

The film was to be shot in Spain, and Luigi would visit every week or so. I accepted those minimum terms since Luigi was financing the film. He had the clout, due to his reputation among distributors around Europe, to presell the film even before the shooting started.

I flew to New York to meet with Eli and his agent to work out a deal. His agent asked for a heap of wampum. I didn't mind at all, but Luigi had to okay it. I called him in Rome and he said he'd be in New York the following day, not to worry, Eli will be in the film. He arrived and within five minutes agreed to everything Eli's agent demanded.

If Luigi had given me the okay over the phone I could have closed the deal. But I supposed it was a shrewd move flying to New York, because he sure impressed Eli as a hands-on producer.

I got Luigi to promise that I would work on the screenplay with the Italian writers. I knew there were low-level screenwriters who would work for peanuts and hand in like value. I also knew how Luigi operated: Once the cast and financing were set, his main concern was to save time and money, not the quality of the film. Two weeks after our conversation, he sprung the screenplay on me. He had paid the equivalent of eight thousand dollars (!) for two writers and the result was not particularly funny or dramatic, or even coherent. Luigi's promise was worthless.

I called Eli and told him my view of the screenplay. He asked what we could do about it and I said we would rewrite the dialogue as we shot. But I knew the problem was more than the dialogue. It was a hell of a way to begin my career as a film producer.

Franco Nero began his movie career as a western hero. He was young, attractive, and ambitious. The westerns he had made gave him a name in the industry. He was hired to costar with Eli.

Franco had met Vanessa Redgrave when they worked on *Camelot* together in Hollywood and they had become lovers. We needed an actress for our film and Franco suggested we hire Vanessa's sister, Lynn Redgrave, who was an excellent actress. And that was our cast, three solid film names.

Through all the years I've worked in the world of films there was never a production that didn't have serious problems. And we were no exception. One of the most important elements in making a movie is the choice of director. In Italy, after Sergio Leone, the most competent western director was Sergio Cobucci, a jovial, easygoing, technically sound director. I had worked with him and the one drawback (there's always one of those) was he rarely got to the set on time. He could be two or three hours late. Shooting outdoors, time is limited by the light, but he worked fast once he got to the set and he would keep, more or less, on schedule.

The other problem was that Sergio Corbucci was blackballed by Franco Nero. Franco had worked with Corbucci previously and got pissed off, claiming Corbucci paid more attention to his costar. He agreed that Corbucci was the best man for the job, but he would rather quit the film than work with him.

Duccio Tassari was a well-dressed gentleman, always pleasant and in a good humor, but he was not born to be a film director. He had little to say to actors and was not very adept technically. But he loved the job; the camaraderie, the status it gave him and the chance to fight young bulls. So he was ready to accept any film shot in Spain. And Franco didn't object, while acknowledging Duccio's lack of talent.

I must admit, Duccio had courage when facing the small bulls, but he also liked to celebrate every night when he hung out with bull-fighters, rolling into his hotel as late as four in the morning to catch a couple of hours sleep. He had a great time on the film, but what little skill he had as a director was lost in the fog of a hangover

Most directors working on a western come dressed for the job; usually jeans or something casual, but not Duccio. He wore a suit, shirt, and tie every day, including a fresh carnation pinned to his jacket lapel.

One morning, we had a scene involving several actors. Duccio seemed to be lost, incapable of knowing where to place the camera. He took me aside and said he needed four cameras to shoot the scene properly. "Have you lost your mind, Duccio? It's a simple scene, why do you need four goddamn cameras?—not that we have them."

"Oh, I want to cover every angle, understand?"

"No, I don't, but I'll give you two cameras and let's get this scene before the sun leaves for New York."

Eli and Lynn, two pros, had few complaints and diligently did their work. Franco, for half the film was, to all intents and purposes, absent. He and Vanessa Redgrave had had an ugly fight over her new boyfriend, so Franco's body was present but not his mind. Each evening I could hear him from across the courtyard of the hotel shouting angrily on the phone at Vanessa, insisting that she come to Madrid to meet with him. Finally, she agreed. I breathed a sigh of relief, hoping that Vanessa would cool Franco's passion so he could concentrate on the film.

Lynn picked Vanessa up at the airport and when they got to the hotel, Franco insisted she come up to his room. At first she refused, then, eager to get it over with, reluctantly agreed.

They talked, but Vanessa had dumped Franco for her new lover—end of story. She left and Franco, resigned, accepted the fait accompli and began acting the role he had signed to do.

Luigi would bring a paper bag to the set every week with twenty grand in it to pay certain expenses. It meant we had to sit in a hot trailer on the set and count it. It was more like a ritual because Luigi, having purposely shortchanged the twenty grand by about thirty bucks, it had to be recounted.

The completed film was ragged, had no pace and made little sense. The humor created by Eli and Lynn was its only saving grace.

The title in Italian and Spanish was *Viva la Muerta Tua*, a lousy title in English: *Long Live Your Death*. Eli came up with a much better title: *Don't Turn the Other Cheek*. Why? Because part of the plot was tattooed on Eli's buttock—half of a map to a hidden treasure.

The film had to be profitable for Luigi. He was given the funds in advance to pay for the shooting of the film and after that was paid off his participation in the gross receipts of the tickets sold from around Europe was all gravy.

He kept delaying opening his books to my lawyer to ascertain the value of my ten percent. And get this, my lawyer was conveniently out of town when Luigi seemed willing to show him the numbers. As the years passed, I gave up. My lawyer and Luigi were obviously in cahoots. I never saw a lire from my percentage.

Why not take it to court? The case wouldn't come up for at least seven years and Luigi was far too clever for me to get a favorable ruling.

That was the end of my film-producing career. The Italian motion picture producers are much too wily for an American innocent abroad. But I had a hell of a good time while it lasted.

1975 New York—Rome

Mailer and Leone, an unlikely mix.

W hen I had worked with Sergio Leone, he talked about making a gangster movie (*Once Upon a Time In America*) and said he needed an American writer. He wanted my advice. I had suggested Norman, and Sergio asked me to arrange a meeting.

Sergio, Norman, and I met in New York. Sergio briefed Norman on what kind of movie he wanted to make. He had bought the rights to a minor book written by an ex-hood. The value of the book was in the background details. Norman's agent, Scott Meredith, and Leone's lawyer made the deal and Norman was set to come to Rome to start writing the screenplay.

Norman had met Norris, his future wife, earlier in 1975 and she came along with him to Rome later that year. A friend of mine, Michela Prodan, fluent in English and Italian and had done my typing, became his secretary. Norman went to work in an office in Leone's suite in EUR, Mussolini's gift to Rome: a modern suburb, but an ugly representation of ancient Rome's heroic architecture. Having been designed by Italians, however, classier than the architectural monstrosity Stalin imposed on Moscow and East Berlin.

In Rome, Norman went to that office six days a week. Michela typed and subsequently began to translate the script from English into Italian. A few weeks later Leone sprung the surprise: He planned on making two films, not unlike the first two *Godfathers* and he expected Norman to write enough material for both films. Norman balked; an adjustment was in order. Finally he turned in a fat script spread over two films. Hollywood filmmakers had much to learn from Leone.

Leone was a master at framing images on the screen to tell his story. Sound easy?—It isn't. It takes great skill.

However, Leone's stories came from his childhood fantasies of western heroes and villains. His movies were more intense than American westerns. And he used the close-up effectively, enhancing the drama. His influence can be seen in westerns directed by Clint Eastwood and others.

Leone worshipped John Ford, the main reason we went to Monument Valley, Ford's preferred location, to shoot much of the exteriors. But there's a vast difference between Leone and Ford; Leone would never consider making a *Grapes of Wrath*, or any movie that had a social idea at its base. Yet Ford made that film and *The Informer* despite his political bent to the right.

Mailer's screenplay gave Leone a dish he couldn't possibly eat; it had serious social content. Mailer was due a payment after completing the screenplay (over two hundred pages). Leone and Grimaldi, Leone's coproducer, refused to honor the contract and make the payment. Norman's lawyer sued them in New York.

The Italian equivalent of *Time* magazine, *Express*, had an article quoting Signore Grimaldi, saying Mailer had written much of the treatment on toilet paper in his hotel room, and that work didn't merit further payment. To put it mildly, I was outraged; after all, I introduced Leone to Mailer. I called Leone and asked him if he was aware of what Grimaldi was plotting. He denied everything in the article. I had a right to grill him; I could see his Machiavellian hand guiding Grimaldo.

I then called Grimaldi and asked him if he had read the screenplay in English (the Italian translation wasn't near being completed),

I was sure he hadn't read it, his English was, for all practical purposes, inadequate.

He avoided answering, but I pressed him and he finally admitted that he hadn't read it, but he denied unrolling the toilet paper story, saying *Express* had invented it. I didn't believe him, it was well within the scope of Sergio's style; the more unlikely the lie, the more believable.

I wrote *Express* a letter that they published. In effect, I said all in the article was false and demanded a retraction. They didn't retract, but printed a vague, unclear response from Grimaldi.

Before the case went to trial, Leone called me exactly five times in one day, requesting I bear witness that Norman was negligent in writing the screenplay. He wasn't subtle in declaring that it would be worth my while. Five times I told him he was wrong; how the hell could he judge a script in English? I told him he'd be laughed out of the courtroom. Shut up and pay up, was my advice. Norman won the case.

As they say in Yiddish, "It's tough to make a living."

1976 New York—Rome—Paris—Santo Domingo

William Friedkin remakes the French Wages of Fear *into* Sorcerer.

I first met William Friedkin in New York at Elaine's Restaurant in the mid 1970s. He was sitting at a table in back of me and tapped me on the shoulder: "You're Mickey Knox and you were in . . ." and he rattled off many of the films I'd acted in. I asked him who he was and when he told me, I praised his direction of *The French Connection*. It was a hell of a good movie and I meant it.

A year later, he was in Rome and invited me to join him in his hotel for a chat. The chat was a job offer; he was going to do a remake of a French movie, *Wages of Fear,* an exact translation of the French title, *Salaire de la peur*, used when distributed in America several years earlier. Friedkin had made a very successful film, *The Exorcist*. It cleaned up at the box office, so he renamed *Wages of Fear* to *Sorcerer*, hoping I imagine, "exorcist" and "sorcerer," two eight-letter, similar sounding titles would be lucky for *Sorcerer*.

Roy Scheider was the lead but most of the other actors were French, Italian, Spanish, Arab. Fredkin wanted me as the dialogue director, to work with those actors so they could convincingly act in English.

He told me he had met Henri-George Clouzot (half the French nation has two first names), the French director of the original film, and suggested he remake his famous movie. Clouzot replied, "But

Monsier Friedkin, I have already made my film, why don't you remake it?"

Friedkin took the advice, obtained the rights and when he next met Clouzot he told him he would like to dedicate the movie to him. The Frenchman replied, "I would like to see the film first." Well, he didn't live to see the finished movie, but Freidkin, intent on keeping his word, if not Clouzat's caveat, dedicated *Sorcerer* to the Master. The movie, I believe, was not up to Friedkin's previous successes. It lacked the French feel, subtlety, and attitude for the subject. In fact, not many French films lend themselves to the culture and life experience of American directors.

The shooting started in Israel with an action sequence, leaving me in Paris to work with a Spanish and French actor, two principal players. Paris was icing on the cake on this gig; it could only have been more to my liking if we had shot the whole film there. The company returned from Israel and we remained in Paris for a few weeks shooting. Then we left for the Dominican Republic, a new location for me.

The Frazier-Foreman fight was going to be shown on large screen TV in Santo Domingo. The day before the fight, we were shooting deep in a forest, an hour from a phone. (No cellphones then.) Billy, a few of the crew, and I were talking about the fight. "I think Frazier has a chance against Foreman," I said. Foreman was the favorite by a large margin. Frazier had already had his three fights with Ali and was felt to be over the hill. My reasoning? It was probably Frazier's last chance at the big money and he might draw on powers within himself to overcome Foreman.

Billy jumped right in: "Put your money where your mouth is. A hundred bucks, Foreman takes him." I wasn't about to let him have the last word. After all, I didn't ask for a bet. "Seventy-five."

"One hundred!"

"Seventy-five or no bet."

"Okay, seventy-five," Billy finally agreed. We shook on it. I thought that sealed it. Ha!

A bunch of us went to see the fight, but Billy wasn't there. Frazier entered the ring and I knew he was a loser. He had shaved his head. Anything to get lucky. He lacked confidence and he lost the fight.

Back in the deep forest the next day, I handed Billy seventy-five bucks and he said, "Hold it, the bet was a hundred."

"You must be kidding, we agreed on seventy-five."

"Bullshit, you owe me twenty-five more."

I stared at him a moment, looked around for the fellas who heard us. A couple of them came over to see what the talk was about. I asked, "You guys know we bet seventy-five, you heard us yesterday, right?" They looked at each other, one was silent, the second guy shook his head and said, "I didn't hear about the bet." You bet he didn't. He would have been on the next plane out of there if he did.

"If you don't come up with the twenty-five, I'm deducting it from your check tonight." It was Friday, payday.

"I wouldn't do that if I were you." I was surprised at how calm I was. I'm generally confrontational, but somehow he didn't scare me. He could fire me, but he didn't scare me. I knew that if he deducted the twenty-five, I'd quit. Billy, it's still hard to believe, left the set to drive to a phone to notify the accountant to make the deduction. We lost an hour of shooting time.

The check was delivered to me in my hotel room. I opened the envelope; the stub of the check read, "minus twenty-five dollars fink tax." Fink tax? I've been many things, but never a fink.

I called Friedkin and said, "Billy, all my actors are as good as they'll get in English, so I'm not leaving you with a headache, but under the circumstances I have to leave the film."

He surprised me: "I'd do the same thing if I were you. I want you to know I'll always give you the highest recommendation if you ever need it."

I felt victorious, but something nagged at me. I had worked with the foreign actors for about four months and they knew their dialogue and their English was pretty good. Was it his way of cutting me loose without the need to fire me? If that was the case, he must have known a lot more about me than I knew myself. He had practically doubled my previous salary; did he want to cut down on the film's cost?

Early the following morning I got a call from the production office; a cable had come for me. I said to bring it over. The envelope was open; had Billy seen it? It was a cable from Sidney Pollack's casting agent asking if I could come right to Florence, Italy, where he was shooting a film and he needed me. I called the number she had included, and said I'd be on the next plane. Had Billy known about the job offer? In any case, the bet was the best thing that could have happened. No bet, no disagreement, no fink tax and if I hadn't quit the night before, I couldn't have taken the Pollack job. Go figure.

1976 Florence—Paris

Bobby Deerfield *with Al Pacino and Marte Keller, directed by Sidney Pollack.*

Florence is a city I used to visit alone. I'd actually buy a guidebook and follow the paths it laid out. There are small churches with one masterpiece that had to be seen. I'd spend three days walking through the old town, which hasn't changed much since the Renaissance, stopping at museums and churches. Oh, yes, the food. That was a good thing too. Heavier meals than one gets in Rome, but the aromas, the tastes, the bean soup; what the hell, three days of gorging won't kill you—if you walk it off.

I was in Florence to work on *Bobby Deerfield*, directed by Sidney Pollack, starring Al Pacino. Filming had already begun and I was called to specifically work with Marte Keller, the female lead opposite Pacino. I have a "puoblem," she told me (and I mean "puobem"). That's what words with the letter R sounded like when Marte spoke them. She also told me, in effect, to leave her alone. She can't change the way she speaks.

I couldn't go to Sidney and tell him she won't work with me, it's no excuse. I had to figure out how to get her to reasonably pronounce Rs. It took me a couple of days experimenting until the solution came to me. I asked her to give me a chance and listen.

Al Pacino was a race car driver and in the film, she kept saying, you are chasing "uabbits." I trilled the R in rabbit by vibrating my

tongue against my upper teeth and held the trill for about three seconds, then slowly repeated rabbit, cutting the time of the trill to a
split second.

Marte resisted trying it, saying it was "uidiculous," but I pressed
her to give it a shot; come hell or high water, I was determined to get
her to trill. She finally gave it a reluctant effort. I assured her it would
work, "You're an actress, you can do anything, trust me on this, give
it your best effort."

After several serious attempts, Marte got it. But then she said, "It
sounds like an Italian accent." Not at all, I told her; John Gielgud,
the famous English actor, trilled the hell out of his Rs and if she likes
I can get a recording of Hamlet's soliloquies to prove it. She nodded,
smiled, and said, okay and we got along fine for the rest of the film.
Pollack was pleased as Punch, having probably believed she'd never
get it.

I was on the film a couple of months. We moved from Florence to
Paris, and then spent the rest of the time on the racetracks. I even
had a part in the film, just one scene, not expected, but appreciated.

I had little to do with Al Pacino. We didn't speak much. He didn't
speak much to anyone. I understood that. He's a special kind of actor,
extremely talented and serious about his work. Talking on a set dis-
sipates an actor's concentration.

However, a couple of days before the shooting ended, we had a
pleasant chat. He was sitting alone in the hotel coffee shop when I
came in. He asked me to join him. He had been to the Actor's Studio
too, so we had grounds for conversation. When we worked together
again in Rome, he was generous with his hugs and warm in his
friendship.

I got along with Sidney. I has always admired his films, never two
the same genre and his locations always varied; Africa, the Rockies,
Japan, all fascinating, all treated with insight and imagination.

Besides directing, Sidney became an indie producer with considerable power to make films of his choosing. At one time I had an
option on a treatment written by an Italian screenwriter, Ugo Pirro,

who had won two Oscars plus several Cannes and Venice film festival awards.

I thought Sidney might consider it as one of his future projects. It was material he had never done before, about Al Capone as a young man growing up in New York before going to Chicago. The meeting was cordial until I told him I thought, all things being equal, the treatment could be the basis for a successful film. I had touched a nerve. Sidney's eyes stared at me and he said, "You just lost ten points!"

I was offended and speechless. I didn't reply, but Christ, I wouldn't be in his office if I didn't believe the film had the potential to be a winner.

Sidney did read the treatment as did the people that work for him. They gave it serious consideration, but passed.

Is arrogance necessarily an adjunct to power? If Sidney ever reads this and mutters, asshole, there's your answer.

1979 Rome—Dublin—Nice

Terence Young casts me as admiral of the fleet in Inchon.

While living in Italy, my favorite director was Terence Young, not because he was the best director I worked with, but because he always wanted me in his films.

Terence made his name directing the first two James Bond movies. They were enormously successful and he got much of the credit.

On the set, he was a well-bred gentleman. Never angry, a neat English sense of humor, and always dressed as a proper Englishman should be: tailored suits and shirts and expensive Sulka ties, shoes always shined.

I got a call from him one day saying he wanted me for a part in *Inchon*, a movie about the Korean War starring Laurence Olivier as General MacArthur. He said you're the best American actor in Rome. "Oh, sure," I replied, "I'm the only one left, that's why."

I went to Cinecittà, the movie studio, to meet with Terence. He took me aside and whispered, "Name your rate. The Korean government is paying." I doubled my salary.

My role was as the admiral of the fleet. I was sent to the costume department to be fitted for my uniform. *They got it all wrong, I thought, I'm too young to be an admiral.* Then, dressed as the admiral, I looked into a full-length mirror. I stared at the image in disbelief. I was an admiral.

One scene was unforgettable.

The highest-ranking military officers of the American forces in Korea were seated in a large room, waiting for General MacArthur to brief us on his decision to land troops at Inchon, a seaport behind the enemy lines. I was seated in the front row in my admiral uniform.

From the day he arrived in Rome to start the shooting, Olivier appeared to be in poor health, he had a nurse with him at all times, helping him walk and get around. He also thought he had cancer of the leg. When he finally entered the briefing, aided by his nurse, he was hunched over, shuffling to his mark to face us. Terence asked, "Are you ready, Larry?" In a barely audible, weak voice, Olivier answered, "Yes, Terence, I am." He took the corncob pipe out of his mouth and straightened to a ramrod military posture. Olivier waited for several moments after Terence called action, then shifted into high gear. In a loud, full, healthy voice that reverberated throughout the room, he began his speech:

> We are going to land on the Inchon beach in force. And we shall succeed! We have God on our side, he is with us and we cannot fail. I will not tolerate failure! And gentlemen, you will aid me in this noble action. And we shall succeed!

And so on. They aren't the exact words but they're close enough.

His actor's energy was startling. He brought tears to my eyes and sent shivers down my spine. When he finished the speech, which was long for any actor, he slumped down once again and was helped out of the room.

I was puzzled. At breakfast where the company ate together in the hotel restaurant, he was jolly and ate a grand breakfast: kippers, eggs, bacon, potatoes, several slices of toast, a fruit cup, a snifter of brandy. The works. He also swam far out in the Mediterranean every morning. "Good for me leg," he said.

I told Olivier I had seen him do *Richard the Third* in London during the war. He was genuinely pleased and said it was his favorite performance. I mentioned that his duel to the death with Richmond was still in my memory. Ralph Richardson, who played Richmond, was an actor I had always admired. "Oh, dear, old Ralph, he had been rehearsing for Richmond most of his life," Olivier said cutely.

I had a week's work filming in Rome, then about a month later, out of the beautiful blue, I got a call from Terence, asking if I was free to come to Dublin for a week to shoot an added scene. Oh boy, was I free!

Another week's work in Dublin, paid in cash by a serious Korean who spoke no English. He was clearly pained as he counted out the green. I almost gave it back to him. Then I came to my senses.

Old Terence knew the ropes. He probably made enough during that week to pay his expenses for the year. He was a high liver.

Pub crawling is a fine Irish sport. Sport because the sporty Irishman will drink until loaded enough to test his pugilistic skills. There's always a reason to fight: losing an argument, disliking a drinking companion, angry at a pub owner, or just feeling the itch to throw a punch.

In Dublin, one evening, I found myself standing at the bar next to a small elderly gent, his cap set at a rakish angle. He had merry eyes, talked a blue streak, and bought me a drink. I returned the compliment. After a couple of rounds, he turned to me, his eyes bright, and challenged me. "Let's you and me go outside and mix it up, eh lad?"

Delighted with himself, he smiled and cocked his head. The last thing I wanted that evening was a fight with a jolly Irishman. "I don't fight people I don't know. Gotta know 'em to fight 'em, right?"

He looked me in the eye, laughed and agreed, "Right, me lad." We drank on it and I staggered back to the hotel.

Inchon had a short run. In order to attract an audience, the Korean producers declared they would give a million dollars to the ticket holder who got the lucky number. Even that didn't help and the film died. I never heard of anyone winning the million.

Fifteen years earlier, in 1964, Terence had been shooting a film in the South of France for the United Nations called, *A Poppy is More than a Flower*. He called me in Rome and asked if I could come to Nice and do some dubbing for him. The U.N. was paying my expenses but no salary, so I went to Nice.

It was a film dramatizing the danger of drugs, especially heroin. It was a full-length movie starring many name actors who had volunteered to act in the film without pay.

I did get a bonus, if no salary. One of my favorite actors, Trevor Howard, was in the film. He was a superb actor with style and panache. We soon became drinking mates (except for his morning double-shot).

Among the scenes I had to dub was one with Marcello Mastroianni and Amadeo Nazzari, a well-known Italian actor. They spoke Italian in the scene and I had to dub them into English. I was going to revoice Nazzari. I asked Terence, "Who's going to revoice Marcello?"

"You," he said. "But I'm doing Nazzari. You want me to do both actors talking to each other?"

"Sure, you can do it," he said and walked out of the dubbing room. I revoiced the two actors and felt like I was talking to myself.

1980 Rome

Acting with Sophia Loren in her life story.

S ophia Loren was the sweetheart of the western world during three decades. She had worked with major American movie stars: Cary Grant, Clark Gable, and Frank Sinatra lead the list. Sophia and Marcello Mastroianni were a delightful film couple (the Italian Spencer Tracy and Katherine Hepburn), and were loved by all Italian filmgoers.

How could you not love Sophia, a woman who must have found a role in many a man's fantasies? A beautiful, intelligent face and a lush disconcerting figure were partly responsible for her long career as an actress, but her natural acting talent did not hurt.

Peter Katz, the American producer of *The Sophia Loren Story*, a film for TV, hired me in Rome to act in it. The script started in the 1920s when a Hollywood producer had gone to Italy in search of a Garbo look-a-like. I played that producer. Sophia played her mother, and later in the story played herself.

I was in the first day's shooting, a scene in which I was interviewing Sophia, playing the mother. After a couple of takes the director admonished Sophia in front of the cast and crew, "Listen, Sophia, cut the 'ands,' 'buts,' 'ahs,' and pauses, when speaking your dialogue. Okay?"

Sophia stared at him hard, then walked off the set.

In her dressing room, she met with Peter Katz, Carlo Ponti's son, the Italian producer, and others involved in the production. She wanted the director fired but she was talked out of it. Fire the director on the first day? He had many credits and wasn't a newcomer. It's bad news to fire an experienced director. They would have to go to Hollywood to recruit someone else. The production would be shut down until someone came aboard. The cost would be considerable.

She returned to work. I had a long speech in that scene. After the first take, the director told me exactly what he told Sophia: "I don't want you to uh . . . uh, add any ahs, buts, uh . . . uh, and, and . . . and no pauses. And . . . oh . . . don't wrinkle your forehead . . . uh . . . you got that?"

Is he nuts? I thought. I told him, "While telling me not to use ahs ands and buts, you interrupted yourself several times with ahs and ands. That's the way people generally speak. You just proved it."

"Just do as I . . . ah . . . ah, say, okay." he said, as he ground his teeth. Sophia and I exchanged complicit looks.

When Sophia greeted me the following morning, she gently pulled my head to her ample bosom and held it there, assuring me of our complicity.

Sophia had the best qualities of the Italian woman—warm, earthy, intelligence, nourished by female instinct, the freedom to express emotions, and the love of laughter. Add actor's talent and you have Sophia Loren.

I had one very good scene, two days work and paid on the spot. It was the kind of job that goosed my spirits and sent me home a happy actor.

1981 Hollywood

The Italian "divo," Luciano Pavarotti, makes his first film.

T he pleasant side of being an itinerant film worker is you get calls that break up the monotony and offer a new adventure each time out. Of course the daily monotony is broken by anxiety when those calls do not come. This call came from Alain Bernheim, a very old friend.

He contacted me in Rome from Hollywood to tell me he was producitng Luciano Pavarotti's first film, *Ciao Giorgio*. Shooting had already begun, but after seeing the first few days work, Alain, Franklin Shafner, the director, and the MGM execs were troubled by Luciano's poor English. Hence the call from Alain.

Alain was French and came to the States after the Nazi Army occupied Paris, where he and his family lived. Paris was not the place to be for Jews. The Bernheims were fortunate to make their way to Marseilles, then sail to North Africa. From there they eventually went to Portugal and finally, America. Alain joined the Free French Army where he was trained as a paratrooper and sent back to North Africa. Being bilingual, he was assigned to the First Airborn Division as an interpreter.

We were both in our twenties when we met in Hollywood. He became a very good and successful literary agent before graduating to being a producer.

My first day on the set I watched Pavarotti act in front of the camera. After the scene was over, he took me aside and wanted to know my reaction (we spoke Italian at all times). I hid my embarrassment and dodged the question. He sensed what I was thinking and offered this explanation: "No one told me I had to walk and talk at the same time."

Of course! It was a punch line to actor jokes. But Luciano didn't know that. He meant it. Opera singers rarely, if ever, walk as they sing or speak when they perform. I had seen Luciano sing in opera on television and when he had to walk across the stage he never spoke or sang until he was firmly planted.

He was a hell of a tenor, but not a persuasive actor. Talented actors are eager to do anything to enrich their performance. Most of the actors I coached worked hard to achieve the perception that they spoke English well even though they had an accent. Many of them, Italian, French, German, and Spanish could not even converse in simple English, but you wouldn't know that watching them perform.

Pavarotti was unwilling to give me time to work with him, which created a serious problem. His answer to my frustration: "I work hard all year performing in concerts and opera. This film is my vacation. They are paying me half a million dollars to rest from opera and enjoy myself and that is what I intend on doing."

"But aren't you concerned with your performance in this film?" I asked.

He shrugged, Italian style, meaning, yes . . . sort of. Then said, "Singing is my only concern." Oh boy, they brought me here from Rome to get this guy to act in reasonably good English and the first day on the job, I hit a brick wall. It's the first time I heard someone claim that making a movie, as the lead actor, is being on vacation.

I tried getting him ten minutes at a time. I didn't want to overwork the great tenor; he'd give me five minutes and quit for the day. He learned nothing. It was a problem I had never faced before as a dialogue director and it frustrated me. I did something I only did once before; I asked the director to intervene. Franklin Shafner spoke to Luciano, but it was useless.

I finally resorted to the tape recorder. I had used the recorder when my time was limited to work with an actor. But Luciano rarely used it.

Pavarotti had charm and was friendly as long as I didn't bother him with that goddamn English.

1981–82 Soviet Union

The making of the Ten Days that Shook the World. *Discovering the hard facts of life in the Soviet Union.*

Ten years before the fall of the Soviet Union, I flew into the Moscow airport to start work on a movie. An Italian film company had made a coproduction deal with Mosfilm, the Soviet Union's film entity, to make *Ten Days that Shook the World*, adapted from John Reed's book. (Warren Beatty's version of Reed's experience during the Russian revolutions, *Reds*, had opened to excellent reviews in the States a couple of months earlier.)

The Italians had hired me to work on the screenplay, adapt all the dialogue into English from Italian, coach the actors, and play Lincoln Steffens, one of the first American muckraking journalists. He wrote from the late 1800s into the 1930s to disturb and disrupt the politics of his time.

Lincoln Steffens, on a visit to Russia soon after the victorious Bolshevik revolution, made his memorable, if untimely, observation: "I have seen the future and it works." He was John Reed's mentor and inspiration.

At the Moscow airport, right off the bat, I had an encounter with a minor Soviet customs officer. He picked *Time* magazine out of my carry-on, flipped through the pages, suddenly froze, his mouth and eyes opened in disbelief. He then pointed to a cartoon of Brezhnev looking like a gorilla.

The custom officer growled ugly sounds of disgust, then proceeded to lecture me in Russian, waving his finger in my face. No doubt, he kept the magazine to show his buddies for a good comradely laugh.

Moscow was only a stop on the way to Leningrad where for the next three months much of the film was to be shot. Leningrad had suffered enormous destruction during the two-year siege by the German Army in World War II. After the war, it had been rebuilt exactly the way it was before the war, a beautiful city.

A bit of history: Peter the Great, in 1703, decided to create a city on marshland on the Gulf of Finland. The new city would be a major port and the capital of Russia, St. Petersburg. Italian and French architects were brought in to design a spacious city of classical beauty.

Given the slow and casual pace of shooting the film, I had time to walk much of the city. The days were mostly gray and in my mind's eye I still see Leningrad as the gray city. The people were friendly and forthcoming, identifying me as an American no matter where I went. The women were, for the most part, chunky, due to their crappy diets, but they were generally cheery. The men were pasty-looking, many serious vodka drinkers and usually glum. Most of the young people I met were openly anti-Soviet and unafraid to speak out.

One of the wonders of the city is the Hermitage, the world famous art museum. It was formerly the Czar's winter palace, stormed by the Bolsheviks in 1917, a turning point of the Russian Revolution. The takeover of the Winter Palace was re-created for the movie by thousands of Soviet soldiers and local workers, a scene I will always remember for the intensity of its players.

The soldiers transformed into the sailors, peasants, and workers of the period, clamoring emotionally to force the gates of the winter palace. They weren't only re-creating that day, they were living it.

The Mosfilm people treated me like royalty, giving me a good-sized suite in one of the old, attractive hotels and supplying me with fresh caviar during my time in Leningrad. I had a refrigerator that held hard-boiled eggs, sour cream, vodka, and caviar. That was my breakfast—fit for a czar.

Sergei Bondarchuk, the well-known director of the Russian-made movie, *War and Peace,* was assigned to direct the film. He was an amiable man but a pedestrian director, thus making life easy for us in the crew and cast. He would rarely get to work before ten or eleven in the morning and we'd quit early. It took him four years to make *War and Peace!*

But he was a good Communist and a member of the Soviet governing body. As an important Party member, he had a spacious apartment, a cook, and a chauffeur-driven car. And he had power. I was denied a visa for the Soviet Union when I was in Rome. Bundarchuk called the Soviet Embassy and demanded that they give me the visa or he would not begin the filming. It was in my hands that day.

The Hermitage was closed to the public for a few days while we shot the interior scenes. I wandered around the empty museum and was struck by its wonder: alone in a room of Rembrandts, one fully senses the genius of the man; two rooms, (not usually available to the public) contained the final Picasso paintings—all scenes of startling sun colors in the South of France, radiating warmth and the "lightness of being."

There were also many of my favorite impressionist painters; paintings I hadn't seen before. I learned that being alone in a roomful of such beauty is a rare gift. For reasons I can't fathom, that intimacy seems to give life that is palpable to those paintings.

I wandered in the basement of the Hermitage and it pissed me off to see several Marc Chagall paintings leaning against the wall, willy-nilly. Why weren't they hung in the daylight of the upper floors? Did the ugly head of anti-Semitism condemn those lovely paintings of Russian Jewish life into darkness?

I went to the museum of the revolution and there it was as clear as day: a three-foot-square "loose-leaf notebook" fastened to the wall so the leaves could swing back and forth freely. They contained hundreds of photographs of "Heroes of Revolution," each noting their birth and death. It was no surprise that among so many of those who died (executed?) during the years (late 1930s) of the infamous Stalinist-instigated trials, many were Jewish "heroes."

Leon Trotsky's name was nowhere to be found in the Museum of Heroes, or anywhere else in Soviet literature, or journalism, yet he had been undoubtedly a leading "hero" of the revolution.

After Lenin died in 1924, Trotsky lost power to Stalin, who finally had him deported in 1929. He was assassinated by a Stalinist agent in Mexico in 1940. In the Soviet Union, Trotsky was a nonperson since his exile.

It surprised me when I was handed a scene of John Reed interviewing Trotsky, which is in his book, but the scene written for the film was a complete fabrication. It was crudely translated from Russian into English. I had to clean it up and adapt it to make some sense of it.

How did Bondarchuk get the okay to shoot a scene with Trotsky? Though he had considerable muscle in the party, I was convinced the decision to keep the scene in the film would be made in the upper levels of the government hierarchy.

The day came to shoot the scene and the surprises never ended. There was Trotsky in the flesh, well, someone else's flesh, but to use an old cliché, he was the spitting image of Trotsky. The actor must have been trained in the Stanislavsky method; he seemed absorbed in conveying an unsmiling, grim character long before the scene even started. Although Trotsky was reported to have had a keen sense of humor, this actor paced the sound stage, stern-faced, his hands clasped behind his back, looking or speaking to no one.

But that was part of the game: the scene starts with Trotsky seated at a desk, his forehead cupped in his hands as he listens to John Reed. He then slowly stands and goes to the window, his fingers caressing his temples as if in some pain. He returns to the desk and stares at Reed, as he rubs his forehead. And when he speaks, it is in a halting, mumbling, low voice.

He was playing a mentally disabled Trotsky! A mad Trotsky! A planned, inaccurate portrait of the real man. How else was Bondarchuk allowed to even suggest Trotsky's rise to power as the head of the Soviet army (he was in uniform in the scene). The sequence was not in the finished film. Was it filmed for the archives as the real McCoysky to prove that Trotsky was a dangerous madman? After all, the actor playing John Reed, Franco Nero, was only photographed from behind and could easily be accepted as the John Reed.

We left Leningrad for Moscow to complete the film. But I felt weird in Moscow, I experienced a free floating sense of fear. The strangeness, the "Easternness" of the Kremlin, the onion bulbs, for some crazy reason unnerved me. The long silent lines of bundled-up men and women in fur hats, in subfreezing weather, waiting to gaze, in passing at Lenin's dead face gave me shivers. I didn't join that line. I didn't want to enter that tomb. I looked on the gray, solid ugliness of the Stalin-style architecture, including my huge hotel, with dismay. Although, for the most part, the people on the streets were friendly, they seemed alien to me.

The scene I was in, as Lincoln Steffens, was shot on the Gulf of Finland on a strip of the coast that had summer homes. It was supposed to represent Provincetown, where Steffens, Reed, and Eugene O'Neill spent time together. Unfortunately that scene was cut out, and joined the Trotsky sequence somewhere in the mysterious corridors of the Soviet Union.

For months after I returned to Rome, the moments, sights, and encounters I experienced in the Soviet Union kept replaying in my mind's eye. I had a view of the country one could only get by living and working there. However, I was there during the harsh Russian winter when everything looked bleak, but I have to admit that the Russians I got to know were resilient and their spirits generally high.

1983 Rome—London—Spain
Working with John and Bo Derek.

The Golden Couple—John Derek and Ursula Andress. They were beautiful to look at walking down the Via Veneto in Rome during the 1960s, their arms around each other's lower waist, her hand deep in his back pocket, his hand cupping her buttock. It wasn't offensive. Rather it had a slight sexual charm. The Via Veneto, made famous by Fellini's film, *La Dolca Vita,* was at its height of popularity. The "Beautiful People" crowded the outdoor cafes. They were a sophisticated bunch, blasé to everyone but themselves. But even they could not resist staring at the Golden Couple in admiration as they sashayed down the Veneto.

Sometime in 1983, John called me in Rome from Los Angeles. He was then married to Bo, wittingly creating a second-generation "Golden Couple." They had met in 1973. She was sixteen, and if you saw the film *Ten* you know how unbelievably alluring she was. I had met her once when they were in Rome and the three of us had lunch. John did most of the talking. Bo was mostly silent. I was impressed. John had changed. He was open, confident, assertive, unlike thirty-five years earlier when we first worked together on the movie *Knock on Any Door.*

He had called to ask about Fabio Testi, an Italian stuntman turned actor. Fabio was handsome and had a pleasant demeanor. He had become one of Italy's leading men after appearing in several films.

John wanted to know if Fabio was a good actor. He was thinking about hiring him for the male lead in a picture he was scheduled to make. Fabio had come to acting by good looks and chance. But I told John he was an improved actor. I had seen him in the latest picture he had made, playing a Neapolitan gangster and he was surprisingly good. He had a pretty good director, which helped.

It wasn't difficult to figure out how John knew about Fabio, a purely Italian invention, made for Italy. He was Ursula Andress's former lover. She suggested him for the role. After hearing from me, he hired Fabio.

John and Bo asked if I would join them as the dialogue director. The movie was called *Bolero*. Yes, taken from the music in *Ten*, Bo's big hit. It made sense; it contributed to the success of the film. Why not title the film *Bolero*?

We started shooting in London. Night shooting. First scene: Bo in a limo with a girlfriend in a rather long dialogue scene. John was not only the director, he was also the lighting cameraman and camera operator. He was a hell of a good photographer. To wit; his sensual, on-the-edge layouts in *Playboy* of Ursula and Bo (not the same issue). But he took on a heavy load in *Bolero*.

Just being a camera operator, a key job, is tough enough. It takes years of training and experience to achieve the necessary skills. John did know about lighting, but that too is a full-time job. A committed director is totally involved in bringing a screenplay to life on film. That too is a full-time job, but John saw everything in life as a challenge to be conquered.

Whatever the reason, the first night of shooting started off badly. John was tense, nervous. He had the normal kind of trouble lighting the interior of the limo at night. After watching a couple of rehearsals through the camera, he knocked me for a loop by the harsh criticism he hurled at Bo. To put it mildly, he wasn't pleased with the way she had played the scene and ended by threatening to quit: ". . . and get yourself another director!" John shouted to make sure everyone on the set knew exactly how he felt. Bo scrambled out of the limo, pale-faced, desperately holding back tears and ran to her trailer.

I had never seen that side of John. Of course I hadn't seen much of him during all those years since we had played brothers in *Saturday's Hero* in 1949. I knew he loved Bo deeply, so his outburst surprised and puzzled me.

Well, I thought, one day into the movie and home I go. I was standing in back of John musing about staying over in London for a couple of days before returning to Rome.

John suddenly whirled, still gripped by the tentacles of simmering rage. He stared at me and shouted, "Got any goddamn ideas?"

"Sure. I'll talk to her," I answered, being well-known for my quick, bright responses.

I trudged over to her trailer, wondering what the hell was going on. I knocked and was let in by Bo's mother who, on this job, was also her makeup artist.

Bo was crying.

I stood in the trailer feeling extraneous. Finally, I sat down facing her and spoke to her about acting and how I might be able to help if she'd let me talk her through the scene as John shot it and to hell with the sound. We can always dub her voice in later.

After working in Italian films for so many years, I learned how useful it was to coach an actor as he's performing. All the great Italian directors were marvelous at it: De Sica, Rosselini, and Fellini talked their actors and nonactors through their scenes whenever necessary.

She must have felt reassured and dried her tears. Her mother fixed her makeup and she walked back to the set with a determined step.

I told John what I was going to do. He said, "Do what you gotta do. We'll dub the sound in later."

The scene came to life. Bo gained confidence as I whispered for her to take her time, to listen, not to anticipate her dialogue. More energy. Look at her girlfriend, listen to what she's saying. Don't hurry, think before responding.

As the scene progressed, she seemed to grasp how to really listen, to respond. It worked and John, although silent, went on to the next setup. He was his old self once again; polite, respectful.

That night, I think, I gave Bo the feeling that she could do it. I believe she began to understand how she could use a tool or two I gave her when acting. It's tough on actors who have had no formal training, unless one is a born actor (Marlon Brando). Actors need to learn how to concentrate, to listen, to recall life experiences that can be used in a scene. Of course that's only the beginning; acting is a complicated process but with experience the complications fall away and you do it. Acting, finally, is doing.

The filming went along fairly smoothly. We were in Spain when the first unwelcome situation developed. Fabio Testi came to Madrid, bursting with his own importance. He told me that he felt confident his first appearance in the big American film would surely make him an international star.

Fabio had changed. He was playing the star. A big mistake. It was "faccia"—front—very Roman. A bit of humility would have gone a long way.

Fabio was shooting his first scene. I had noticed a sore on his upper lip. Herpes? I didn't say anything. Bo hadn't noticed it and I'm surprised that John hadn't seen it while peering through the finder. Finally, Bo called out to Dere (short for Derek).

"Dere, you see the sore on Fabio's lip?" John sprinted to join her in examining Fabio's upper lip. Fabio weakly said he cut himself shaving, but it was clearly not a cut. The makeup lady said he sent her out to find some medicine for herpes that morning. The shooting was suspended for the day. Fabio was sent to visit a doctor. The doc said the herpes test will take a few days, but it sure looked like herpes. Since the script called for intimate lovemaking scenes between Bo and Fabio, and since herpes is highly contagious, John and Bo decided to send Fabio back to Rome.

There's nothing like a hot shower to wash away the day's dust. I made the mistake of answering the phone (fancy hotels have phones in the bathroom). I was bare-assed, dripping hot water and Bo's voice was urgent: "John and Fabio are going to get into a fight. Come down right away!"

"I'm taking a shower. Give me five minutes," I said.

In the lobby, Fabio was seated and weeping. John stood over him, surprised at the tears, but unrelenting. Fabio wiped the tears away and pleaded with John to keep him on the film. No dice.

Now comes the good part: Bo tells us that soon after arriving in Madrid, Fabio made a serious play for her body. He told her he had worked with most European leading ladies and they were all delighted with his performance, especially in the bedroom.

Fabio went back to Rome nursing his wounded ego.

Bo, John, and I had a meeting. Who will replace him? It's difficult to shoot around the part because of the logistics. We were due to move to various locations around Spain, which meant a new actor had to be found "yesterday" as every producer likes to say when in trouble.

I usually get brilliant ideas in times of crises, like "Come to Rome and I'll find you an actor in a minute." The Dereks believed me. Well, not unlike Ralph Kramden, I opened my big mouth once again.

I called several actors' agents I knew in Rome to line up the prospects. One of the agents suggested a young actor with a pretty name: Andrea Occhipinti. I told him he was way too young. The man in the film should be in his forties. That's what the story called for—a young girl falls for a middle-aged bullfighter. Occhipinti was in his midtwenties. The agent begged me to see Andrea as a personal favor. So I said, okay, but I doubted he'll be seen by the Dereks.

So we flew to Rome. Bo and John checked into a hotel around the corner from my apartment. The actors were to be interviewed in my living room.

Fifteen interviews—fifteen strike-outs. The gloom in my living room was palpable. Not one of them impressed the Dereks. In fact, except for the few name actors, almost all comedians, there wasn't a pool of good actors in Rome. I knew that, but I believed in small miracles.

I had Occhipinti sit outside on the terrace. I forgot about him. All the other actors were gone. John and Bo were silent, deflated. What the hell to do? They couldn't afford a major name and time was awasting, costing a goodly sum every day. Feeling guilty, I kept my mouth shut.

Facing the terrace were two large picture windows. Bo saw Andrea on the terrace and asked who he was. I said he was too young. His agent insisted we see him. I had Andrea come into the living room to introduce him and Bo and John before leaving. Bo poked John and said, "Isn't he the actor we saw on television in that Italian movie a couple of months ago? You remember, we thought he was good-looking and a pretty good actor." (That movie was adapted from the book *Charterhouse of Palma,* by Henri Stendhal.)

John was one of the best-looking actors when he started in the movies. And he had an eye for beauty. To wit; his wives, however, he didn't want Occhipinti, a handsome young actor, because the part demanded a middle-aged man.

Painted into a corner, he had no choice. We had to get back to Spain and shoot the movie. He finally agreed. He'd rewrite the script to accommodate a younger leading man.

The small miracle. I was off the hook. (But hang on: Folly was not to be denied.)

Back in Spain, Andrea had, we thought, an easy scene for the first day. He was in the stables, tending to his horses. He answered the phone, but he was incapable of speaking in a normal voice. He was 'acting.' It sounded as if he was pretending to talk to someone. John shot a few takes and quit. Frustration had turned him red. I wondered if he had high blood pressure. Into the breach once again. I offered to talk to Andrea.

(The Dereks saw him on TV, but it wasn't Andrea's voice. He was dubbed by a professional American actor.)

I took him aside and talked about acting. He seemed puzzled so I went to the basics. He still didn't get it. I had struck out.

I patted him on the shoulder and sent him back into action. After the first take, I took a walk.

At the production office in Madrid that evening, Andrea sat looking up timidly at the fuming Derek standing over him. "Why the fuck didn't you tell me you couldn't act when I hired you?" he shouted.

I stared at him in disbelief, then burst out laughing: "John are you fucking crazy? You wanted him to tell you he couldn't act? Shit man, ease up, will ya?"

I think if Andrea had made a move to get at John, John would have strangled him.

There was no choice but to continue with Andrea. It was impossible to search for another actor. John turned to me. "Okay, you direct him, I'll just handle the camera. You do all the talking."

More or less, that's the way it went. Andrea, after a time, got some confidence and didn't do badly.

We got to the final scene, in which Bo and Andrea were nude, simulating lovemaking. Before we even got started, John was unhappy with Andrea's body; too slim, not enough muscle definition. As I said, John loved beauty. Bo was beautiful with a terrific body and he demanded that the lovemaking scene have a gorgeous look.

I told him Andrea was wiry and strong. He beat everyone at armwrestling. "I don't give a shit, I want to see definition," he said.

"Okay, send him to Hollywood to a bodybuilder, that'll do it." I was kidding. John wasn't. He sent Andrea to Hollywood for two weeks of body building.

The production shut down while we all waited for Andrea to come back carrying sufficient muscle. I went to Rome to await the call to return to the front.

After two weeks, I got the call from the production manager. I didn't know why he was whispering until I heard him say: "Occhipinti came back with fifteen pounds of added muscle . . . and herpes." Herpes? Oh shit.

The bodybuilding worked as John said it would. He knew the

bodybuilder at MGM to be a whiz at quickly creating lats, pecs, biceps, triceps, etc. But what whiz bequeathed herpes to Andrea? (Exactly where Fabio's sore was.) When they signed Andrea, he was examined by the insurance doctor who made him swear that he never had herpes. We'll never know if he told the truth or picked it up in Hollywood. However, the makeup artist found a way to effectively cover the sore up.

Back to Madrid: The only people allowed on the set were Bo, Andrea, John, me, and the soundman. After all, Bo was bare-assed naked. It was the hottest day ever in Madrid. Andrea dripped sweat. Nerves added to heat, he was bathed in it. Bo, of course, refused to kiss him on the mouth, aside from hating the way he smelled.

"Give the guy a break," I told her, "he's nervous and it's hot." John shot the love scene from all angles, getting complete coverage of two people who heartily disliked each other making love.

At one point, the film was going to be called, *Ecstasy*, based on that scene. Needless to say, *Ecstasy* lost its glow and *Bolero* won out.

The experience on that film was unique for me—the producers were also the creators on the set. How does one juggle time to fulfill all roles? The answer—all roles suffer.

1985 Rome

Let's Hope It's a Girl, *with Catherine Deneuve, Liv Ullmann, and Stefania Sandrelli. A feminist film, Italian style.*

I must have adapted close to a hundred and fifty screenplays and treatments from Italian into English during all the years I lived in Italy, but there were few memorable scripts. One of them was *Let's Hope it's a Girl*.

The Italian feminist movement was on its way to being a tidal wave in 1984 and its influence on social and cultural life was substantial and growing. During my first stay in Italy in 1952, the woman's place was in the home, a condition unchanged for centuries. Women were married young and quickly donned the ubiquitous black dress with few trimmings. After all, women were supposed to bear children (please God, make it a boy) and work the fields if married to a farmer.

By the time I left Italy in 1995, after living in Rome for nearly thirty-five years, women were a force in politics (a woman was president of the lower house of parliament); in the labor movement; in literature and film as writers and directors.

Let's Hope it's a Girl was a direct result of femme power. They changed the Italian frame of mind. It became—please God, make it a girl.

The film's cast was superb. Among them was Stefania Sandrelli, a natural-born actress who, at the age of eighteen was the young wife of Marcello Mastoianni in the brilliant *Divorce Italian Style*.

Also included in the cast were Catherine Deneuve and Liv Ullman, two internationally known actresses, and Philippe Noiret, one of France's finest actors who appeared in many Italian films.

I was hired to coach the actors in English. Each scene was to be filmed in Italian, then in English. The two versions would then be dubbed into Italian and English. For distribution outside of Italy, the English version was obligatory.

Liv Ullman arrived in Rome a few days before shooting began. We met in her hotel to confer about dialogue. She had originally turned the movie down after reading the previous English version of the script. She didn't know Italian and had made her decision based on the English translation. She found the dialogue poorly written. However, when she read my English version (apologies for the lack of modesty), she agreed to be in the film. She told me she felt at ease with my English dialogue and was pleased because she loved the story.

I had no chance to meet with Deneuve before the shooting started because she flew in from Paris on her first day's work. I offered to help with any problems she might have with the English dialogue, but she flatly refused, saying she wasn't sure she wanted to do the English version. I told her I had been hired to oversee the English version, therefore if she wanted any modifications I would be available. She coolly brushed all that aside.

I was struck by her coldness. I believe she never overcame her love for Mastroianni (she had his child). The end of the affair must have embittered her. (As we used to say in Brooklyn—dat guy is a hellofa lady killer.) She was incredibly beautiful and as a young girl probably suffered the cost of being the best-looking girl on the block.

Mario Monicelli, the director of the film, was among the most talented and creative directors in Italy. Off the set, he was taciturn and self contained. He didn't have the personal flair of Fellini, de Sica, or Rossellini, but he had flair in his films. And penetrating humor. Two of his films are among the best I've ever seen: *La Grande Guerra* (*The Great War*), set during the first World War, and *I Soliti Ignoti* (*Big*

Deal on Madonna Street), a very funny movie about a gang of petty thieves. It had a very successful run in the States.

On the set, he was all business—a tough demanding director. Oddly enough, he rarely smiled or laughed.

Deneuve spoke in French in her first scene, rather than Italian. When Monicelli asked her to do it in English, Deneuve stuck it into me. "The English dialogue is not quite right," she said.

I responded, "I'm here to work with you, as I suggested earlier. If something in the dialogue doesn't please you, I can adjust it or make any changes you feel are necessary."

Her English was close to excellent, so I knew she could handle the language. But she simply didn't want to act in English. I can understand that. Generally, actors faced with a language not their own find it difficult to concentrate on the essence of the scene. However, in Deneuve's case, she knew the film would be dubbed, so why go through the effort of memorizing her part in English?

Deneuve's answer to Monicelli was sharp, decisive: "I have already done it in French and that will have to do."

Monicelli erupted, "Do it in Chinese or whatever you like, but I want another take." So Deneuve did another take—in Italian. Not nearly as good as her English.

Having been married to a French girl, I became aware of the rapport French women have with each other, how they adore being together. The subtext: Men are the enemy, and they learn that early on.

Those who have been to Paris must have noticed that when two or more women are seated together in a café or restaurant, they talk, they laugh, their eyes sparkle, and they seem delighted to be with each other. I have rarely seen a married couple in public, speak much or laugh or be at all intimate. Silence usually reigns.

Deneuve was most relaxed and congenial with the other women on the set, and except for Philippe Noiret, an actor approachable by all, she was remote and even wary of the men.

We hardly said a word to each other while she was on the film. I was not unhappy to see her go.

Stefania Sandrelli's presence saved the day for me. She, her boyfriend, and I became long-lasting friends. She's a beautiful actress—in looks, in talent, and as a woman. Although one of Italy's major movie stars over many years, she's modest and warm with most everyone. The man in her life is a youngish movie director, a jolly character, ready for a fun time at any hour of the day or night. It was always a delight to be with them.

Liv Ullman, being Scandinavian, had a low temperature, emotionally and socially. She is a talented and intelligent actress and we were friends until a greedy restauranteur soured our friendship.

Liv was engaged to be married to a wealthy hotel owner from Boston. He came to Rome to be wed in the ancient city. Liv had invited about sixty family members and friends from Norway and Sweden for the wedding dinner. She asked me to find a typical Roman trattoria.

I had the perfect place; rustic, beamed ceiling, and simple but good Roman food—il Grappolo d'Oro once again. Carlo, the owner, had come through perfectly for Ambassador Burt and his bride earlier in the year. For Liv's dinner I told him there would be over sixty people. He said he'd close the joint to the public. He also offered to give me a commission of a couple hundred bucks. I refused, saying I'm not in the business of seeking commissions. He didn't press the matter.

In 1985, prices in Rome were still reasonable. Carlo suggested the equivalent of twenty bucks (in lire) a guest, including drinks and wine. The menu was pasta, chicken, meat or fish, salad and dessert. Not a bad deal for Liv or Carlo.

The dinner was hugely successful. A lot of laughter, and good cheer. And then Liv asked me to come with her to pay the bill. But Carlo wanted thirty bucks a head instead of the twenty agreed upon. I asked him why he was doing that and he said a lot of wine was consumed, but I knew the cost to the restaurant for Italian table wine was no more than a buck a bottle.

I nearly burst a blood vessel trying to contain my anger. However,

I quietly argued with him not to do it. It made me look real bad. I knew, being Italian, he'd understand that. He did understand, but the extra money was irresistible.

Although I do have some paranoia, I felt that Liv thought I was getting a cut. Our friendship went out the window and Carlo lost a frequent customer.

Grappolo d'Oro—"cluster of gold." I finally understood Carlo's drive, enrich the cluster!

1986 New York

Mailer is president of PEN.

P resident Mailer? Well, yes and no. He wasn't president of the
United States but he was president of PEN (poets, essayists,
novelists). He had a two-year term that began in 1984. Being
an active president, it took much of his time. One of his efforts was
to raise money for PEN. But how? His plan was apt: Use the talent
in the room. He arranged for a series of eight readings, presented
more or less every two weeks; each evening would field two well-
known authors.

Sometime in mid-1986, Norman dialed me in Rome, told me of
the readings and asked me to feel Gore out about appearing in one of
them. He could choose his partner. Norman was available.

I went to see Gore and told him what Norman was doing. Would
Gore be interested in participating in one of the readings? His
answer: Perhaps. "Perhaps" meant Gore intended to accept.

I called Norman and told him Gore was onboard. He wrote Gore
a letter that Gore asked me to read. It was a gracious letter, and he
chose to appear at the reading with Norman.

I flew to New York. That performance I would not miss. It took
place on November, 17, 1986 at the Booth theater. The house was
full, including students invited to attend as standees. Gore was very
well prepared. He opened with a funny joke about Reagan rescuing

his coloring book from a White House fire, and he was off and running.

Norman didn't prepare; he was going to rely on his wits and wing it. Gore made a speech decrying Imperial America and read some of his writings. Then Norman spoke and read some recent writings; they did not have a colloquy.

After the intermission, they were going to answer written questions from the audience. Norman suggested to the moderator, Murray Kempton, that he and Gore debate, no written questions. They would face each other center stage and argue their ideas. Kempton brushed it aside and the evening slid downward. The written questions weren't provocative or that interesting.

In 1987 Norris and Norman Mailer went to Moscow for an international writers' conference where they ran into Gore Vidal and they spent some friendly time together. When Gore returned to Rome, he told me how much Norris impressed him; in effect he gave her a rave notice.

Norris is formidable. A beautiful, tall redhead; a talented painter, writer, and actress. She taught art in high school, has written a novel, *Windchill Summer*, that got excellent reviews around the country. I acted with her and can attest to her talent.

Norman had his misses, but Norris was a hit. I knew Norman's five ex-wives and she is Norman's home run. The marriage is more than twenty-five years old to date (January 2002).

I didn't see much of Norman during the years I lived in Rome. We kept in touch through the mail, the phone, or on my visits to the States. I missed his run in 1969 for the mayor of New York.

Mayor Mailer would have, at the least, created an exciting time. He had the quixotic but sensible notion that New York City should become the 51st state. He's a battler but he would have run into a brick wall on that and many other issues. Nonetheless, there are issues where he would have prevailed, making for a better New York. We'll never know.

Norman and I have had, in recent years, hot political arguments.

I know I should keep my mouth shut, but I argue with everyone about politics; it seems I'm not left enough of or too far left, depending on whom I talk to.

Now, January, 2002, Norman and I have been friends for fifty-three years. Except for a two-year stretch of silence between us, he's been loyal and a good friend to have.

In an interview, I once remarked that at times Norman tends to be tougher on his friends than on his enemies and it pissed him off. Many years ago we were discussing the belief in God and Norman said words to the effect that the better we become, the better God becomes.

1988 Various Locations

A second adventure with John and Bo Derek takes us to foreign lands.

J oin the Dereks and see the world. 1988 was another traveling year for the second movie I worked on with Bo and John. We filmed in Hong Kong, the Maldive Islands, Sri Lanka, New York City, and Jackson Hole, Wyoming.

John was allergic to Hollywood. He had little respect for those that ran the film industry. He was bitter after his experience directing *Tarzan* for a major studio: MGM. He felt the studio execs continuous interference prevented him from doing his best work. That and other considerations took him to foreign locations for his next and last film. John and Bo managed to get independent financing with the proviso that the Dereks have complete artistic control.

The ticket that took us to exotic places was, *Ghosts Can't Do It*, written by John after he had a mild heart attack. The attack stirred his imagination to write about a loving, macho husband who suddenly is hit by congestive heart failure. He is bedridden and all his activities are emphatically curtailed. Since he had had an energetic sexual life and a successful worldwide business, he cannot accept a situation that, in his mind, isolates him from his adoring wife. So what does a macho hombre do? He blows his brains out.

But hold on—it's only the beginning—he returns from the dead as a shade. Only his wife can hear and talk to her husband's ghost. However, he is invisible to her.

John envisions a benign god who will allow the dead husband to return to the world of the living if his wife discovers a healthy and handsome young man so the ghost can come back to inhabit the young man's body. But here's the caveat: the poor chap must expire first and the metamorphosis must take place within a set time.

The wife (Bo) travels to the Far East to run her dead husband's business as his invisible ghost cues her during business meetings. All the while she's on the lookout for the handsome young man. John died in 1998 and if he were prescient, Bo is not being produced by a future young John Derek.

We had filmed all of the movie except for the part of the husband and we were finally on our way to Jackson Hole, Wyoming, to shoot the husband's sequences before he puts his trusty six-shooter to his head.

A rare event! An actor asks to be replaced. He told John he was miscast as Bo's husband. John didn't need to be persuaded, but a replacement had to be found immediately.

If the reader recalls the casting change when we began *Bolero* it's that old cliché, déjà vu. But this time I came through like gangbusters: Anthony Quinn.

Quinn was a superb actor and macho to boot—just what the part demanded. The idea appealed to John and Bo, but they were skeptical; would Quinn accept a role that was central to the plot but little more than a cameo on-screen, and just as important, would he accept the money available in the budget role?

I called Tony, filled him in on the deal. The idea of playing Bo's husband intrigued him. After all Bo was beautiful and much younger than he. Not bad for an aging actor's ego.

After negotiations, Tony was set. The Dereks were relieved and thankful to have an actor who had two Oscars on his mantelpiece and sure to give a powerful performance. That he did. He then recorded his dialogue that would be spliced in the scenes already shot with Bo when Tony was the voice of an invisible ghost.

• • •

Bo, who was also the producer of the film, got Donald Trump to offer his business suite in Trump Towers to shoot a sequence involving high finance types. She also persuaded Donald to appear in the scene.

The camera intimidated him! It surprised me. Trump was so up front, in control of a conversation, sure of his abilities and strengths. He had a few speeches in a scene that should have been his playground—a business meeting. He faltered, his voice was flat and weak.

John, peering through the camera, shot me a puzzled look. I glanced at Bo, there was a hint of dismay in her eye. So, unfailingly, me and my big mouth stepped in:

"Donald. I saw you on the phone earlier, your voice had authority; tough but persuasive. You sounded unsure of yourself in the scene, your voice was not your normal voice. You weren't convincing. You are Donald Trump in this scene, man, not some show salesman. Relax—and be The Donald."

I could hear Bo gasp. Trump stared daggers at me, but controlled his scorn and unlike his usual self, kept his mouth shut. John fucked around with the camera for a bit, then called action.

I'll be a sonofabitch, Trump's voice dominated the scene; he played a born bullshit artist and brought the scene alive. But later he did approach me, smile and say, "hey, you know your business."

Shmoozing with John and Bo in their large, hard-earned ranch house in the Santa Ynez hills north of Santa Barbara, I offered a thought: if John could ever shuck the husk of machismo he'd discover the heart of a poet.

His eye for beauty in people and the things he lived with, and the gentle manner when we first met as young men, and then, many years later, when we spent so much time working together, the poet in John would, now and then, peek through.

After Bo made *Ten*, she became an instant star. John, in all good faith, made decisions, with Bo, which, in effect, kept her out of the hands of the major studios. He knew what could happen to a young woman in the Hollywood studios.

And Bo, young and inexperienced, willingly listened to John's advice. Any of the major studios would have signed her and surrounded her with the best writers, cast, and directors. Within three years she would have been the queen of the Hollywood firmament. And at that point, John and Bo could have formed a strong independent company making it easier to finance their projects. However, underlying that rosy scenario was John's core antagonism toward Hollywood.

He was accused by many of being a Svengali, an ambiguous soubriquet at best. But Bo was a babe in the Hollywood woods and she relied on John's judgement.

John was caught in a pitiless web spun by the lords of Filmland and couldn't cut his way out. When he told me on his first starring film that he would rather be with horses on a ranch than on a movie set, his fate was sealed unless he split then and there.

1999 Los Angeles

Joseph Heller, the author of Catch-22, *the key to understanding the 20th Century.*

J oseph Heller wasn't an easy friend, he could nail a half-baked idea, a false assumption or hypocritical note the moment it was heard coming out of your mouth. It was impossible for him to suffer ignorant bias and at times he could be gruff. But, as the rabbi would say, "on the other hand" he could be most understanding of your failings or pain. He was a *mensch* and I had a lot of affection for him.

We met in 1970 in Sidney Cohen's office. I got to know Sidney when he married John Garfield's widow, Robbie. Sidney was a well-known labor lawyer who helped or tried to help those blacklisted get off the blacklist. He was also Joe's personal lawyer (Joe was not on any blacklist).

A couple of times I was invited to spend a few days as a guest of the Hellers in East Hampton on Long Island. Like most homes in the Hamptons, the Heller home was comfortable and not ostentatious. They did have a guesthouse, which is a hell of a lot better than a guest room except in the dead of winter. For fear of pipes freezing, the Hellers shut the water off in the guesthouse. Valerie, Joe's wife-extraordinaire handed me a pot to piss in. (actually a vase) and told me to empty it in the morning in the wooded area behind the guesthouse. Having been in the U.S. Army over three years, that seemed civilized.

Joe worked during much of the day and we got together in the evenings. He had frosted martini glasses in the freezer, ready for the nightly dry martini (or two). Nothing better to oil a conversation. At times he reminded me of a scornful, grumpy comic as he punctured hypocritical politicians or told a couple of very funny jokes. He could be curt in destroying a stupid idea, but behind it all, being a softy, he would laugh to ease the sting. Joe was an innately generous man and could be surprisingly shy, but he was adept at covering up his shyness, making it difficult to see.

Joe and his laughter-loving wife always enjoyed coming to Rome. He liked good food, cooked properly. And what place better than Rome? The owner of Marcello's, a good restaurant, was a great admirer of the Heller books.

Joe enjoyed going to Marcello's restaurant where Marcello would quote passages he had learned by heart, in Italian, of Joe's prose. Joe would bring him an inscribed copy of his latest book. Marcello, delighted by the gift, would hover around our table and personally serve us.

One night, the Hellers and I went to a small Emiliano trattoria (the province of Emilia Romagna, in Northern Italy, is noted for its excellent kitchen) Federico Fellini was dining a couple of tables away. I told Joe that Fellini, during World War II, used to sketch people by the Spanish Steps in Rome to earn a few lire. Joe, then in the U.S. Army Airforce, in Italy, told me that Fellini had sketched him. I immediately took Joe to Fellini's table and introduced him to Heller. Lo and behold, Fellini knew he had sketched Joe. (He probably remembered him after *Catch-22* was published in Italian and had a photo of Joe in uniform, had a flash of memory and said to himself, I know that boy, he overpaid for that sketch I drew of him.) Joe told him he still had the drawing. It was a brief, polite meeting. Famous people are cautious with each other. No fawning there.

Joe Heller and I were not longtime buddies but the news of his death of a heart attack on December 12, 1999 was a hard hit. I valued the occasions we spent together (perhaps a dozen times). He took friendship seriously and we always had a fine time together.

I was not part of his inner circle, however, there was some kinship. We were both born and raised in Coney Island (Brooklyn) and went to the same grammar school, P.S. 188, at the same time. Although we lived within half a mile of each other, we never met as kids.

I had much admiration for his talent, his unique view of life, and how he used humor to expose fear and corruption during wartime. They guy was fun to be with and I deeply regret that he isn't around anymore. However, *Catch-22* made its way into the English dictionary and plugged a neglected hole. We all have a Catch-22 in our lives. But that was Heller's genius—he aired the complexities of much of life to make some sense of the nonsensical.

End Word

After living in Rome continuously for thirty-three years, I finally returned to Los Angeles in 1995 with some reluctance. Of all the major cities I have lived and worked in, Los Angeles is last on my list. How in hell can one live in a city where having a car is as important as having a place to live in. But my two daughters were living there, and I knew I wanted to be, for the time allotted me, within fifteen minutes of them.

Unlike Europe, where I had the luxury of refusing work, there was little to do in L.A. Yes, old friends cast me in a few TV movies and series, but the movie capital is a youth-oriented town and my youth is long gone.

The thought of writing some sort of memoir started to nag me. I lived with it as the seeds began to sprout and during the latter part of 1998 I asked Norman Mailer for his take on it; after all he had known me for exactly fifty years at that point and I valued his judgment. "Write it," he said, "you will find out whether or not you can write." He hit the right button. What he said was not what I expected, but it turned me on. I had translated and adapted about a hundred and fifty screenplays and screen treatments from Italian (and a couple of French scripts) into English, but it's a specialized kind of writing that had no connection to my life experience or thoughts and reflections on that experience.

And so I sat down and began tentatively typing on the last word processor being sold, having been overcome by computers. Almost four years later I had a stack of about six hundred manuscript pages. A writer I knew said, only one half of one percent of those wanting to write "their" book ever finish it. One can say being in that one half percent ain't all that half bad.

Acknowledgments

The author is grateful to: Patrick McGilligan, who was always available when I needed his good thinking. His encouragement, his optimism and expert advice was essential while writing the manuscript.

And Ruth Baldwin, who read the manuscript during a weekend and recommended that Nation Books publish it. She stayed with it and proved to be a perceptive editor and had the patience to hear me out during the months before publication

Index